Praise for *Effective C#, Second Edition*

"Being an effective .NET developer requires one to have a deep understanding of the language of their choice. Wagner's book provides the reader with that knowledge via well-reasoned arguments and insight. Whether you're new to C# or you've been using it for years, you'll learn something new when you read this book."

—Jason Bock, Principal Consultant, Magenic

"If you're at all like me, you have collected a handful of C# language pearls that have immediately transformed your abilities as a professional developer. What you hold in your hands is quite possibly the best collection of these tips that have ever been assembled. Bill has managed to exceed my wildest expectations with the latest edition in his eponymous *Effective C#*."

—Bill Craun, Principal Consultant, Ambassador Solutions

"*Effective C#, Second Edition,* is a must-read for anyone building high performance and/or highly scalable applications. Bill has that rare and awesome ability to take an amazingly complex problem and break it down into human, digestible, and understandable chunks."

—Josh Holmes, Architect Evangelist, Microsoft

"Bill has done it again. This book is a concise collection of invaluable tips for any C# developer. Learn one tip every day, and you'll become a much better C# developer after fifty days!"

—Claudio Lassala, Lead Developer, EPS Software/CODE Magazine

"A fountain of knowledge and understanding of the C# language. Bill gives insight to what happens under the covers of the .NET runtime based on what you write in your code and teaches pragmatic practices that lead to cleaner, easier to write, and more understandable code. A great mix of tips, tricks, and deep understanding—including things true since C# 1.0 up through new capabilities in C# 4.0—that every C# developer should read."

—Brian Noyes, Chief Architect, IDesign Inc. (www.idesign.net)

"*Effective C#* is a must-have for every C# developer. Period. Its pragmatic advice on code design is invaluable."

—Shawn Wildermuth, Microsoft MVP (C#), Author, Trainer, and Speaker

"In this book Bill Wagner provides practical explanations of how to use the most important features in the C# language. His deep knowledge and sophisticated communication skills illuminate the new features in C# so that you can use them to write programs that are more concise and easier to maintain."

—Charlie Calvert, Microsoft C# Community Program Manager

Effective C#

Second Edition

Effective C#

50 Specific Ways to Improve Your C#

Second Edition

Bill Wagner

✦✦ Addison-Wesley

Upper Saddle River, NJ • Boston • Indianapolis • San Francisco
New York • Toronto • Montreal • London • Munich • Paris • Madrid
Capetown • Sydney • Tokyo • Singapore • Mexico City

Many of the designations used by manufacturers and sellers to distinguish their products are claimed as trademarks. Where those designations appear in this book, and the publisher was aware of a trademark claim, the designations have been printed with initial capital letters or in all capitals.

The author and publisher have taken care in the preparation of this book, but make no expressed or implied warranty of any kind and assume no responsibility for errors or omissions. No liability is assumed for incidental or consequential damages in connection with or arising out of the use of the information or programs contained herein.

The publisher offers excellent discounts on this book when ordered in quantity for bulk purchases or special sales, which may include electronic versions and/or custom covers and content particular to your business, training goals, marketing focus, and branding interests. For more information, please contact:

DEC 0 7 2010

U.S. Corporate and Government Sales
(800) 382-3419
corpsales@pearsontechgroup.com

For sales outside the United States please contact:

005.133
C1112w2

International Sales
international@pearson.com

Visit us on the Web: informit.com/aw

Library of Congress Cataloging-in-Publication Data
Wagner, Bill.
    Effective C# : 50 specific ways to improve your C# / Bill Wagner.–2nd ed.
        p.   cm.
    Includes index.
    ISBN 978-0-321-65870-8 (pbk. : alk. paper)
  1. C# (Computer program language) 2. Database management. 3. Microsoft .NET Framework.
I. Title.
    QA76.73.C154W343 2010
    005.13'3–dc22

                                                                                2009052199

ISBN-13: 978-0-321-65870-8
ISBN-10:   0-321-65870-1
Text printed in the United States on recycled paper at Courier in Stoughton, Massachusetts.
First printing, March 2010

To my parents, Bill and Alice Wagner.
They continue to demonstrate great strength and inspiration.

Contents at a Glance

Contents

Introduction

The C# community is very different in 2010 than it was in 2004 when the first edition of *Effective C#* was published. There are many more developers using C#. A large contingent of the C# community is now seeing C# as their first professional language. They aren't approaching C# with a set of ingrained habits formed using a different language. The community has a much broader range of experience. New graduates all the way to professionals with decades of experience are using C#.

The C# language has also grown in the last five years. The language I covered in the first edition did not have generics, lambda expressions, LINQ, and many of the other features we now take for granted. C# 4.0 adds new features that change our toolset again. And yet, even with all the growth in the C# language, much of the original advice is as relevant now as it was in the C# 1.x days. Viewed in hindsight, the changes to the C# language appear to be natural and obvious extensions to what we had in C# 1.0. New editions give us new ways of solving problems, without invalidating previous idioms.

I organized this second edition of *Effective C#* by taking into account both the changes in the language and the changes in the C# community. *Effective C#* does not take you on a historical journey through the changes in the language. Rather, I provide advice on how to use the current C# language. The items that have been removed from this second edition are those that aren't as relevant in today's C# language. The new items cover the new language and framework features, and those practices the community has learned from building several versions of software products using C#. Overall, these items are a set of recommendations that will help you use C# 4.0 more effectively as a professional developer.

This book covers C# 4.0, but it is not an exhaustive treatment of the new language features. Like all books in the Effective Software Development Series, this book offers practical advice on how to use these features to solve problems you're likely to encounter every day. Many of the items are equally valid in the 3.0 and even earlier versions of the language.

Who Should Read This Book?

Effective C# was written for professional developers who use C# as part of their daily toolset. It assumes you are familiar with the C# syntax and the language's features. The second edition assumes you understand the new syntax added in C# 4.0, as well as the syntax available in the previous versions of the language. This book does not include tutorial instruction on language features. Instead, this book discusses how you can integrate all the features of the current version of the C# language into your everyday development.

In addition to language features, I assume you have some knowledge of the Common Language Runtime (CLR) and Just-In-Time (JIT) compiler.

About the Content

There are language constructs you'll use every day in almost every C# program you write. Chapter 1, "C# Language Idioms," covers those language idioms you'll use so often they should feel like well-worn tools in your hands. These are the building blocks of every type you create and every algorithm you implement.

Working in a managed environment doesn't mean the environment absolves you of all your responsibilities. You still must work with the environment to create correct programs that satisfy the stated performance requirements. It's not just about performance testing and performance tuning. Chapter 2, ".NET Resource Management," teaches you the design idioms that enable you to work with the environment to achieve those goals before detailed optimization begins.

In many ways, we write programs to satisfy human readers rather than a compiler. All the compiler cares about is that a program is valid. Our colleagues want to understand our intent as well. Chapter 3, "Expressing Designs in C#," discusses how the C# language can be applied to express your design intent. There are always several ways to solve a problem. The recommendations in Chapter 3 will help you choose the solution that best expresses your design intent to fellow developers.

C# is a small language, supported by a rich framework library. Chapter 4, "Working with the Framework," covers the portions of the .NET Base Class Library (BCL) that support your core algorithms. In addition, I cover some of the common idioms that you'll encounter throughout the framework. Multicore processors are a way of life, and the Parallel Task Library provides a step forward in creating multithreaded programs on the .NET platform. I cover the most common practices for the Parallel Task Library in this chapter.

Chapter 5, "Dynamic Programming in C#," discusses how to use C# as a dynamic language. C# is a strongly typed, statically typed language. However, more and more programs contain both dynamic and static typing. C# provides ways for you to leverage dynamic programming idioms without losing the benefits of static typing throughout your entire program. You'll learn how to use dynamic features and how to avoid having dynamic types leak through your entire program.

Chapter 6, "Miscellaneous," covers those items that somehow continue to defy classification. These are the techniques you'll use often to create robust programs that are easier to maintain and extend.

Code Conventions

We no longer look at code in monochrome, and we shouldn't in books either. While it's impossible to replicate the experience of using a modern IDE on paper, I've tried to provide a better experience reading the code in the book. Where the medium supports it, the code samples use the standard Visual Studio IDE colors for all code elements. Where I am pointing to particular changes in samples, those changes are highlighted.

Showing code in a book still requires making some compromises for space and clarity. I've tried to distill the samples down to illustrate the particular point of the sample. Often that means eliding other portions of a class or a method. Sometimes that will include eliding error recovery code for space. Public methods should validate their parameters and other inputs, but that code is usually elided for space. Similar space considerations remove validation of method calls, and `try`/`finally` clauses that would often be included in complicated algorithms.

I also usually assume most developers can find the appropriate namespace when samples use one of the common namespaces. You can safely assume that every sample implicitly includes the following using statements:

```
using System;
using System.Collections.Generic;
```

```
using System.Linq;
using System.Text;
using System.Dynamic;
using System.Threading;
```

Finally, I use the #region/#endregion directives to denote interface implementations. While that's not necessary, and some dislike the region directive in code, it does make it easy to see which methods implement interface methods in static text. Any other option would be nonstandard and take more space.

Providing Feedback

Despite my best efforts, and the efforts of the people who have reviewed the text, errors may have crept into the text or samples. If you believe you have found an error, please contact me at bill.wagner@srtsolutions.com. Errata will be posted at http://srtsolutions.com/blogs/effectivecsharp. Many of the items in this book, and *More Effective C#*, are the result of email conversations with other C# developers. If you have questions or comments about the recommendations, please contact me. Discussions of general interest will be covered on my blog at http://srtsolutions.com/blogs/billwagner.

Acknowledgments

There are many people to whom I owe thanks for their contributions to this book. I've been privileged to be part of an amazing C# community over the years. Everyone on the C# Insiders mailing list (whether inside or outside Microsoft) has contributed ideas and conversations that made this a better book.

I must single out a few members of the C# community who directly helped me with ideas, and with turning ideas into concrete recommendations. Conversations with Charlie Calvert, Eric DeCarufel, Justin Etheredge, Marc Gravell, Mike Gold, and Doug Holland are the basis for many new ideas in this edition.

I also had great email conversations with Stephen Toub and Michael Wood on the Parallel Task Library and its implications on C# idioms.

I had a wonderful team of technical reviewers for this edition. Jason Bock, Claudio Lassala, and Tomas Petricek pored over the text and the samples to ensure the quality of the book you now hold. Their reviews were thorough and complete, which is the best anyone can hope for. Beyond that, they added recommendations that helped me explain many of the topics better.

The team at Addison-Wesley is a dream to work with. Joan Murray is a fantastic editor, taskmaster, and the driving force behind anything that gets done. She leans on Olivia Basegio heavily, and so do I. Their contributions created the quality of the finished manuscript from the front cover to the back, and everything in between. Curt Johnson and Brandon Prebynski continue to do an incredible job marketing technical content. No matter what format you chose, Curt and Brandon have had something to do with its existence for this book. Geneil Breeze poured over the entire manuscript improving explanations and clarifying the wording in several places.

It's an honor, once again, to be part of Scott Meyer's series. He goes over every manuscript and offers suggestions and comments for improvement. He is incredibly thorough, and his experience in software, although not in C#, means he finds any areas where I haven't explained an item clearly or fully justified a recommendation. His feedback, as always, is invaluable.

I've also had the privilege of bouncing ideas off the other consultants at SRT Solutions. From the most experienced to the youngest, they are an incredibly smart group of people with great insight. They are also not afraid to express their opinions. Countless conversations with Ben Barefield, Dennis Burton, Marina Fedner, Alex Gheith, Darrell Hawley, Chris Marinos, Dennis Matveyev, Anne Marsan, Dianne Marsh, Charlie Sears, Patrick Steele, Mike Woelmer, and Jay Wren sparked ideas and samples. Later conversations helped clarify how to explain and justify different recommendations.

As always, my family gave up time with me so that I could finish this manuscript. My children Lara, Sarah, and Scott, put up with the times I hid in the home office and didn't join in other activities. My wife, Marlene, gave up countless hours while I went off to write or create samples. Without their support, I never would have finished this or any other book. Nor would it be as satisfying to finish.

About the Author

With more than twenty years of experience, Bill Wagner, SRT Solutions cofounder, is a recognized expert in software design and engineering, specializing in C#, .NET, and the Azure platform. He serves as Michigan's Regional Director for Microsoft and is a multiyear winner of Microsoft's MVP award. An internationally recognized writer, Bill is the author of the first edition of this book and *More Effective C#* (Addison-Wesley, 2009) and currently writes a column on the Microsoft C# Developer Center. Bill earned a B.S. in computer science from the University of Illinois at Champaign-Urbana.

1 | C# Language Idioms

Why should you change what you are doing today if it works? The answer is that you can be better. You change tools or languages because you can be more productive. You don't realize the expected gains if you don't change your habits. This is harder when the new language, C#, has so much in common with a familiar language, such as C++ or Java. C# is another curly braced language, making it easy to fall into the same idioms you used in other languages in the same family. That will prevent you from getting the most out of C#. The C# language has evolved since its first commercial release in 2001. It's now much farther removed from C++ or Java than it was in its original release. If you are approaching C# from another language, you need to learn the C# idioms so that the language works with you, rather than against you. This chapter discusses the habits that you should change—and what you should do instead.

Item 1: Use Properties Instead of Accessible Data Members

Properties have always been first-class citizens in the C# language. Several enhancements since the 1.0 release of the C# language have made properties even more expressive. You can specify different access restrictions on the getter and setter. Implicit properties minimize the hand typing for properties instead of data members. If you're still creating public variables in your types, stop now. If you're still creating get and set methods by hand, stop now. Properties let you expose data members as part of your public interface and still provide the encapsulation you want in an object-oriented environment. Properties are language elements that are accessed as though they are data members, but they are implemented as methods.

Some members of a type really are best represented as data: the name of a customer, the x,y location of a point, or last year's revenue. Properties enable you to create an interface that acts like data access but still has all the benefits of a method. Client code accesses properties as though they are accessing public fields. But the actual implementation uses methods, in which you define the behavior of property accessors.

1

The .NET Framework assumes that you'll use properties for your public data members. In fact, the data binding classes in the .NET Framework support properties, not public data members. This is true for all the data binding libraries: WPF, Windows Forms, Web Forms, and Silverlight. Data binding ties a property of an object to a user interface control. The data binding mechanism uses reflection to find a named property in a type:

```
textBoxCity.DataBindings.Add("Text",
    address, "City");
```

The previous code binds the Text property of the textBoxCity control to the City property of the address object. It will not work with a public data member named City; the Framework Class Library designers did not support that practice. Public data members are bad practice, so support for them was not added. Their decision simply gives you yet another reason to follow the proper object-oriented techniques.

Yes, data binding applies only to those classes that contain elements that are displayed in your user interface logic. But that doesn't mean properties should be used exclusively in UI logic. You should use properties for other classes and structures. Properties are far easier to change as you discover new requirements or behaviors over time. You might soon decide that your customer type should never have a blank name. If you used a public property for Name, that's easy to fix in one location:

```
public class Customer
{
    private string name;
    public string Name
    {
        get { return name; }
        set
        {
            if (string.IsNullOrEmpty(value))
                throw new ArgumentException(
                    "Name cannot be blank",
                    "Name");
            name = value;
        }
        // More Elided.
    }
}
```

If you had used public data members, you're stuck looking for every bit of code that sets a customer's name and fixing it there. That takes more time—much more time.

Because properties are implemented with methods, adding multithreaded support is easier. You can enhance the implementation of the get and set accessors to provide synchronized access to the data:

```
public class Customer
{
    private object syncHandle = new object();

    private string name;
    public string Name
    {
        get
        {
            lock (syncHandle)
                return name;
        }
        set
        {
            if (string.IsNullOrEmpty(value))
                throw new ArgumentException(
                    "Name cannot be blank",
                    "Name");
            lock (syncHandle)
                name = value;
        }
    }
    // More Elided.
}
```

Properties have all the language features of methods. Properties can be virtual:

```
public class Customer
{
    public virtual string Name
    {
        get;
```

```
        set;
    }
}
```

You'll notice that the last examples use the C# 3.0 implicit property syntax. Creating a property to wrap a backing store is a common pattern. Often, you won't need validation logic in the property getters or setters. The language supports the simplified implicit property syntax to minimize typing needed to expose a simple field as a property. The compiler creates a private member field (typically called a backing store) for you and implements the obvious logic for both the get and set accessors.

You can extend properties to be abstract and define properties as part of an interface definition, using similar syntax to implicit properties. The example below shows a property definition in a generic interface. Note that while the syntax is consistent with implicit properties, the interface definition below does not include any implementation. It defines a contract that must be satisfied by any type that implements this interface.

```
public interface INameValuePair<T>
{
    string Name
    {
        get;
    }

    T Value
    {
        get;
        set;
    }
}
```

Properties are full-fledged, first-class language elements that are an extension of methods that access or modify internal data. Anything you can do with member functions, you can do with properties.

The accessors for a property are two separate methods that get compiled into your type. You can specify different accessibility modifiers to the get and set accessors in a property in C#. This gives you even greater control over the visibility of those data elements you expose as properties:

```
public class Customer
{
    public virtual string Name
    {
        get;
        protected set;
    }
    // remaining implementation omitted
}
```

The property syntax extends beyond simple data fields. If your type should contain indexed items as part of its interface, you can use indexers (which are parameterized properties). It's a useful way to create a property that returns the items in a sequence:

```
public int this[int index]
{
    get { return theValues[index]; }
    set { theValues[index] = value; }
}


// Accessing an indexer:
int val = someObject[i];
```

Indexers have all the same language support as single-item properties: They are implemented as methods you write, so you can apply any verification or computation inside the indexer. Indexers can be virtual or abstract, can be declared in interfaces, and can be read-only or read-write. Single-dimension indexers with numeric parameters can participate in data binding. Other indexers can use noninteger parameters to define maps and dictionaries:

```
public Address this[string name]
{
    get { return adressValues[name]; }
    set { adressValues[name] = value; }
}
```

In keeping with the multidimensional arrays in C#, you can create multidimensional indexers, with similar or different types on each axis:

```
public int this[int x, int y]
{
```

```
    get { return ComputeValue(x, y); }
}

public int this[int x, string name]
{
    get { return ComputeValue(x, name); }
}
```

Notice that all indexers are declared with the `this` keyword. You cannot name an indexer in C#. Therefore, every different indexer in a type must have distinct parameter lists to avoid ambiguity. Almost all the capabilities for properties apply to indexers. Indexers can be virtual or abstract; indexers can have separate access restrictions for setters and getters. You cannot create implicit indexers as you can with properties.

This property functionality is all well and good, and it's a nice improvement. But you might still be tempted to create an initial implementation using data members and then replace the data members with properties later when you need one of those benefits. That sounds like a reasonable strategy—but it's wrong. Consider this portion of a class definition:

```
// using public data members, bad practice:
public class Customer
{
    public string Name;

    // remaining implementation omitted
}
```

It describes a customer, with a name. You can get or set the name using the familiar member notation:

```
string name = customerOne.Name;
customerOne.Name = "This Company, Inc.";
```

That's simple and straightforward. You are thinking that you could later replace the Name data member with a property, and the code would keep working without any change. Well, that's sort of true. Properties are meant to look like data members when accessed. That's the purpose behind the syntax. But properties are not data. A property access generates different Microsoft Intermediate Language (MSIL) instructions than a data access.

Although properties and data members are source compatible, they are not binary compatible. In the obvious case, this means that when you change from a public data member to the equivalent public property, you must recompile all code that uses the public data member. C# treats binary assemblies as first-class citizens. One goal of the language is that you can release a single updated assembly without upgrading the entire application. The simple act of changing a data member to a property breaks binary compatibility. It makes upgrading single assemblies that have been deployed much more difficult.

While looking at the IL for a property, you probably wonder about the relative performance of properties and data members. Properties will not be faster than data member access, but they might not be any slower. The JIT compiler does inline some method calls, including property accessors. When the JIT compiler does inline property accessors, the performance of data members and properties is the same. Even when a property accessor has not been inlined, the actual performance difference is the negligible cost of one function call. That is measurable only in a small number of situations.

Properties are methods that can be viewed from the calling code like data. That puts some expectations into your users' heads. They will see a property access as though it was a data access. After all, that's what it looks like. Your property accessors should live up to those expectations. Get accessors should not have observable side effects. Set accessors do modify the state, and users should be able to see those changes.

Property accessors also have performance expectations for your users. A property access looks like a data field access. It should not have performance characteristics that are significantly different than a simple data access. Property accessors should not perform lengthy computations, or make cross-application calls (such as perform database queries), or do other lengthy operations that would be inconsistent with your users' expectations for a property accessor.

Whenever you expose data in your type's public or protected interfaces, use properties. Use an indexer for sequences or dictionaries. All data members should be private, without exception. You immediately get support for data binding, and you make it much easier to make any changes to the implementation of the methods in the future. The extra typing to encapsulate any variable in a property amounts to one or two minutes of your day. Finding that you need to use properties later to correctly express your designs will take hours. Spend a little time now, and save yourself lots of time later.

Item 2: Prefer `readonly` to `const`

C# has two different versions of constants: **compile-time** constants and **runtime** constants. They have very different behaviors, and using the wrong one will cost you performance or correctness. Neither problem is a good one to have, but if you must pick one, a slower, correct program is better than a faster, broken program. For that reason, you should prefer runtime constants over compile-time constants. Compile-time constants are slightly faster, but far less flexible, than runtime constants. Reserve the compile-time constants for when performance is critical and the value of the constant will never change between releases.

You declare runtime constants with the `readonly` keyword. Compile-time constants are declared with the `const` keyword:

```
// Compile time constant:
public const int Millennium = 2000;


// Runtime constant:
public static readonly int ThisYear = 2004;
```

The code above shows both kinds of constants at the class or `struct` scope. Compile-time constants can also be declared inside methods. Read-only constants cannot be declared with method scope.

The differences in the behavior of compile-time and runtime constants follow from how they are accessed. A compile-time constant is replaced with the value of that constant in your object code. This construct:

```
if (myDateTime.Year == Millennium)
```

compiles to the same IL as if you had written this:

```
if (myDateTime.Year == 2000)
```

Runtime constants are evaluated at runtime. The IL generated when you reference a read-only constant references the `readonly` variable, not the value.

This distinction places several restrictions on when you are allowed to use either type of constant. Compile-time constants can be used only for primitive types (built-in integral and floating-point types), enums, or strings. These are the only types that enable you to assign meaningful constant values in initializers. These primitive types are the only ones that can be replaced with literal values in the compiler-generated IL. The following construct does not compile. You cannot initialize a compile-time constant using the new operator, even when the type being initialized is a value type:

```
// Does not compile, use readonly instead:
private const DateTime classCreation = new
    DateTime(2000, 1, 1, 0, 0, 0);
```

Compile-time constants are limited to numbers and strings. Read-only values are also constants, in that they cannot be modified after the constructor has executed. But read-only values are different in that they are assigned at runtime. You have much more flexibility in working with runtime constants. For one thing, runtime constants can be any type. You must initialize them in a constructor, or you can use an initializer. You can make readonly values of the DateTime structures; you cannot create DateTime values with const.

You can use readonly values for instance constants, storing different values for each instance of a class type. Compile-time constants are, by definition, static constants.

The most important distinction is that readonly values are resolved at runtime. The IL generated when you reference a readonly constant references the readonly variable, not the value. This difference has far-reaching implications on maintenance over time. Compile-time constants generate the same IL as though you've used the numeric constants in your code, even across assemblies: A constant in one assembly is still replaced with the value when used in another assembly.

The way in which compile-time and runtime constants are evaluated affects runtime compatibility. Suppose you have defined both const and readonly fields in an assembly named Infrastructure:

```
public class UsefulValues
{
    public static readonly int StartValue = 5;
    public const int EndValue = 10;
}
```

In another assembly, you reference these values:

```
for (int i = UsefulValues.StartValue;
    i < UsefulValues.EndValue; i++)
    Console.WriteLine("value is {0}", i);
```

If you run your little test, you see the following obvious output:

```
Value is 5
Value is 6
. . .
Value is 9
```

Time passes, and you release a new version of the Infrastructure assembly with the following changes:

```
public class UsefulValues
{
    public static readonly int StartValue = 105;
    public const int EndValue = 120;
}
```

You distribute the Infrastructure assembly without rebuilding your Application assembly. You expect to get this:

```
Value is 105
Value is 106
. . .
Value is 119
```

In fact, you get no output at all. The loop now uses the value 105 for its start and 10 for its end condition. The C# compiler placed the const value of 10 into the Application assembly instead of a reference to the storage used by EndValue. Contrast that with the StartValue value. It was declared as readonly: It gets resolved at runtime. Therefore, the Application assembly makes use of the new value without even recompiling the Application assembly; simply installing an updated version of the Infrastructure assembly is enough to change the behavior of all clients using that value. Updating the value of a public constant should be viewed as an interface change. You must recompile all code that references that constant. Updating the value of a read-only constant is an implementation change; it is binary compatible with existing client code.

On the other hand, sometimes you really mean for a value to be determined at compile time. For example, consider a set of constants to mark different versions of an object in its serialized form (see Item 27). Persistent values that mark specific versions should be compile-time constants; they never change. The current version should be a runtime constant, changing with each release.

```
private const int Version1_0 = 0x0100;
private const int Version1_1 = 0x0101;
private const int Version1_2 = 0x0102;
// major release:
private const int Version2_0 = 0x0200;

// check for the current version:
private static readonly int CurrentVersion =
    Version2_0;
```

You use the runtime version to store the current version in each saved file:

```
// Read from persistent storage, check
// stored version against compile-time constant:
protected MyType(SerializationInfo info,
  StreamingContext cntxt)
{
    int storedVersion = info.GetInt32("VERSION");
    switch (storedVersion)
    {
        case Version2_0:
            readVersion2(info, cntxt);
            break;
        case Version1_1:
            readVersion1Dot1(info, cntxt);
            break;

        // etc.
    }
}


// Write the current version:
[SecurityPermissionAttribute(SecurityAction.Demand,
 SerializationFormatter = true)]
void ISerializable.GetObjectData(SerializationInfo inf,
    StreamingContext cxt)
{
    // use runtime constant for current version:
    inf.AddValue("VERSION", CurrentVersion);

    // write remaining elements...
}
```

The final advantage of using const over readonly is performance: Known constant values can generate slightly more efficient code than the variable accesses necessary for readonly values. However, any gains are slight and should be weighed against the decreased flexibility. Be sure to profile performance differences before giving up the flexibility.

You'll encounter similar tradeoffs between runtime and compile-time processing of constant values when you use named and optional parameters. The default values for optional parameters are placed in the call site just like the default value for compile-time constants (those declared with const). Like working with readonly and const values, you'll want to be careful with changes to the values of optional parameters. (See Item 10.)

const must be used when the value must be available at compile time: attribute parameters and enum definitions, and those rare times when you mean to define a value that does not change from release to release. For everything else, prefer the increased flexibility of readonly constants.

Item 3: Prefer the is or as Operators to Casts

By embracing C#, you've embraced strong typing. That is almost always a good thing. Strong typing means you expect the compiler to find type mismatches in your code. That also means your applications do not need to perform as much type checking at runtime. But sometimes, runtime type checking is unavoidable. There will be times in C# when you write functions that take object parameters because the framework defines the method signature for you. You likely need to attempt to cast those objects to other types, either classes or interfaces. You've got two choices: Use the as operator or force the compiler to bend to your will using a cast. You also have a defensive variant: You can test a conversion with is and then use as or casts to convert it.

The correct choice is to use the as operator whenever you can because it is safer than blindly casting and is more efficient at runtime. The as and is operators do not perform any user-defined conversions. They succeed only if the runtime type matches the sought type; they never construct a new object to satisfy a request.

Take a look at an example. You write a piece of code that needs to convert an arbitrary object into an instance of MyType. You could write it this way:

```
object o = Factory.GetObject();

// Version one:
MyType t = o as MyType;

if (t != null)
{
    // work with t, it's a MyType.
}
else
{
    // report the failure.
}
```

Or, you could write this:

```
object o = Factory.GetObject();

// Version two:
try
{
    MyType t;
    t = (MyType)o;
    // work with T, it's a MyType.
}
catch (InvalidCastException)
{
    // report the conversion failure.
}
```

You'll agree that the first version is simpler and easier to read. It does not have the `try`/`catch` clause, so you avoid both the overhead and the code. Notice that the cast version must check `null` in addition to catching exceptions. `null` can be converted to any reference type using a cast, but the `as` operator returns `null` when used on a `null` reference. So, with casts, you need to check `null` and catch exceptions. Using `as`, you simply check the returned reference against `null`.

The biggest difference between the `as` operator and the `cast` operator is how user-defined conversions are treated. The `as` and `is` operators examine the runtime type of the object being converted; they do not perform any other operations. If a particular object is not the requested type or is derived from the requested type, they fail. Casts, on the other hand, can use conversion operators to convert an object to the requested type. This includes any built-in numeric conversions. Casting a long to a short can lose information.

The same problems are lurking when you cast user-defined types. Consider this type:

```
public class SecondType
{
    private MyType _value;

    // other details elided

    // Conversion operator.
    // This converts a SecondType to
    // a MyType, see item 9.
    public static implicit operator
      MyType(SecondType t)
    {
        return t._value;
    }
}
```

Suppose an object of SecondType is returned by the Factory.GetObject() function in the first code snippet:

```
object o = Factory.GetObject();

// o is a SecondType:
MyType t = o as MyType; // Fails. o is not MyType

if (t != null)
{
    // work with t, it's a MyType.
}
else
{
    // report the failure.
}
```

```
// Version two:
try
{
    MyType t1;
    t1 = (MyType)o; // Fails. o is not MyType
    // work with t1, it's a MyType.
}
catch (InvalidCastException)
{
    // report the conversion failure.
}
```

Both versions fail. But I told you that casts will perform user-defined conversions. You'd think the cast would succeed. You're right—it should succeed if you think that way. But it fails because your compiler is generating code based on the compile-time type of the object, o. The compiler knows nothing about the runtime type of o; it views o as an instance of object. The compiler sees that there is no user-defined conversion from object to MyType. It checks the definitions of object and MyType. Lacking any user-defined conversion, the compiler generates the code to examine the runtime type of o and checks whether that type is a MyType. Because o is a SecondType object, that fails. The compiler does not check to see whether the actual runtime type of o can be converted to a MyType object.

You could make the conversion from SecondType to MyType succeed if you wrote the code snippet like this:

```
object o = Factory.GetObject();

// Version three:
SecondType st = o as SecondType;
try
{
    MyType t;
    t = (MyType)st;
    // work with T, it's a MyType.
}
catch (InvalidCastException)
{
    // report the failure.
}
```

You should never write this ugly code, but it does illustrate a common problem. Although you would never write this, you can use an `object` parameter to a function that expects the proper conversions:

```
object o = Factory.GetObject();
DoStuffWithObject(o);

private static void DoStuffWithObject(object o)
{
    try
    {
        MyType t;
        t = (MyType)o; // Fails. o is not MyType
        // work with T, it's a MyType.
    }
    catch (InvalidCastException)
    {
        // report the conversion failure.
    }
}
```

Remember that user-defined conversion operators operate only on the compile-time type of an object, not on the runtime type. It does not matter that a conversion between the runtime type of o and MyType exists. The compiler just doesn't know or care. This statement has different behavior, depending on the declared type of st:

```
t = (MyType)st;
```

This next statement returns the same result, no matter what the declared type of st is. So, you should prefer as to casts—it's more consistent. In fact, if the types are not related by inheritance, but a user-defined conversion operator exists, the following statement will generate a compiler error:

```
t = st as MyType;
```

Now that you know to use as when possible, let's discuss when you can't use it. The as operator does not work on value types. This statement won't compile:

```
object o = Factory.GetValue();
int i = o as int; // Does not compile.
```

That's because `int`s are value types and can never be `null`. What value of `int` should be stored in i if o is not an integer? Any value you pick might also be a valid integer. Therefore, `as` can't be used. You're stuck using the cast syntax. It's actually a boxing/unboxing conversion (see Item 45):

```
object o = Factory.GetValue();
int i = 0;
try
{
    i = (int)o;
}
catch (InvalidCastException)
{
    i = 0;
}
```

Using exceptions as a flow control mechanism should strike you as a terrible practice. (See Item 47.) But you're not stuck with the behaviors of casts. You can use the `is` statement to remove the chance of exceptions or conversions:

```
object o = Factory.GetValue();
int i = 0;
if (o is int)
    i = (int)o;
```

If o is some other type that can be converted to an `int`, such as a `double`, the `is` operator returns false. The `is` operator always returns false for null arguments.

The `is` operator should be used only when you cannot convert the type using `as`. Otherwise, it's simply redundant:

```
// correct, but redundant:
object o = Factory.GetObject();

MyType t = null;
if (o is MyType)
    t = o as MyType;
```

The previous code is the same as if you had written the following:

```
// correct, but redundant:
object o = Factory.GetObject();
```

```
MyType t = null;
if (o is MyType)
    t = o as MyType;
```

That's inefficient and redundant. If you're about to convert a type using as, the is check is simply not necessary. Check the return from as against null; it's simpler.

Now that you know the difference among is, as, and casts, which operator do you suppose the foreach loop uses? Foreach loops can operate on nongeneric IEnumerable sequences and have the type coercion built into the iteration. (You should prefer the type-safe generic versions whenever possible. The nongeneric version exists for historical purposes, and to support some late binding scenarios.)

```
public void UseCollection(IEnumerable theCollection)
{
  foreach (MyType t in theCollection)
    t.DoStuff( );
}
```

foreach uses a cast operation to perform conversions from an object to the type used in the loop. The code generated by the foreach statement roughly equates to this hand-coded version:

```
public void UseCollectionV2(IEnumerable theCollection)
{
    IEnumerator it = theCollection.GetEnumerator();
    while (it.MoveNext())
    {
        MyType t = (MyType)it.Current;
        t.DoStuff();
    }
}
```

foreach needs to use casts to support both value types and reference types. By choosing the cast operator, the foreach statement exhibits the same behavior, no matter what the destination type is. However, because a cast is used, foreach loops can cause an InvalidCastException to be thrown.

Because IEnumerator.Current returns a System.Object, which has no conversion operators, none is eligible for this test. A collection of SecondType objects cannot be used in the previous UseCollection() function because the conversion fails, as you already saw. The `foreach` statement (which uses a cast) does not examine the casts that are available in the runtime type of the objects in the collection. It examines only the conversions available in the System.Object class (the type returned by IEnumerator.Current) and the declared type of the loop variable (in this case, MyType).

Finally, sometimes you want to know the exact type of an object, not just whether the current type can be converted to a target type. The `is` operator returns true for any type derived from the target type. The GetType() method gets the runtime type of an object. It is a more strict test than the `is` or `as` statement provides. GetType() returns the type of the object and can be compared to a specific type.

Consider this function again:

```
public void UseCollectionV3(IEnumerable theCollection)
{
    foreach (MyType t in theCollection)
        t.DoStuff();
}
```

If you made a NewType class derived from MyType, a collection of NewType objects would work just fine in the UseCollection function:

```
public class NewType : MyType
{
    // contents elided.
}
```

If you mean to write a function that works with all objects that are instances of MyType, that's fine. If you mean to write a function that works only with MyType objects exactly, you should use the exact type for comparison. Here, you would do that inside the `foreach` loop. The most common time when the exact runtime type is important is when doing equality tests (see Item 6). In most other comparisons, the `.isinst` comparisons provided by `as` and `is` are semantically correct.

The .NET Base Class Library (BCL) contains a method for converting elements in a sequence using the same type of operations: Enumerable .Cast<T>() converts each element in a sequence that supports the classic IEnumerable interface:

```
IEnumerable collection = new List<int>()
    {1,2,3,4,5,6,7,8,9,10};
```

```
var small = from int item in collection
            where item < 5
            select item;

var small2 = collection.Cast<int>().Where(item => item < 5).
    Select(n => n);
```

The query generates the same method calls as the last line of code above. In both cases, the Cast<T> method converts each item in the sequence to the target type. The Enumerable.Cast<T> method uses an old style cast rather than the as operator. Using the old style cast means that Cast<T> does not need to have a class constraint. Using the as operator would be limiting, and rather than implement different Cast<T> methods, the BCL team chose to create a single method using the old style cast operator. It's a tradeoff you should consider in your code as well. On those occasions where you need to convert an object that is one of the generic type parameters, you'll need to weigh the necessity of a class constraint against the different behavior of using the cast operator.

In C# 4.0, the type system can be circumvented even more by using dynamic and runtime type checking. That's the subject of Chapter 5, "Dynamic Programming in C#." There are quite a few ways to treat objects based on expectations of known behavior rather than knowing anything about a particular type or interface supplied. You'll learn about when to use those techniques and when to avoid them.

Good object-oriented practice says that you should avoid converting types, but sometimes there are no alternatives. If you can't avoid the conversions, use the language's as and is operators to express your intent more clearly. Different ways of coercing types have different rules. The is and as operators are almost always the correct semantics, and they succeed only when the object being tested is the correct type. Prefer those statements to cast operators, which can have unintended side effects and succeed or fail when you least expect it.

Item 4: Use Conditional Attributes Instead of #if

#if/#endif blocks have been used to produce different builds from the same source, most often debug and release variants. But these have never been a tool we were happy to use. #if/#endif blocks are too easily abused, creating code that is hard to understand and harder to debug. Language designers have responded by creating better tools to produce different machine code for different environments. C# has added the Conditional attribute to indicate whether a method should be called based on an environment setting. It's a cleaner way to describe conditional compilation than #if/#endif. The compiler understands the Conditional attribute, so it can do a better job of verifying code when conditional attributes are applied. The conditional attribute is applied at the method level, so it forces you to separate conditional code into distinct methods. Use the Conditional attribute instead of #if/#endif blocks when you create conditional code blocks.

Most veteran programmers have used conditional compilation to check pre- and post-conditions in an object. You would write a private method to check all the class and object invariants. That method would be conditionally compiled so that it appeared only in your debug builds.

```
private void CheckStateBad()
{
    // The Old way:
#if DEBUG
    Trace.WriteLine("Entering CheckState for Person");

    // Grab the name of the calling routine:
    string methodName =
      new StackTrace().GetFrame(1).GetMethod().Name;

    Debug.Assert(lastName != null,
      methodName,
      "Last Name cannot be null");

    Debug.Assert(lastName.Length > 0,
      methodName,
      "Last Name cannot be blank");

    Debug.Assert(firstName != null,
      methodName,
      "First Name cannot be null");

    Debug.Assert(firstName.Length > 0,
      methodName,
      "First Name cannot be blank");
```

```
    Trace.WriteLine("Exiting CheckState for Person");
#endif
}
```

Using the #if and #endif pragmas, you've created an empty method in your release builds. The CheckState() method gets called in all builds, release and debug. It doesn't do anything in the release builds, but you pay for the method call. You also pay a small cost to load and JIT the empty routine.

This practice works fine but can lead to subtle bugs that appear only in release builds. The following common mistake shows what can happen when you use pragmas for conditional compilation:

```
public void Func()
{
    string msg = null;

#if DEBUG
    msg = GetDiagnostics();
#endif
    Console.WriteLine(msg);
}
```

Everything works fine in your debug build, but your release builds happily print a blank message. That's not your intent. You goofed, but the compiler couldn't help you. You have code that is fundamental to your logic inside a conditional block. Sprinkling your source code with #if/#endif blocks makes it hard to diagnose the differences in behavior with the different builds.

C# has a better alternative: the Conditional attribute. Using the Conditional attribute, you can isolate functions that should be part of your classes only when a particular environment variable is defined or set to a certain value. The most common use of this feature is to instrument your code with debugging statements. The .NET Framework library already has the basic functionality you need for this use. This example shows how to use the debugging capabilities in the .NET Framework Library, to show you how conditional attributes work and when to add them to your code.

When you build the Person object, you add a method to verify the object invariants:

```
private void CheckState()
{
    // Grab the name of the calling routine:
    string methodName =
        new StackTrace().GetFrame(1).GetMethod().Name;

    Trace.WriteLine("Entering CheckState for Person:");
    Trace.Write("\tcalled by ");
    Trace.WriteLine(methodName);

    Debug.Assert(lastName != null,
        methodName,
        "Last Name cannot be null");

    Debug.Assert(lastName.Length > 0,
        methodName,
        "Last Name cannot be blank");

    Debug.Assert(firstName != null,
        methodName,
        "First Name cannot be null");

    Debug.Assert(firstName.Length > 0,
        methodName,
        "First Name cannot be blank");

    Trace.WriteLine("Exiting CheckState for Person");
}
```

You might not have encountered many library functions in this method, so let's go over them briefly. The StackTrace class gets the name of the calling method using Reflection. It's rather expensive, but it greatly simplifies tasks, such as generating information about program flow. Here, it determines the name of the method called CheckState. There is a minor risk here if the calling method is inlined, but the alternative is to have each method that calls CheckState() pass in the method name using Method-Base.GetCurrentMethod(). You'll see shortly why I decided against that strategy.

The remaining methods are part of the System.Diagnostics.Debug class or the System.Diagnostics.Trace class. The Debug.Assert method tests a condition and stops the program if that condition is false. The remaining parameters define messages that will be printed if the condition is false. Trace.WriteLine writes diagnostic messages to the debug console. So, this method writes messages and stops the program if a person object is invalid. You would call this method in all your public methods and properties as a precondition and a post-condition:

```
public string LastName
{
    get
    {
        CheckState();
        return lastName;
    }
    set
    {
        CheckState();
        lastName = value;
        CheckState();
    }
}
```

CheckState fires an assert the first time someone tries to set the last name to the empty string, or null. Then you fix your set accessor to check the parameter used for LastName. It's doing just what you want.

But this extra checking in each public routine takes time. You'll want to include this extra checking only when creating debug builds. That's where the Conditional attribute comes in:

```
[Conditional("DEBUG")]
private void CheckState()
{
    // same code as above
}
```

The Conditional attribute tells the C# compiler that this method should be called only when the compiler detects the DEBUG environment variable. The Conditional attribute does not affect the code generated for the CheckState() function; it modifies the calls to the function. If the DEBUG symbol is defined, you get this:

```csharp
public string LastName
{
    get
    {
        CheckState();
        return lastName;
    }
    set
    {
        CheckState();
        lastName = value;
        CheckState();
    }
}
```

If not, you get this:

```csharp
public string LastName
{
    get
    {
        return lastName;
    }
    set
    {
        lastName = value;
    }
}
```

The body of the CheckState() function is the same, regardless of the state of the environment variable. This is one example of why you need to understand the distinction made between the compilation and JIT steps in .NET. Whether the DEBUG environment variable is defined or not, the CheckState() method is compiled and delivered with the assembly. That might seem inefficient, but the only cost is disk space. The CheckState() function does not get loaded into memory and JITed unless it is called. Its presence in the assembly file is immaterial. This strategy increases flexibility and does so with minimal performance costs. You can get a deeper understanding by looking at the Debug class in the .NET Framework. On any machine with the .NET Framework installed, the System.dll assembly does have all the code for all the methods in the Debug class. Environment variables control whether they get called when callers are compiled. Using the Conditional directive enables you to create libraries with debugging features embedded. Those features can be enabled or disabled at runtime.

You can also create methods that depend on more than one environment variable. When you apply multiple conditional attributes, they are combined with OR. For example, this version of CheckState would be called when either DEBUG or TRACE is true:

```
[Conditional("DEBUG"),
 Conditional("TRACE")]
private void CheckState()
```

To create a construct using AND, you need to define the preprocessor symbol yourself using preprocessor directives in your source code:

```
#if ( VAR1 && VAR2 )
#define BOTH
#endif
```

Yes, to create a conditional routine that relies on the presence of more than one environment variable, you must fall back on your old practice of `#if`. All `#if` does is create a new symbol for you. But avoid putting any executable code inside that pragma.

Then, you could write the old version of CheckState this way:

```
private void CheckStateBad()
{
    // The Old way:
#if BOTH
    Trace.WriteLine("Entering CheckState for Person");

    // Grab the name of the calling routine:
    string methodName =
      new StackTrace().GetFrame(1).GetMethod().Name;

    Debug.Assert(lastName != null,
      methodName,
      "Last Name cannot be null");

    Debug.Assert(lastName.Length > 0,
      methodName,
      "Last Name cannot be blank");
```

```
    Debug.Assert(firstName != null,
      methodName,
       "First Name cannot be null");

    Debug.Assert(firstName.Length > 0,
      methodName,
       "First Name cannot be blank");

    Trace.WriteLine("Exiting CheckState for Person");
#endif
}
```

The Conditional attribute can be applied only to entire methods. In addition, any method with a Conditional attribute must have a return type of void. You cannot use the Conditional attribute for blocks of code inside methods or with methods that return values. Instead, create carefully constructed conditional methods and isolate the conditional behavior to those functions. You still need to review those conditional methods for side effects to the object state, but the Conditional attribute localizes those points much better than `#if`/`#endif`. With `#if` and `#endif` blocks, you can mistakenly remove important method calls or assignments.

The previous examples use the predefined DEBUG or TRACE symbols. But you can extend this technique for any symbols you define. The Conditional attribute can be controlled by symbols defined in a variety of ways. You can define symbols from the compiler command line, from environment variables in the operating system shell, or from pragmas in the source code.

You may have noticed that every method shown with the Conditional attribute has been a method that has a void return type and takes no parameters. That's a practice you should follow. The compiler enforces that conditional methods must have the void return type. However, you could create a method that takes any number of reference type parameters. That can lead to practices where an important side effect does not take place. Consider this snippet of code:

```
Queue<string> names = new Queue<string>();
names.Enqueue("one");
names.Enqueue("two");
names.Enqueue("three");
```

```
string item = string.Empty;
SomeMethod(item = names.Dequeue());
Console.WriteLine(item);
```

SomeMethod has been created with a Conditional attribute attached:

```
[Conditional("DEBUG")]
private static void SomeMethod(string param)
{

}
```

That's going to cause very subtle bugs. The call to SomeMethod() only happens when the DEBUG symbol is defined. If not, that call doesn't happen. Neither does the call to names.Dequeue(). Because the result is not needed, the method is not called. Any method marked with the Conditional attribute should not take any parameters. The user could use a method call with side effects to generate those parameters. Those method calls will not take place if the condition is not true.

The Conditional attribute generates more efficient IL than `#if/#endif` does. It also has the advantage of being applicable only at the function level, which forces you to better structure your conditional code. The compiler uses the Conditional attribute to help you avoid the common errors we've all made by placing the `#if` or `#endif` in the wrong spot. The Conditional attribute provides better support for you to cleanly separate conditional code than the preprocessor did.

Item 5: Always Provide ToString()

System.Object.ToString() is one of the most-used methods in the .NET environment. You should write a reasonable version for all the clients of your class. Otherwise, you force every user of your class to use the properties in your class and create a reasonable human-readable representation. This string representation of your type can be used to easily display information about an object to users: in Windows Presentation Foundation (WPF) controls, Silverlight controls, Web Forms, or console output. The string representation can also be useful for debugging. Every type that you create should provide a reasonable override of this method. When you create more complicated types, you should implement the more sophisticated IFormattable.ToString(). Face it: If you don't override this routine, or if you write a poor one, your clients are forced to fix it for you.

The System.Object version returns the fully qualified name of the type. It's useless information: "System.Drawing.Rect", "MyNamespace.Point", "SomeSample.Size" is not what you want to display to your users. But that's what you get when you don't override ToString() in your classes. You write a class once, but your clients use it many times. A little more work when you write the class pays off every time you or someone else uses it.

Let's consider the simplest requirement: overriding System.Object.ToString(). Every type you create should override ToString() to provide the most common textual representation of the type. Consider a Customer class with three public properties:

```
public class Customer
{
    public string Name
    {
        get;
        set;
    }
    public decimal Revenue
    {
        get;
        set;
    }
    public string ContactPhone
    {
        get;
        set;
    }

    public override string ToString()
    {
        return Name;
    }
}
```

The inherited version of Object.ToString() returns "Customer". That is never useful to anyone. Even if ToString() will be used only for debugging purposes, it should be more sophisticated than that. Your override of Object.ToString() should return the textual representation most likely to be used by clients of that class. In the Customer example, that's the name:

```
public override string ToString()
{
    return Name;
}
```

If you don't follow any of the other recommendations in this item, follow that exercise for all the types you define. It will save everyone time immediately. When you provide a reasonable implementation for the Object .ToString() method, objects of this class can be more easily added to WPF controls, Silverlight controls, Web Form controls, or printed output. The .NET BCL uses the override of Object.ToString() to display objects in any of the controls: combo boxes, list boxes, text boxes, and other controls. If you create a list of customer objects in a Windows Form or a Web Form, you get the name displayed as the text System.Console.WriteLine() and System.String.Format() as well as ToString() internally. Anytime the .NET BCL wants to get the string representation of a customer, your customer type supplies that customer's name. One simple three-line method handles all those basic requirements.

In C# 3.0, the compiler creates a default ToString() for all anonymous types. The generated ToString() method displays the value of each scalar property. Properties that represent sequences are LINQ query results and will display their type information instead of each value. This snippet of code:

```
int[] list = new int[] { 1, 2, 3, 4, 5, 6, 7, 8, 9, 10 };
var test = new { Name = "Me",
    Numbers = from l in list select l };
Console.WriteLine(test);
```

will display:

```
{ Name = Me, Numbers =
    System.Linq.Enumerable+WhereSelectArrayIterator`2
    [System.Int32,System.Int32] }
```

Even compiler-created anonymous types display a better output than your user-defined types unless you override ToString(). You should do a better job of supporting your users than the compiler does for a temporary type with a scope of one method.

This one simple method, ToString(), satisfies many of the requirements for displaying user-defined types as text. But sometimes, you need more.

The previous customer type has three fields: the name, the revenue, and a contact phone. The System.ToString() override uses only the name. You can address that deficiency by implementing the IFormattable interface on your type. IFormattable contains an overloaded ToString() method that lets you specify formatting information for your type. It's the interface you use when you need to create different forms of string output. The customer class is one of those instances. Users will want to create a report that contains the customer name and last year's revenue in a tabular format. The IFormattable.ToString() method provides the means for you to let users format string output from your type. The IFormattable.ToString() method signature contains a format string and a format provider:

```
string System.IFormattable.ToString(string format,
    IFormatProvider formatProvider)
```

You can use the format string to specify your own formats for the types you create. You can specify your own key characters for the format strings. In the customer example, you could specify n to mean the name, r for the revenue, and p for the phone. By allowing the user to specify combinations as well, you would create this version of IFormattable.ToString():

```
// supported formats:
// substitute n for name.
// substitute r for revenue
// substitute p for contact phone.
// Combos are supported:  nr, np, npr, etc
// "G" is general.
string System.IFormattable.ToString(string format,
    IFormatProvider formatProvider)
{
    if (formatProvider != null)
    {
        ICustomFormatter fmt = formatProvider.GetFormat(
          this.GetType())
          as ICustomFormatter;
        if (fmt != null)
            return fmt.Format(format, this, formatProvider);
    }

    switch (format)
    {
```

```
case "r":
    return Revenue.ToString();
case "p":
    return ContactPhone;
case "nr":
    return string.Format("{0,20}, {1,10:C}",
        Name, Revenue);
case "np":
    return string.Format("{0,20}, {1,15}",
        Name, ContactPhone);
case "pr":
    return string.Format("{0,15}, {1,10:C}",
        ContactPhone, Revenue);
case "pn":
    return string.Format("{0,15}, {1,20}",
        ContactPhone, Name);
case "rn":
    return string.Format("{0,10:C}, {1,20}",
        Revenue, Name);
case "rp":
    return string.Format("{0,10:C}, {1,20}",
        Revenue, ContactPhone);
case "nrp":
    return string.Format("{0,20}, {1,10:C}, {2,15}",
        Name, Revenue, ContactPhone);
case "npr":
    return string.Format("{0,20}, {1,15}, {2,10:C}",
        Name, ContactPhone, Revenue);
case "pnr":
    return string.Format("{0,15}, {1,20}, {2,10:C}",
        ContactPhone, Name, Revenue);
case "prn":
    return string.Format("{0,15}, {1,10:C}, {2,15}",
        ContactPhone, Revenue, Name);
case "rpn":
    return string.Format("{0,10:C}, {1,15}, {2,20}",
        Revenue, ContactPhone, Name);
case "rnp":
    return string.Format("{0,10:C}, {1,20}, {2,15}",
        Revenue, Name, ContactPhone);
```

```
        case "n":
        case "G":
        default:
            return Name;
    }
}
```

Adding this function gives your clients the capability to specify the presentation of their customer data:

```
IFormattable c1 = new Customer();
Console.WriteLine("Customer record: {0}",
  c1.ToString("nrp", null));
```

Any implementation of IFormattable.ToString() is specific to the type, but you must handle certain cases whenever you implement the IFormattable interface. First, you must support the general format, "G". Second, you must support the empty format in both variations: "" and null. All three format specifiers must return the same string as your override of the Object.ToString() method. The .NET Base Class Library (BCL) calls IFormattable.ToString() instead of Object.ToString() for every type that implements IFormattable. The .NET BCL usually calls IFormattable. ToString() with a null format string, but a few locations use the "G" format string to indicate the general format. If you add support for the IFormattable interface and do not support these standard formats, you've broken the automatic string conversions in the BCL. You can see that supporting IFormattable can quickly get out of hand. You can't anticipate all the possible format options that your type might support. At most, pick a few of the most likely formats. Client code should make up all the edge cases.

The second parameter to IFormattable.ToString() is an object that implements the IFormatProvider interface. This object lets clients provide formatting options that you did not anticipate. If you look at the previous implementation of IFormattable.ToString(), you will undoubtedly come up with any number of format options that you would like but that you find lacking. That's the nature of providing human-readable output. No matter how many different formats you support, your users will one day want some format that you did not anticipate. That's why the first few lines of the method look for an object that implements IFormatProvider and delegate the job to its ICustomFormatter.

Shift your focus now from class author to class consumer. You find that you want a format that is not supported. For example, you have customers whose names are longer than 20 characters, and you want to modify the format to provide a 50-character width for the customer name. That's why the IFormatProvider interface is there. You create a class that implements IFormatProvider and a companion class that implements ICustomFormatter to create your custom output formats. The IFormatProvider interface defines one method: GetFormat(). GetFormat() returns an object that implements the ICustomFormatter interface. The ICustomFormatter interface specifies the method that does the actual formatting. The following pair creates modified output that uses 50 columns for the customer name:

```csharp
// Example IFormatProvider:
public class CustomFormatter : IFormatProvider
{
    #region IFormatProvider Members
    // IFormatProvider contains one method.
    // This method returns an object that
    // formats using the requested interface.
    // Typically, only the ICustomFormatter
    // is implemented
    public object GetFormat(Type formatType)
    {
        if (formatType == typeof(ICustomFormatter))
            return new CustomerFormatProvider();
        return null;
    }
    #endregion

    // Nested class to provide the
    // custom formatting for the Customer class.
    private class CustomerFormatProvider : ICustomFormatter
    {
        #region ICustomFormatter Members
        public string Format(string format, object arg,
          IFormatProvider formatProvider)
        {
            Customer c = arg as Customer;
            if (c == null)
                return arg.ToString();
            return string.Format("{0,50}, {1,15}, {2,10:C}",
              c.Name, c.ContactPhone, c.Revenue);
        }
```

```
    #endregion
  }
}
```

The GetFormat() method creates the object that implements the ICustomFormatter interface. The ICustomFormatter.Format() method does the actual work of formatting the output in the requested manner. That one method translates the object into a string format. You can define the format strings for ICustomFormatter.Format() so that you can specify multiple formats in one routine. The FormatProvider will be the IFormatProvider object from the GetFormat() method.

To specify your custom format, you need to explicitly call string.Format() with the IFormatProvider object:

```
Console.WriteLine(string.Format(new CustomFormatter(),
    "", c1));
```

You can create IFormatProvider and ICustomFormatter implementations for classes whether or not the class implemented the IFormattable interface. So, even if the class author didn't provide reasonable ToString() behavior, you can make your own. Of course, from outside the class, you have access to only the public properties and data members to construct your strings. Writing two classes, IFormatProvider and ICustomFormatter, is a lot of work just to get text output. But implementing your specific text output using this form means that it is supported everywhere in the .NET Framework.

So now step back into the role of class author again. Overriding Object.ToString() is the simplest way to provide a string representation of your classes. You should provide that every time you create a type. It should be the most obvious, most common representation of your type. It must not be too verbose. It may end up in controls, HTML pages, or other human-readable locations. On those rare occasions when your type is expected to provide more sophisticated output, you should take advantage of implementing the IFormattable interface. It provides the standard way for users of your class to customize the text output for your type. If you leave these out, your users are left with implementing custom formatters. Those solutions require more code, and because users are outside of your class, they cannot examine the internal state of the object. But of course, publishers cannot anticipate all potential formats.

Eventually, people consume the information in your types. People understand text output, so you want to provide it in the simplest fashion possible: Override ToString() in all your types. Make the ToString() output short and reasonable.

Item 6: Understand the Relationships Among the Many Different Concepts of Equality

When you create your own types (either classes or `structs`), you define what equality means for that type. C# provides four different functions that determine whether two different objects are "equal":

```
public static bool ReferenceEquals
    (object left, object right);
public static bool Equals
    (object left, object right);
public virtual bool Equals(object right);
public static bool operator ==(MyClass left, MyClass right);
```

The language enables you to create your own versions of all four of these methods. But just because you can doesn't mean that you should. You should never redefine the first two static functions. You'll often create your own instance Equals() method to define the semantics of your type, and you'll occasionally override operator==(), typically for performance reasons in value types. Furthermore, there are relationships among these four functions, so when you change one, you can affect the behavior of the others. Yes, needing four functions to test equality is complicated. But don't worry—you can simplify it.

Of course, those four methods are not the only options for equality. Types that override Equals() should implement IEquatable<T>. Types that implement value semantics should implement the IStructuralEquality interface. That means six different ways to express equality.

Like so many of the complicated elements in C#, this one follows from the fact that C# enables you to create both value types and reference types. Two variables of a reference type are equal if they refer to the same object, referred to as object identity. Two variables of a value type are equal if they are the same type and they contain the same contents. That's why equality tests need so many different methods.

Let's start with the two functions you should never change. Object
.ReferenceEquals() returns true if two variables refer to the same object—
that is, the two variables have the same object identity. Whether the types
being compared are reference types or value types, this method always tests
object identity, not object contents. Yes, that means that ReferenceEquals()
always returns false when you use it to test equality for value types. Even
when you compare a value type to itself, ReferenceEquals() returns false.
This is due to boxing, which is covered in Item 45.

```
int i = 5;
int j = 5;
if (Object.ReferenceEquals(i, j))
    Console.WriteLine("Never happens.");
else
    Console.WriteLine("Always happens.");

if (Object.ReferenceEquals(i, i))
    Console.WriteLine("Never happens.");
else
    Console.WriteLine("Always happens.");
```

You'll never redefine Object.ReferenceEquals() because it does exactly what
it is supposed to do: tests the object identity of two different variables.

The second function you'll never redefine is static Object.Equals(). This
method tests whether two variables are equal when you don't know the
runtime type of the two arguments. Remember that System.Object is the
ultimate base class for everything in C#. Anytime you compare two variables, they are instances of System.Object. Value types and reference types
are instances of System.Object. So how does this method test the equality
of two variables, without knowing their type, when equality changes its
meaning depending on the type? The answer is simple: This method delegates that responsibility to one of the types in question. The static
Object.Equals() method is implemented something like this:

```
public static new bool Equals(object left, object right)
{
    // Check object identity
    if (Object.ReferenceEquals(left, right) )
        return true;
    // both null references handled above
```

```
    if (Object.ReferenceEquals(left, null) ||
        Object.ReferenceEquals(right, null))
        return false;
    return left.Equals(right);
}
```

This example code introduces a method I have not discussed yet: namely, the instance Equals() method. I'll explain that in detail, but I'm not ready to end my discussion of the static Equals() just yet. For right now, I want you to understand that static Equals() uses the instance Equals() method of the left argument to determine whether two objects are equal.

As with ReferenceEquals(), you'll never overload or redefine your own version of the static Object.Equals() method because it already does exactly what it needs to do: determines whether two objects are the same when you don't know the runtime type. Because the static Equals() method delegates to the left argument's instance Equals(), it uses the rules for that type.

Now you understand why you never need to redefine the static ReferenceEquals() and static Equals() methods. It's time to discuss the methods you will override. But first, let's briefly discuss the mathematical properties of an equality relation. You need to make sure that your definition and implementation are consistent with other programmers' expectations. This means that you need to keep in mind the mathematical properties of equality: Equality is reflexive, symmetric, and transitive. The reflexive property means that any object is equal to itself. No matter what type is involved, a == a is always true. The symmetric property means that order does not matter: If a == b is true, b == a is also true. If a == b is false, b == a is also false. The last property is that if a == b and b == c are both true, then a == c must also be true. That's the transitive property.

Now it's time to discuss the instance Object.Equals() function, including when and how you override it. You create your own instance version of Equals() when the default behavior is inconsistent with your type. The Object.Equals() method uses object identity to determine whether two variables are equal. The default Object.Equals() function behaves exactly the same as Object.ReferenceEquals(). But wait—value types are different. System.ValueType does override Object.Equals(). Remember that ValueType is the base class for all value types that you create (using the `struct` keyword). Two variables of a value type are equal if they are the same type and they have the same contents. ValueType.Equals() implements that behavior. Unfortunately, ValueType.Equals() does not have an efficient implementation. ValueType.Equals() is the base class for all value types. To provide the correct behavior, it must compare all the member variables in any derived type, without knowing the runtime type of the object. In C#, that means using reflection. As you'll see in Item 43, there are many disadvantages to reflection, especially when performance is a goal. Equality is one of those fundamental constructs that gets called frequently in programs, so performance is a worthy goal. Under almost all circumstances, you can write a much faster override of Equals() for any value type. The recommendation for value types is simple: Always create an override of ValueType.Equals() whenever you create a value type.

You should override the instance Equals() function only when you want to change the defined semantics for a reference type. A number of classes in the .NET Framework Class Library use value semantics instead of reference semantics for equality. Two string objects are equal if they contain the same contents. Two DataRowView objects are equal if they refer to the same DataRow. The point is that if your type should follow value semantics (comparing contents) instead of reference semantics (comparing object identity), you should write your own override of instance Object.Equals().

Now that you know when to write your own override of Object.Equals(), you must understand how you should implement it. The equality relationship for value types has many implications for boxing and is discussed in Item 45. For reference types, your instance method needs to follow predefined behavior to avoid strange surprises for users of your class. Whenever you override Equals(), you'll want to implement IEquatable<T> for that type. I'll explain why a little further into this item. Here is the standard pattern for overriding System.Object.Equals. The highlight shows the changes to implement IEquatable<T>.

```csharp
public class Foo : IEquatable<Foo>
{
    public override bool Equals(object right)
    {
        // check null:
        // this pointer is never null in C# methods.
        if (object.ReferenceEquals(right, null))
            return false;

        if (object.ReferenceEquals(this, right))
            return true;
```

```
        // Discussed below.
        if (this.GetType() != right.GetType())
            return false;

        // Compare this type's contents here:
        return this.Equals(right as Foo);
    }


    #region IEquatable<Foo> Members
    public bool Equals(Foo other)
    {
        // elided.
        return true;
    }
    #endregion
}
```

First, Equals() should never throw exceptions—it doesn't make much sense. Two variables are or are not equal; there's not much room for other failures. Just return false for all failure conditions, such as null references or the wrong argument types. Now, let's go through this method in detail so you understand why each check is there and why some checks can be left out. The first check determines whether the right-side object is null. There is no check on this reference. In C#, this is never null. The CLR throws an exception before calling any instance method through a null reference. The next check determines whether the two object references are the same, testing object identity. It's a very efficient test, and equal object identity guarantees equal contents.

The next check determines whether the two objects being compared are the same type. The exact form is important. First, notice that it does not assume that this is of type Foo; it calls this.GetType(). The actual type might be a class derived from Foo. Second, the code checks the exact type of objects being compared. It is not enough to ensure that you can convert the right-side parameter to the current type. That test can cause two subtle bugs. Consider the following example involving a small inheritance hierarchy:

```
public class B : IEquatable<B>
{
    public override bool Equals(object right)
    {
        // check null:
```

```csharp
        if (object.ReferenceEquals(right, null))
            return false;

        // Check reference equality:
        if (object.ReferenceEquals(this, right))
            return true;

        // Problems here, discussed below.
        B rightAsB = right as B;
        if (rightAsB == null)
            return false;

        return this.Equals(rightAsB);
    }

    #region IEquatable<B> Members

    public bool Equals(B other)
    {
        // elided
        return true;
    }

    #endregion
}

public class D : B, IEquatable<D>
{
    // etc.
    public override bool Equals(object right)
    {
        // check null:
        if (object.ReferenceEquals(right, null))
            return false;

        if (object.ReferenceEquals(this, right))
            return true;

        // Problems here.
        D rightAsD = right as D;
```

```
            if (rightAsD == null)
                return false;

            if (base.Equals(rightAsD) == false)
                return false;

            return this.Equals(rightAsD);
    }

    #region IEquatable<D> Members
    public bool Equals(D other)
    {
        // elided.
        return true; // or false, based on test
    }
    #endregion
}


//Test:
B baseObject = new B();
D derivedObject = new D();

// Comparison 1.
if (baseObject.Equals(derivedObject))
    Console.WriteLine("Equals");
else
    Console.WriteLine("Not Equal");

// Comparison 2.
if (derivedObject.Equals(baseObject))
    Console.WriteLine("Equals");
else
    Console.WriteLine("Not Equal");
```

Under any possible circumstances, you would expect to see either Equals or Not Equal printed twice. Because of some errors, this is not the case with the previous code. The second comparison will never return true. The base object, of type B, can never be converted into a D. However, the first comparison might evaluate to true. The derived object, of type D, can be implicitly converted to a type B. If the B members of the right-side argument match the B members of the left-side argument, B.Equals() considers the objects equal. Even though the two objects are different types, your method has considered them equal. You've broken the symmetric property of Equals. This construct broke because of the automatic conversions that take place up and down the inheritance hierarchy.

When you write this, the D object is explicitly converted to a B:

```
baseObject.Equals(derived)
```

If baseObject.Equals() determines that the fields defined in its type match, the two objects are equal. On the other hand, when you write this, the B object cannot be converted to a D object:

```
derivedObject.Equals(base)
```

The derivedObject.Equals() method always returns false. If you don't check the object types exactly, you can easily get into this situation, in which the order of the comparison matters.

All of the examples above also showed another important practice when you override Equals(). Overriding Equals() means that your type should implement IEquatable<T>. IEquatable<T> contains one method: Equals(T other). Implemented IEquatable<T> means that your type also supports a type-safe equality comparison. If you consider that the Equals() should return true only in the case where the right-hand side of the equation is of the same type as the left side, IEquatable<T> simply lets the compiler catch numerous occasions where the two objects would be not equal.

There is another practice to follow when you override Equals(). You should call the base class only if the base version is not provided by System.Object or System.ValueType. The previous code provides an example. Class D calls the Equals() method defined in its base class, Class B. However, Class B does not call baseObject.Equals(). It calls the version defined in System.Object, which returns true only when the two arguments refer to the same object. That's not what you want, or you wouldn't have written your own method in the first place.

The rule is to override Equals() whenever you create a value type, and to override Equals() on reference types when you do not want your reference type to obey reference semantics, as defined by System.Object. When you write your own Equals(), follow the implementation just outlined. Overriding Equals() means that you should write an override for GetHashCode(). See Item 7 for details.

We're almost done. operator==() is simple. Anytime you create a value type, redefine operator==(). The reason is exactly the same as with the instance Equals() function. The default version uses reflection to compare the contents of two value types. That's far less efficient than any implementation that you would write, so write your own. Follow the recommendations in Item 46 to avoid boxing when you compare value types.

Notice that I didn't say that you should write operator==() whenever you override instance Equals(). I said to write operator==() when you create value types. You should rarely override operator==() when you create reference types. The .NET Framework classes expect operator==() to follow reference semantics for all reference types.

Finally, you come to IStructuralEquality, which is implemented on System.Array and the Tuple<> generic classes. It enables those types to implement value semantics without enforcing value semantics for every comparison. It is doubtful that you'll ever create types that implement IStructuralEquality. It is needed only for those lightweight types. Implementing IStructuralEquality declares that a type can be composed into a larger object that implements value-based semantics.

C# gives you numerous ways to test equality, but you need to consider providing your own definitions for only two of them, along with supporting the analogous interfaces. You never override the static Object.ReferenceEquals() and static Object.Equals() because they provide the correct tests, regardless of the runtime type. You always override instance Equals() and operator==() for value types to provide better performance. You override instance Equals() for reference types when you want equality to mean something other than object identity. Anytime you override Equals() you implement IEquatable<T>. Simple, right?

Item 7: Understand the Pitfalls of GetHashCode()

This is the only item in this book dedicated to one function that you should avoid writing. GetHashCode() is used in one place only: to define the hash value for keys in a hash-based collection, typically the HashSet<T> or Dictionary<K,V> containers. That's good because there are a number of problems with the base class implementation of GetHashCode(). For reference types, it works but is inefficient. For value types, the base class version is often incorrect. But it gets worse. It's entirely possible that you cannot write GetHashCode() so that it is both efficient and correct. No single function generates more discussion and more confusion than GetHashCode(). Read on to remove all that confusion.

If you're defining a type that won't ever be used as the key in a container, this won't matter. Types that represent window controls, Web page controls, or database connections are unlikely to be used as keys in a collection. In those cases, do nothing. All reference types will have a hash code that is correct, even if it is very inefficient. Value types should be immutable (see Item 20), in which case, the default implementation always works, although it is also inefficient. In most types that you create, the best approach is to avoid the existence of GetHashCode() entirely.

One day, you'll create a type that is meant to be used as a hash key, and you'll need to write your own implementation of GetHashCode(), so read on. Hash-based containers use hash codes to optimize searches. Every object generates an integer value called a hash code. Objects are stored in buckets based on the value of that hash code. To search for an object, you request its key and search just that one bucket. In .NET, every object has a hash code, determined by System.Object.GetHashCode(). Any overload of GetHashCode() must follow these three rules:

1. If two objects are equal (as defined by operator==), they must generate the same hash value. Otherwise, hash codes can't be used to find objects in containers.
2. For any object A, A.GetHashCode() must be an instance invariant. No matter what methods are called on A, A.GetHashCode() must always return the same value. That ensures that an object placed in a bucket is always in the right bucket.
3. The hash function should generate a random distribution among all integers for all inputs. That's how you get efficiency from a hash-based container.

Writing a correct and efficient hash function requires extensive knowledge of the type to ensure that rule 3 is followed. The versions defined in System.Object and System.ValueType do not have that advantage. These versions must provide the best default behavior with almost no knowledge of your particular type. Object.GetHashCode() uses an internal field in the System.Object class to generate the hash value. Each object created is assigned a unique object key, stored as an integer, when it is created. These keys start at 1 and increment every time a new object of any type gets created. The object identity field is set in the System.Object constructor and cannot be modified later. Object.GetHashCode() returns this value as the hash code for a given object.

Now examine Object.GetHashCode() in light of those three rules. If two objects are equal, Object.GetHashCode() returns the same hash value, unless you've overridden operator==. System.Object's version of operator==() tests object identity. GetHashCode() returns the internal object identity field. It works. However, if you've supplied your own version of operator==, you must also supply your own version of GetHashCode() to ensure that the first rule is followed. See Item 6 for details on equality.

The second rule is followed: After an object is created, its hash code never changes.

The third rule, a random distribution among all integers for all inputs, does not hold. A numeric sequence is not a random distribution among all integers unless you create an enormous number of objects. The hash codes generated by Object.GetHashCode() are concentrated at the low end of the range of integers.

This means that Object.GetHashCode() is correct but not efficient. If you create a hashtable based on a reference type that you define, the default behavior from System.Object is a working, but slow, hashtable. When you create reference types that are meant to be hash keys, you should override GetHashCode() to get a better distribution of the hash values across all integers for your specific type.

Before covering how to write your own override of GetHashCode, this section examines ValueType.GetHashCode() with respect to those same three rules. System.ValueType overrides GetHashCode(), providing the default behavior for all value types. Its version returns the hash code from the first field defined in the type. Consider this example:

```
public struct MyStruct
{
    private string msg;
    private int id;
    private DateTime epoch;
}
```

The hash code returned from a MyStruct object is the hash code generated by the msg field. The following code snippet always returns true, assuming msg is not null:

```
MyStruct s = new MyStruct();
s.SetMessage("Hello");
return s.GetHashCode() == s.GetMessage().GetHashCode();
```

The first rule says that two objects that are equal (as defined by operator==()) must have the same hash code. This rule is followed for value types under most conditions, but you can break it, just as you could with for reference types. ValueType.operator==() compares the first field in the struct, along with every other field. That satisfies rule 1. As long as any override that you define for operator== uses the first field, it will work. Any struct whose first field does not participate in the equality of the type violates this rule, breaking GetHashCode().

The second rule states that the hash code must be an instance invariant. That rule is followed only when the first field in the struct is an immutable field. If the value of the first field can change, so can the hash code. That breaks the rules. Yes, GetHashCode() is broken for any struct that you create when the first field can be modified during the lifetime of the object. It's yet another reason why immutable value types are your best bet (see Item 20).

The third rule depends on the type of the first field and how it is used. If the first field generates a random distribution across all integers, and the first field is distributed across all values of the struct, then the struct generates an even distribution as well. However, if the first field often has the same value, this rule is violated. Consider a small change to the earlier struct:

```
public struct MyStruct
{
    private DateTime epoch;
    private string msg;
    private int id;
}
```

If the epoch field is set to the current date (not including the time), all MyStruct objects created in a given date will have the same hash code. That prevents an even distribution among all hash code values.

Summarizing the default behavior, Object.GetHashCode() works correctly for reference types, although it does not necessarily generate an efficient distribution. (If you have overridden Object.operator==(), you can break

GetHashCode()). ValueType.GetHashCode() works only if the first field in your `struct` is read-only. ValueType.GetHashCode() generates an efficient hash code only when the first field in your `struct` contains values across a meaningful subset of its inputs.

If you're going to build a better hash code, you need to place some constraints on your type. Ideally, you'd create an immutable value type. The rules for a working GetHashCode() are simpler for immutable value types than they are for unconstrained types. Examine the three rules again, this time in the context of building a working implementation of GetHashCode().

First, if two objects are equal, as defined by operator==(), they must return the same hash value. Any property or data value used to generate the hash code must also participate in the equality test for the type. Obviously, this means that the same properties used for equality are used for hash code generation. It's possible to have properties participate in equality that are not used in the hash code computation. The default behavior for System.ValueType does just that, but it often means that rule 3 usually gets violated. The same data elements should participate in both computations.

The second rule is that the return value of GetHashCode() must be an instance invariant. Imagine that you defined a reference type, Customer:

```
public class Customer
{
    private string name;
    private decimal revenue;

    public Customer(string name)
    {
        this.name = name;
    }

    public string Name
    {
        get { return name; }
        set { name = value; }
    }

    public override int GetHashCode()
    {
```

```
        return name.GetHashCode();
    }
}
```

Suppose that you execute the following code snippet:

```
Customer c1 = new Customer("Acme Products");
myHashMap.Add(c1, orders);
// Oops, the name is wrong:
c1.Name = "Acme Software";
```

c1 is lost somewhere in the hash map. When you placed c1 in the map, the hash code was generated from the string "Acme Products". After you change the name of the customer to "Acme Software", the hash code value changed. It's now being generated from the new name: "Acme Software". c1 is stored in the bucket defined by "Acme Products", but it should be in the bucket defined for "Acme Software". You've lost that customer in your own collection. It's lost because the hash code is not an object invariant. You've changed the correct bucket after storing the object.

The earlier situation can occur only if Customer is a reference type. Value types misbehave differently, but they still cause problems. If customer is a value type, a copy of c1 gets stored in the hash map. The last line changing the value of the name has no effect on the copy stored in the hash map. Because boxing and unboxing make copies as well, it's very unlikely that you can change the members of a value type after that object has been added to a collection.

The only way to address rule 2 is to define the hash code function to return a value based on some invariant property or properties of the object. System.Object abides by this rule using the object identity, which does not change. System.ValueType hopes that the first field in your type does not change. You can't do better without making your type immutable. When you define a value type that is intended for use as a key type in a hash container, it must be an immutable type. If you violate this recommendation, then the users of your type will find a way to break hashtables that use your type as keys. Revisiting the Customer class, you can modify it so that the customer name is immutable. The highlight shows the changes to make a customer's name immutable:

```
public class Customer
{
```

```csharp
private string name;
private decimal revenue;

public Customer(string name)
{
    this.name = name;
}

public string Name
{
    get { return name; }
    // Name is readonly
}

public decimal Revenue
{
    get { return revenue; }
    set { revenue = value; }
}

public override int GetHashCode()
{
    return name.GetHashCode();
}

public Customer ChangeName(string newName)
{
    return new Customer(newName) { Revenue = revenue };
}
}
```

ChangeName() creates a new Customer object, using the constructor and object initialize syntax to set the current revenue. Making the name immutable changes how you must work with customer objects to modify the name:

```csharp
Customer c1 = new Customer("Acme Products");
myDictionary.Add(c1, orders);
// Oops, the name is wrong:
Customer c2 = c1.ChangeName("Acme Software");
Order o = myDictionary[c1];
```

```
myDictionary.Remove(c1);
myDictionary.Add(c2, o);
```

You have to remove the original customer, change the name, and add the new Customer object to the dictionary. It looks more cumbersome than the first version, but it works. The previous version allowed programmers to write incorrect code. By enforcing the immutability of the properties used to calculate the hash code, you enforce correct behavior. Users of your type can't go wrong. Yes, this version is more work. You're forcing developers to write more code, but only because it's the only way to write the correct code. Make certain that any data members used to calculate the hash value are immutable.

The third rule says that GetHashCode() should generate a random distribution among all integers for all inputs. Satisfying this requirement depends on the specifics of the types you create. If a magic formula existed, it would be implemented in System.Object, and this item would not exist. A common and successful algorithm is to XOR all the return values from GetHashCode() on all fields in a type. If your type contains some mutable fields, exclude those fields from the calculations.

GetHashCode() has very specific requirements: Equal objects must produce equal hash codes, and hash codes must be object invariants and must produce an even distribution to be efficient. All three can be satisfied only for immutable types. For other types, rely on the default behavior, but understand the pitfalls.

Item 8: Prefer Query Syntax to Loops

There is no lack of support for different control structures in the C# language: `for`, `while`, `do / while`, and `foreach`, are all part of the language. It's doubtful the language designers missed any amazing looping construct from the past history of computer language design. But there's often a much better way: query syntax.

Query syntax enables you to move your program logic from a more imperative model to a declarative model. Query syntax defines what the answer is and defers the decision about how to create that answer to the particular implementation. Throughout this item, where I refer to query syntax, you can get the same benefits through the method call syntax as you can from the query syntax. The important point is that the query syntax, and by extension, the method syntax that implements the query expression pattern, provides a cleaner expression of your intent than imperative looping constructs.

This code snippet shows an imperative method of filling an array and then printing its contents to the Console:

```
int[] foo = new int[100];

for (int num = 0; num < foo.Length; num++)
    foo[num] = num * num;

foreach (int i in foo)
    Console.WriteLine(i.ToString());
```

Even this small example focuses too much on how actions are performed than on what actions are performed. Reworking this small example to use the query syntax creates more readable code and enables reuse of different building blocks.

As a first step, you can change the generation of the array to a query result:

```
int[] foo = (from n in Enumerable.Range(0, 100)
                select n * n).ToArray();
```

You can then do a similar change to the second loop, although you'll also need to write an extension method to perform some action on all the elements:

```
foo.ForAll((n) => Console.WriteLine(n.ToString()));
```

The .NET BCL has a ForAll implementation in List<T>. It's just as simple to create one for IEnumerable<T>:

```
public static class Extensions
{
    public static void ForAll<T>(
        this IEnumerable<T> sequence,
        Action<T> action)
    {
        foreach (T item in sequence)
            action(item);
    }
}
```

It may not look that significant, but it can enable more reuse. Anytime you are performing work on a sequence of elements, ForAll can do the work.

This is a small, simple operation, so you may not see much benefit. In fact, you're probably right. Let's look at some different problems.

Many operations require you to work through nested loops. Suppose you need to generate (X,Y) pairs for all integers from 0 through 99. It's obvious how you would do that with nested loops:

```
private static IEnumerable<Tuple<int, int>> ProduceIndices()
{
    for (int x = 0; x < 100; x++)
        for (int y = 0; y < 100; y++)
            yield return Tuple.Create(x, y);
}
```

Of course, you could produce the same objects with a query:

```
private static IEnumerable<Tuple<int, int>> QueryIndices()
{
    return from x in Enumerable.Range(0, 100)
           from y in Enumerable.Range(0, 100)
           select Tuple.Create(x, y);
}
```

They look similar, but the query syntax keeps its simplicity even as the problem description gets more difficult. Change the problem to generating only those pairs where the sum of X and Y is less than 100. Compare these two methods:

```
private static IEnumerable<Tuple<int, int>> ProduceIndices2()
{
    for (int x = 0; x < 100; x++)
        for (int y = 0; y < 100; y++)
            if (x + y < 100)
                yield return Tuple.Create(x, y);
}


private static IEnumerable<Tuple<int, int>> QueryIndices2()
{
    return from x in Enumerable.Range(0, 100)
           from y in Enumerable.Range(0, 100)
```

```
        where x + y < 100
        select Tuple.Create(x, y);
}
```

It's still close, but the imperative syntax starts to hide its meaning under the necessary syntax used to produce the result. So let's change the problem a bit again. Now, add that you must return the points in decreasing order based on their distance from the origin.

Here are two different methods that would produce the correct result:

```
private static IEnumerable<Tuple<int, int>> ProduceIndices3()
{
    var storage = new List<Tuple<int, int>>();

    for (int x = 0; x < 100; x++)
        for (int y = 0; y < 100; y++)
            if (x + y < 100)
                storage.Add(Tuple.Create(x, y));

    storage.Sort((point1, point2) =>
        (point2.Item1*point2.Item1 +
         point2.Item2 * point2.Item2).CompareTo(
        point1.Item1 * point1.Item1 +
        point1.Item2 * point1.Item2));
    return storage;
}
private static IEnumerable<Tuple<int, int>> QueryIndices3()
{
    return from x in Enumerable.Range(0, 100)
           from y in Enumerable.Range(0, 100)
           where x + y < 100
           orderby (x*x + y*y) descending
           select Tuple.Create(x, y);
}
```

Something clearly changed now. The imperative version is much more difficult to comprehend. If you looked quickly, you almost certainly did not notice that the arguments on the comparison function got reversed. That's to ensure that the sort is in descending order. Without comments, or other supporting documentation, the imperative code is much more difficult to read.

Even if you did spot where the parameter order was reversed, did you think that it was an error? The imperative model places so much more emphasis on how actions are performed that it's easy to get lost in those actions and lose the original intent for what actions are being accomplished.

There's one more justification for using query syntax over looping constructs: Queries create a more composable API than looping constructs can provide. Query syntax naturally leads to constructing algorithms as small blocks of code that perform one operation on a sequence. The deferred execution model for queries enables developers to compose these single operations into multiple operations that can be accomplished in one enumeration of the sequence. Looping constructs cannot be similarly composed. You must either create interim storage for each step, or create methods for each combination of operations on a sequence.

That last example shows how this works. The operation combines a filter (the where clause) with a sort (the orderby clause) and a projection (the select clause). All of these are accomplished in one enumeration operation. The imperative version creates an interim storage model and separates the sort into a distinct operation.

I've discussed this as query syntax, though you should remember that every query has a corresponding method call syntax. Sometimes the query is more natural, and sometimes the method call syntax is more natural. In the example above, the query syntax is much more readable. Here's the equivalent method call syntax:

```
private static IEnumerable<Tuple<int, int>> MethodIndices3()
{
    return Enumerable.Range(0, 100).
        SelectMany(x => Enumerable.Range(0,100),
        (x,y) => Tuple.Create(x,y)).
        Where(pt => pt.Item1 + pt.Item2 < 100).
        OrderByDescending(pt =>
            pt.Item1* pt.Item1 + pt.Item2 * pt.Item2);
}
```

It's a matter of style whether the query or the method call syntax is more readable. In this instance, I'm convinced the query syntax is clearer. However, other examples may be different. Furthermore, some methods do not have equivalent query syntax. Methods such as Take, TakeWhile, Skip, SkipWhile, Min, and Max require you to use the method syntax at some level. Other languages, in particular VB.NET, did define query syntax for many of these keywords.

This is the part of any discussion where someone usually asserts that queries perform more slowly than other loops. While you can certainly create examples where a hand-coded loop will outperform a query, it's not a general rule. You do need to measure performance to determine if you have a specific case where the query constructs don't perform well enough. However, before completely rewriting an algorithm, consider the parallel extensions for LINQ. Another advantage to using query syntax is that you can execute those queries in parallel using the .AsParallel() method. (See Item 35.)

C# began as an imperative language. It continues to include all the features that are part of that heritage. It's natural to reach for the most familiar tools at your disposal. However, those tools might not be the best tools. When you find yourself writing any form of a looping construct, ask yourself if you can write that code as a query. If the query syntax does not work, consider using the method call syntax instead. In almost all cases, you'll find that you create cleaner code than you would using imperative looping constructs.

Item 9: Avoid Conversion Operators in Your APIs

Conversion operators introduce a kind of substitutability between classes. Substitutability means that one class can be substituted for another. This can be a benefit: An object of a derived class can be substituted for an object of its base class, as in the classic example of the shape hierarchy. You create a Shape base class and derive a variety of customizations: Rectangle, Ellipse, Circle, and so on. You can substitute a Circle anywhere a Shape is expected. That's using polymorphism for substitutability. It works because a circle is a specific type of shape. When you create a class, certain conversions are allowed automatically. Any object can be substituted for an instance of System.Object, the root of the .NET class hierarchy. In the same fashion, any object of a class that you create will be substituted implicitly for an interface that it implements, any of its base interfaces, or any of its base classes. The language also supports a variety of numeric conversions.

When you define a conversion operator for your type, you tell the compiler that your type may be substituted for the target type. These substitutions often result in subtle errors because your type probably isn't a perfect substitute for the target type. Side effects that modify the state of the target type won't have the same effect on your type. Worse, if your conversion operator returns a temporary object, the side effects will modify the temporary object and be lost forever to the garbage collector. Finally, the rules for invoking conversion operators are based on the compile-time type of an object, not the runtime type of an object. Users of your type might need to perform multiple casts to invoke the conversion operators, a practice that leads to unmaintainable code.

If you want to convert another type into your type, use a constructor. This more clearly reflects the action of creating a new object. Conversion operators can introduce hard-to-find problems in your code. Suppose that you inherit the code for a library shown in Figure 1.1. Both the Circle class and the Ellipse class are derived from the Shape class. You decide to leave that hierarchy in place because you believe that, although the Circle and Ellipse are related, you don't want to have nonabstract leaf classes in your hierarchy, and several implementation problems occur when you try to derive the Circle class from the Ellipse class. However, you realize that every circle could be an ellipse. In addition, some ellipses could be substituted for circles.

That leads you to add two conversion operators. Every Circle is an Ellipse, so you add an implicit conversion to create a new Ellipse from a Circle. An implicit conversion operator will be called whenever one type needs to be converted to another type. By contrast, an explicit conversion will be called only when the programmer puts a cast operator in the source code.

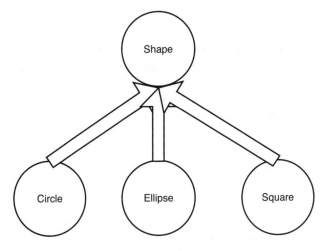

Figure 1.1 Basic shape hierarchy.

```
public class Circle : Shape
{
    private PointF center;
    private float radius;

    public Circle() :
        this(PointF.Empty, 0)
    {
    }

    public Circle(PointF c, float r)
    {
        center = c;
        radius = r;
    }

    public override void Draw()
    {
        //...
    }

    static public implicit operator Ellipse(Circle c)
    {
        return new Ellipse(c.center, c.center,
          c.radius, c.radius);
    }
}
```

Now that you've got the implicit conversion operator, you can use a Circle anywhere an Ellipse is expected. Furthermore, the conversion happens automatically:

```
public static double ComputeArea(Ellipse e)
{
    // return the area of the ellipse.
    return e.R1 * e.R2 * Math.PI;
}


// call it:
Circle c1 = new Circle(new PointF(3.0f, 0), 5.0f);
ComputeArea(c1);
```

This sample shows what I mean by substitutability: A circle has been substituted for an ellipse. The ComputeArea function works even with the substitution. You got lucky. But examine this function:

```
public static void Flatten(Ellipse e)
{
    e.R1 /= 2;
    e.R2 *= 2;
}


// call it using a circle:
Circle c = new Circle(new PointF(3.0f, 0), 5.0f);
Flatten(c);
```

This won't work. The Flatten() method takes an ellipse as an argument. The compiler must somehow convert a circle to an ellipse. You've created an implicit conversion that does exactly that. Your conversion gets called, and the Flatten() function receives as its parameter the ellipse created by your implicit conversion. This temporary object is modified by the Flatten() function and immediately becomes garbage. The side effects expected from your Flatten() function occur, but only on a temporary object. The end result is that nothing happens to the circle, c.

Changing the conversion from implicit to explicit only forces users to add a cast to the call:

```
Circle c = new Circle(new PointF(3.0f, 0), 5.0f);
Flatten((Ellipse)c);
```

The original problem remains. You just forced your users to add a cast to cause the problem. You still create a temporary object, flatten the temporary object, and throw it away. The circle, c, is not modified at all. Instead, if you create a constructor to convert the Circle to an Ellipse, the actions are clearer:

```
Circle c = new Circle(new PointF(3.0f, 0), 5.0f);
Flatten(new Ellipse(c));
```

Most programmers would see the previous two lines and immediately realize that any modifications to the ellipse passed to Flatten() are lost. They would fix the problem by keeping track of the new object:

```
Circle c = new Circle(new PointF(3.0f, 0), 5.0f);
Flatten(c);
```

```
// Work with the circle.
// ...

// Convert to an ellipse.
Ellipse e = new Ellipse(c);
Flatten(e);
```

The variable e holds the flattened ellipse. By replacing the conversion operator with a constructor, you have not lost any functionality; you've merely made it clearer when new objects are created. (Veteran C++ programmers should note that C# does not call constructors for implicit or explicit conversions. You create new objects only when you explicitly use the new operator, and at no other time. There is no need for the `explicit` keyword on constructors in C#.)

Conversion operators that return fields inside your objects will not exhibit this behavior. They have other problems. You've poked a serious hole in the encapsulation of your class. By casting your type to some other object, clients of your class can access an internal variable. That's best avoided for all the reasons discussed in Item 26.

Conversion operators introduce a form of substitutability that causes problems in your code. You're indicating that, in all cases, users can reasonably expect that another class can be used in place of the one you created. When this substituted object is accessed, you cause clients to work with temporary objects or internal fields in place of the class you created. You then modify temporary objects and discard the results. These subtle bugs are hard to find because the compiler generates code to convert these objects. Avoid conversion operators in your APIs.

Item 10: Use Optional Parameters to Minimize Method Overloads

C# now has support for named parameters at the call site. That means the names of formal parameters are now part of the public interface for your type. Changing the name of a public parameter could break calling code. That means you should avoid using named parameters in many situations, and also you should avoid changing the names of the formal parameters on public, or protected methods.

Of course, no language designer adds features just to make your life difficult. Named parameters were added for a reason, and they have positive

uses. Named parameters work with optional parameters to limit the nois-
iness around many APIs, especially COM APIs for Microsoft Office. This
small snippet of code creates a Word document and inserts a small amount
of text, using the classic COM methods:

```
var wasted = Type.Missing;
var wordApp = new
    Microsoft.Office.Interop.Word.Application();
wordApp.Visible = true;
Documents docs = wordApp.Documents;

Document doc = docs.Add(ref wasted,
    ref wasted, ref wasted, ref wasted);

Range range = doc.Range(0, 0);

range.InsertAfter("Testing, testing, testing. . .");
```

This small, and arguably useless, snippet uses the Type.Missing object four
times. Any Office Interop application will use a much larger number of
Type.Missing objects in the application. Those instances clutter up your
application and hide the actual logic of the software you're building.

That extra noise was the primary driver behind adding optional and
named parameters in the C# language. Optional parameters means that
these Office APIs can create default values for all those locations where
Type.Missing would be used. That simplifies even this small snippet:

```
var wordApp = new
    Microsoft.Office.Interop.Word.Application();
wordApp.Visible = true;
Documents docs = wordApp.Documents;

Document doc = docs.Add();

Range range = doc.Range(0, 0);

range.InsertAfter("Testing, testing, testing. . .");
```

Even this small change increases the readability of this snippet. Of course,
you may not always want to use all the defaults. And yet, you still don't
want to add all the Type.Missing parameters in the middle. Suppose you

wanted to create a new Web page instead of new Word document. That's the last parameter of four in the Add() method. Using named parameters, you can specify just that last parameter:

```
var wordApp = new
    Microsoft.Office.Interop.Word.Application();
wordApp.Visible = true;
Documents docs = wordApp.Documents;

object docType = WdNewDocumentType.wdNewWebPage;
Document doc = docs.Add(DocumentType : ref docType);

Range range = doc.Range(0, 0);

range.InsertAfter("Testing, testing, testing. . .");
```

Named parameters mean that in any API with default parameters, you only need to specify those parameters you intend to use. It's simpler than multiple overloads. In fact, with four different parameters, you would need to create 15 different overloads of the Add() method to achieve the same level of flexibility that named and optional parameters provide. Remember that some of the Office APIs have as many as 16 parameters, and optional and named parameters are a big help.

I left the `ref` decorator in the parameter list, but another change in C# 4.0 makes that optional in COM scenarios. That's because COM, in general, passes objects by reference, so almost all parameters are passed by reference, even if they aren't modified by the called method. In fact, the Range() call passes the values (0,0) by reference. I did not include the `ref` modifier there, because that would be clearly misleading. In fact, in most production code, I would not include the `ref` modifier on the call to Add() either. I did above so that you could see the actual API signature.

Of course, just because the justification for named and optional parameters was COM and the Office APIs, that doesn't mean you should limit their use to Office interop applications. In fact, you can't. Developers calling your API can decorate calling locations using named parameters whether you want them to or not.

This method:

```
private void SetName(string lastName, string firstName)
{
```

```
    // elided
}
```

Can be called using named parameters to avoid any confusion on the order:

```
SetName(lastName: "Wagner", firstName: "Bill");
```

Annotating the names of the parameters ensures that people reading this code later won't wonder if the parameters are in the right order or not. Developers will use named parameters whenever adding the names will increase the clarity of the code someone is trying to read. Anytime you use methods that contain multiple parameters of the same type, naming the parameters at the callsite will make your code more readable.

Changing parameter names manifests itself in an interesting way as a breaking change. The parameter names are stored in the MSIL only at the callsite, not at the calling site. You can change parameter names and release the component without breaking any users of your component in the field. The developers who use your component will see a breaking change when they go to compile against the updated version, but any earlier client assemblies will continue to run correctly. So at least you won't break existing applications in the field. The developers who use your work will still be upset, but they won't blame you for problems in the field. For example, suppose you modify SetName() by changing the parameter names:

```
public void SetName(string Last, string First)
```

You could compile and release this assembly as a patch into the field. Any assemblies that called this method would continue to run, even if they contain calls to SetName that specify named parameters. However, when client developers went to build updates to their assemblies, any code like this would no longer compile:

```
SetName(lastName: "Wagner", firstName: "Bill");
```

The parameter names have changed.

Changing the default value also requires callers to recompile in order to pick up those changes. If you compile your assembly and release it as a patch, all existing callers would continue to use the previous default parameter.

Of course, you don't want to upset the developers who use your components either. For that reason, you must consider the names of your parameters as part of the public interface to your component. Changing the names of parameters will break client code at compile time.

In addition, adding parameters (even if they have default values) will break at runtime. Optional parameters are implemented in a similar fashion to named parameters. The callsite will contain annotations in the MSIL that reflect the existence of default values, and what those default values are. The calling site substitutes those values for any optional parameters the caller did not explicitly specify.

Therefore, adding parameters, even if they are optional parameters, is a breaking change at runtime. If they have default values, it's not a breaking change at compile time.

Now, after that explanation, the guidance should be clearer. For your initial release, use optional and named parameters to create whatever combination of overloads your users may want to use. However, once you start creating future releases, you must create overloads for additional parameters. That way, existing client applications will still function. Furthermore, in any future release, avoid changing parameter names. They are now part of your public interface.

Item 11: Understand the Attraction of Small Functions

As experienced programmers, in whatever language we favored before C#, we internalized several practices for developing more efficient code. Sometimes what worked in our previous environment is counterproductive in the .NET environment. This is very true when you try to hand-optimize algorithms for the C# compiler. Your actions often prevent the JIT compiler from more effective optimizations. Your extra work, in the name of performance, actually generates slower code. You're better off writing the clearest code you can create. Let the JIT compiler do the rest. One of the most common examples of premature optimizations causing problems is when you create longer, more complicated functions in the hopes of avoiding function calls. Practices such as hoisting function logic into the bodies of loops actually harm the performance of your .NET applications. It's counterintuitive, so let's go over all the details.

The .NET runtime invokes the JIT compiler to translate the IL generated by the C# compiler into machine code. This task is amortized across the lifetime of your program's execution. Instead of JITing your entire application when it starts, the CLR invokes the JITer on a function-by-function basis. This minimizes the startup cost to a reasonable level, yet keeps the application from becoming unresponsive later when more code needs to be JITed. Functions that do not ever get called do not get JITed. You can minimize the amount of extraneous code that gets JITed by factoring code into more, smaller functions rather than fewer larger functions. Consider this rather contrived example:

```
public string BuildMsg(bool takeFirstPath)
{
    StringBuilder msg = new StringBuilder();
    if (takeFirstPath)
    {
        msg.Append("A problem occurred.");
        msg.Append("\nThis is a problem.");
        msg.Append("imagine much more text");
    }
    else
    {
        msg.Append("This path is not so bad.");
        msg.Append("\nIt is only a minor inconvenience.");
        msg.Append("Add more detailed diagnostics here.");
    }
    return msg.ToString();
}
```

The first time BuildMsg gets called, both paths are JITed. Only one is needed. But suppose you rewrote the function this way:

```
public string BuildMsg2(bool takeFirstPath)
{
    if (takeFirstPath)
    {
        return FirstPath();
    }
    else
    {
        return SecondPath();
    }
}
```

Because the body of each clause has been factored into its own function, that function can be JITed on demand rather than the first time BuildMsg is called. Yes, this example is contrived for space, and it won't make much difference. But consider how often you write more extensive examples: an `if` statement with 20 or more statements in both branches of the `if` statement. You'll pay to JIT both clauses the first time the function is entered. If one clause is an unlikely error condition, you'll incur a cost that you could easily avoid. Smaller functions mean that the JIT compiler compiles the logic that's needed, not lengthy sequences of code that won't be used immediately. The JIT cost savings multiplies for long switch statements, with the body of each case statement defined inline rather than in separate functions.

Smaller and simpler functions make it easier for the JIT compiler to support **enregistration**. Enregistration is the process of selecting which local variables can be stored in registers rather than on the stack. Creating fewer local variables gives the JIT compiler a better chance to find the best candidates for enregistration. The simplicity of the control flow also affects how well the JIT compiler can enregister variables. If a function has one loop, that loop variable will likely be enregistered. However, the JIT compiler must make some tough choices about enregistering loop variables when you create a function with several loops. Simpler is better. A smaller function is more likely to contain fewer local variables and make it easier for the JIT compiler to optimize the use of the registers.

The JIT compiler also makes decisions about **inlining** methods. Inlining means to substitute the body of a function for the function call. Consider this example:

```
// readonly name property:
public string Name { get; private set; }

// access:
string val = Obj.Name;
```

The body of the property accessor contains fewer instructions than the code necessary to call the function: saving register states, executing method prologue and epilogue code, and storing the function return value. There would be even more work if arguments needed to be pushed on the stack as well. There would be far fewer machine instructions if you were to use a public field.

Of course, you would never do that because you know better than to create public data members (see Item 1). The JIT compiler understands your need for both efficiency and elegance, so it inlines the property accessor. The JIT compiler inlines methods when the speed or size benefits (or both) make it advantageous to replace a function call with the body of the called function. The standard does not define the exact rules for inlining, and any implementation could change in the future. Moreover, it's not your responsibility to inline functions. The C# language does not even provide you with a keyword to give a hint to the compiler that a method should be inlined. In fact, the C# compiler does not provide any hints to the JIT compiler regarding inlining. (You can request that a method not be inlined using the System.Runtime.CompilerServices.MethodImpl attribute, specifying the NoInlining option. It's typically done to preserve method names on the callstack for debugging scenarios.)

```
[MethodImpl(MethodImplOptions.NoInlining)]
```

All you can do is ensure that your code is as clear as possible, to make it easier for the JIT compiler to make the best decision possible. The recommendation should be getting familiar by now: Smaller methods are better candidates for inlining. But remember that even small functions that are virtual or that contain try/catch blocks cannot be inlined.

Inlining modifies the principle that code gets JITed when it will be executed. Consider accessing the name property again:

```
string val = "Default Name";
if (Obj != null)
    val = Obj.Name;
```

If the JIT compiler inlines the property accessor, it must JIT that code when the containing method is called.

This recommendation to build smaller and composable methods takes on greater importance in the world of LINQ queries and functional programming. All the LINQ query methods are rather small. Also, most of the predicates, actions, and functions passed to LINQ queries will be small blocks of code. This small, more composable nature means that those methods, and your actions, predicates, and functions, are all more easily reused. In addition, the JIT compiler has a better chance of optimizing that code to create more efficient runtime execution.

It's not your responsibility to determine the best machine-level representation of your algorithms. The C# compiler and the JIT compiler together do that for you. The C# compiler generates the IL for each method, and the JIT compiler translates that IL into machine code on the destination machine. You should not be too concerned about the exact rules the JIT compiler uses in all cases; those will change over time as better algorithms are developed. Instead, you should be concerned about expressing your algorithms in a manner that makes it easiest for the tools in the environment to do the best job they can. Luckily, those rules are consistent with the rules you already follow for good software-development practices. One more time: smaller and simpler functions.

Remember that translating your C# code into machine-executable code is a two-step process. The C# compiler generates IL that gets delivered in assemblies. The JIT compiler generates machine code for each method (or group of methods, when inlining is involved), as needed. Small functions make it much easier for the JIT compiler to amortize that cost. Small functions are also more likely to be candidates for inlining. It's not just smallness: Simpler control flow matters just as much. Fewer control branches inside functions make it easier for the JIT compiler to enregister variables. It's not just good practice to write clearer code; it's how you create more efficient code at runtime.

2 | .NET Resource Management

The simple fact that .NET programs run in a managed environment has a big impact on the kinds of designs that create effective C#. Taking advantage of that environment requires changing your thinking from other environments to the .NET Common Language Runtime (CLR). It means understanding the .NET Garbage Collector. An overview of the .NET memory management environment is necessary to understand the specific recommendations in this chapter, so let's get on with the overview.

The Garbage Collector (GC) controls managed memory for you. Unlike native environments, you are not responsible for most memory leaks, dangling pointers, uninitialized pointers, or a host of other memory-management issues. But the Garbage Collector is not magic: You need to clean up after yourself, too. You are responsible for unmanaged resources such as file handles, database connections, GDI+ objects, COM objects, and other system objects. In addition you can cause objects to stay in memory longer than you'd like because you've created links between them using event handlers or delegates. Queries, which execute when results are requested, can also cause objects to remain referenced longer than you would expect. Queries capture bound variables in closures, and those bound variables are reachable until the containing results have gone out of scope.

Here's the good news: Because the GC controls memory, certain design idioms are much easier to implement. Circular references, both simple relationships and complex webs of objects, are much easier. The GC's Mark and Compact algorithm efficiently detects these relationships and removes unreachable webs of objects in their entirety. The GC determines whether an object is reachable by walking the object tree from the application's root object instead of forcing each object to keep track of references to it, as in COM. The EntitySet class provides an example of how this algorithm simplifies object ownership decisions. An Entity is a collection of objects loaded from a database. Each Entity may contain references to other Entity objects. Any of these entities may also contain links to other entities. Just like the relational database entity sets model, these links and references may be circular.

There are references all through the web of objects represented by different EntitySets. Releasing memory is the GC's responsibility. Because the .NET Framework designers did not need to free these objects, the complicated web of object references did not pose a problem. No decision needed to be made regarding the proper sequence of freeing this web of objects; it's the GC's job. The GC's design simplifies the problem of identifying this kind of web of objects as garbage. The application can stop referencing any entity when it's done. The Garbage Collector will know if the entity is still reachable from live objects in the application. Any objects that cannot be reached from the application are all garbage.

The Garbage Collector runs in its own thread to remove unused memory from your program. It also compacts the managed heap each time it runs. Compacting the heap moves each live object in the managed heap so that the free space is located in one contiguous block of memory. Figure 2.1 shows two snapshots of the heap before and after a garbage collection. All free memory is placed in one contiguous block after each GC operation.

As you've just learned, memory management (for the managed heap) is completely the responsibility of the Garbage Collector. Other system

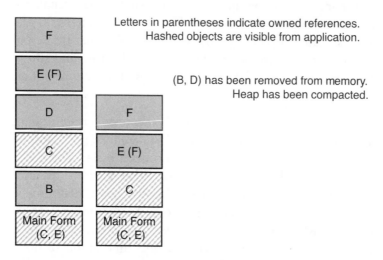

Letters in parentheses indicate owned references.
Hashed objects are visible from application.

(B, D) has been removed from memory.
Heap has been compacted.

Figure 2.1 The Garbage Collector not only removes unused memory, but it also moves other objects in memory to compact used memory and maximize free space.

resources must be managed by developers: you and the users of your classes. Two mechanisms help developers control the lifetimes of unmanaged resources: finalizers and the IDisposable interface. A finalizer is a defensive mechanism that ensures your objects always have a way to release unmanaged resources. Finalizers have many drawbacks, so you also have the IDisposable interface that provides a less intrusive way to return resources to the system in a timely manner.

Finalizers are called by the Garbage Collector. They will be called at some time after an object becomes garbage. You don't know when that happens. All you know is that it happens sometime after your object cannot be reached. That is a big change from C++, and it has important ramifications for your designs. Experienced C++ programmers wrote classes that allocated a critical resource in its constructor and released it in its destructor:

```
// Good C++, bad C#:
class CriticalSection
{
    // Constructor acquires the system resource.
    public CriticalSection()
    {
        EnterCriticalSection();
    }

    // Destructor releases system resource.
    ~CriticalSection()
    {
        ExitCriticalSection();
    }

    private void ExitCriticalSection()
    {
        throw new NotImplementedException();
    }
    private void EnterCriticalSection()
    {
        throw new NotImplementedException();
    }
}
```

```
// usage:
void Func()
{
    // The lifetime of s controls access to
    // the system resource.
    CriticalSection s = new CriticalSection();
    // Do work.

    //...

    // compiler generates call to destructor.
    // code exits critical section.
}
```

This common C++ idiom ensures that resource deallocation is exception-proof. This doesn't work in C#, however—at least, not in the same way. Deterministic finalization is not part of the .NET environment or the C# language. Trying to force the C++ idiom of deterministic finalization into the C# language won't work well. In C#, the finalizer eventually executes, but it doesn't execute in a timely fashion. In the previous example, the code eventually exits the critical section, but, in C#, it doesn't exit the critical section when the function exits. That happens at some unknown time later. You don't know when. You can't know when. Finalizers are the only way to guarantee that unmanaged resources allocated by an object of a given type are eventually released. But finalizers execute at nondeterministic times, so your design and coding practices should minimize the need for creating finalizers, and also minimize the need for executing the finalizers that do exist. Throughout this chapter you'll learn when you must create a finalizer, and how to minimize the negative impact of having one.

Relying on finalizers also introduces performance penalties. Objects that require finalization put a performance drag on the Garbage Collector. When the GC finds that an object is garbage but also requires finalization, it cannot remove that item from memory just yet. First, it calls the finalizer. Finalizers are not executed by the same thread that collects garbage. Instead, the GC places each object that is ready for finalization in a queue and spawns yet another thread to execute all the finalizers. It continues with its business, removing other garbage from memory. On the next GC cycle, those objects that have been finalized are removed from memory. Figure 2.2 shows three different GC operations and the difference in memory usage. Notice that the objects that require finalizers stay in memory for extra cycles.

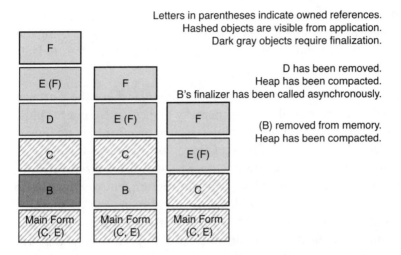

Letters in parentheses indicate owned references.
Hashed objects are visible from application.
Dark gray objects require finalization.

D has been removed.
Heap has been compacted.
B's finalizer has been called asynchronously.

(B) removed from memory.
Heap has been compacted.

Figure 2.2 This sequence shows the effect of finalizers on the Garbage Collector. Objects stay in memory longer, and an extra thread needs to be spawned to run the Garbage Collector.

This might lead you to believe that an object that requires finalization lives in memory for one GC cycle more than necessary. But I simplified things. It's more complicated than that because of another GC design decision. The .NET Garbage Collector defines generations to optimize its work. Generations help the GC identify the likeliest garbage candidates more quickly. Any object created since the last garbage collection operation is a generation 0 object. Any object that has survived one GC operation is a generation 1 object. Any object that has survived two or more GC operations is a generation 2 object. The purpose of generations is to separate local variables and objects that stay around for the life of the application. Generation 0 objects are mostly local variables. Member variables and global variables quickly enter generation 1 and eventually enter generation 2.

The GC optimizes its work by limiting how often it examines first- and second-generation objects. Every GC cycle examines generation 0 objects. Roughly 1 GC out of 10 examines the generation 0 and 1 objects. Roughly 1 GC cycle out of 100 examines all objects. Think about finalization and its cost again: An object that requires finalization might stay in memory for nine GC cycles more than it would if it did not require finalization. If it still has not been finalized, it moves to generation 2. In generation 2, an object lives for an extra 100 GC cycles until the next generation 2 collection.

I've spent some time now explaining why finalizers are not a good solution. But yet, you still need to free resources. You address these issues using the IDisposable interface and the standard dispose pattern. (See Item 17 later in this chapter.)

To close, remember that a managed environment, where the Garbage Collector takes the responsibility for memory management, is a big plus: Memory leaks and a host of other pointer-related problems are no longer your problem. Nonmemory resources force you to create finalizers to ensure proper cleanup of those nonmemory resources. Finalizers can have a serious impact on the performance of your program, but you must write them to avoid resource leaks. Implementing and using the IDisposable interface avoids the performance drain on the Garbage Collector that finalizers introduce. The next section moves on to the specific items that will help you create programs that use this environment more effectively.

Item 12: Prefer Member Initializers to Assignment Statements

Classes often have more than one constructor. Over time, it's easy for the member variables and the constructors to get out of sync. The best way to make sure this doesn't happen is to initialize variables where you declare them instead of in the body of every constructor. You should utilize the initializer syntax for both static and instance variables.

Constructing member variables when you declare that variable is natural in C#. Just initialize the variable when you declare it:

```
public class MyClass
{
    // declare the collection, and initialize it.
    private List<string> labels = new List<string>();
}
```

Regardless of the number of constructors you eventually add to the MyClass type, labels will be initialized properly. The compiler generates code at the beginning of each constructor to execute all the initializers you have defined for your instance member variables. When you add a new constructor, labels get initialized. Similarly, if you add a new member variable, you do not need to add initialization code to every constructor; initializing the variable where you define it is sufficient. Equally important, the initializers are added to the compiler-generated default constructor.

The C# compiler creates a default constructor for your types whenever you don't explicitly define any constructors.

Initializers are more than a convenient shortcut for statements in a constructor body. The statements generated by initializers are placed in object code before the body of your constructors. Initializers execute before the base class constructor for your type executes, and they are executed in the order the variables are declared in your class.

Using initializers is the simplest way to avoid uninitialized variables in your types, but it's not perfect. In three cases, you should not use the initializer syntax. The first is when you are initializing the object to 0, or null. The default system initialization sets everything to 0 for you before any of your code executes. The system-generated 0 initialization is done at a very low level using the CPU instructions to set the entire block of memory to 0. Any extra 0 initialization on your part is superfluous. The C# compiler dutifully adds the extra instructions to set memory to 0 again. It's not wrong—it's just inefficient. In fact, when value types are involved, it's very inefficient.

```
MyValType myVal1;  // initialized to 0
MyValType myVal2 = new MyValType(); // also 0
```

Both statements initialize the variable to all 0s. The first does so by setting the memory containing myVal1 to 0. The second uses the IL instruction initobj, which causes both a box and an unbox operation on the myVal2 variable. This takes quite a bit of extra time (see Item 45).

The second inefficiency comes when you create multiple initializations for the same object. You should use the initializer syntax only for variables that receive the same initialization in all constructors. This version of MyClass has a path that creates two different List objects as part of its construction:

```
public class MyClass2
{
    // declare the collection, and initialize it.
    private List<string> labels = new List<string>();

    MyClass2()
    {
    }
```

```
    MyClass2(int size)
    {
        labels = new List<string>(size);
    }
}
```

When you create a new MyClass2, specifying the size of the collection, you create two array lists. One is immediately garbage. The variable initializer executes before every constructor. The constructor body creates the second array list. The compiler creates this version of MyClass2, which you would never code by hand. (For the proper way to handle this situation, see Item 14.)

```
public class MyClass2
{
    // declare the collection, and initialize it.
    private List<string> labels;

    MyClass2()
    {
        labels = new List<string>();
    }

    MyClass2(int size)
    {
        labels = new List<string>();
        labels = new List<string>(size);
    }
}
```

You can run into the same situation whenever you use implicit properties (see Item 1). Your code does not have access to the compiler-generated backing field, so you can't use an initializer for implicit properties. You have no choice but to initialize data coded in implicit properties using constructors. Using implicit properties is still an advantage when you don't have any validation logic in your data setters. If you migrate from an implicit property to a named backing field with explicitly coded properties, you should update the initialization code to initialize the data members using initializers rather than constructor code. For those data elements where implicit properties are the right choice, Item 14 shows how to minimize any duplication when you initialize data held in implicit properties.

The final reason to move initialization into the body of a constructor is to facilitate exception handling. You cannot wrap the initializers in a `try` block. Any exceptions that might be generated during the construction of your member variables get propagated outside your object. You cannot attempt any recovery inside your class. You should move that initialization code into the body of your constructors so that you implement the proper recovery code to create your type and gracefully handle the exception (see Item 47).

Member initializers are the simplest way to ensure that the member variables in your type are initialized regardless of which constructor is called. The initializers are executed before each constructor you make for your type. Using this syntax means that you cannot forget to add the proper initialization when you add new constructors for a future release. Use initializers when all constructors create the member variable the same way; it's simpler to read and easier to maintain.

Item 13: Use Proper Initialization for Static Class Members

You know that you should initialize static member variables in a type before you create any instances of that type. C# lets you use static initializers and a static constructor for this purpose. A static constructor is a special function that executes before any other methods, variables, or properties defined in that class are accessed for the first time. You use this function to initialize static variables, enforce the singleton pattern, or perform any other necessary work before a class is usable. You should not use your instance constructors, some special private function, or any other idiom to initialize static variables.

As with instance initialization, you can use the initializer syntax as an alternative to the static constructor. If you simply need to allocate a static member, use the initializer syntax. When you have more complicated logic to initialize static member variables, create a static constructor.

Implementing the singleton pattern in C# is the most frequent use of a static constructor. Make your instance constructor private, and add an initializer:

```
public class MySingleton
{
    private static readonly MySingleton theOneAndOnly =
        new MySingleton();
```

```
    public static MySingleton TheOnly
    {
        get { return theOneAndOnly; }
    }

    private MySingleton()
    {
    }


    // remainder elided
}
```

The singleton pattern can just as easily be written this way, in case you have more complicated logic to initialize the singleton:

```
public class MySingleton2
{
    private static readonly MySingleton2 theOneAndOnly;

    static MySingleton2()
    {
        theOneAndOnly = new MySingleton2();
    }

    public static MySingleton2 TheOnly
    {
        get { return theOneAndOnly; }
    }

    private MySingleton2()
    {
    }


    // remainder elided
}
```

As with instance initializers, the static initializers are called before any static constructors are called. And, yes, your static initializers execute before the base class's static constructor.

The CLR calls your static constructor automatically before your type is first accessed in an application space (an AppDomain). You can define only one static constructor, and it must not take any arguments. Because static constructors are called by the CLR, you must be careful about exceptions generated in them. If you let an exception escape a static constructor, the CLR will terminate your program. The situation where the caller catches the exception is even more insidious. Code that tries to create the type will fail until that AppDomain is unloaded. The CLR could not initialize the type by executing the static constructor. It won't try again, and yet the type did not get initialized correctly. Creating an object of that type (or any type derived from it) would not be well defined. Therefore, it is not allowed.

Exceptions are the most common reason to use the static constructor instead of static initializers. If you use static initializers, you cannot catch the exceptions yourself. With a static constructor, you can (see Item 47):

```
static MySingleton2()
{
    try
    {
        theOneAndOnly = new MySingleton2();
    }
    catch
    {
        // Attempt recovery here.
    }
}
```

Static initializers and static constructors provide the cleanest, clearest way to initialize static members of your class. They are easy to read and easy to get correct. They were added to the language to specifically address the difficulties involved with initializing static members in other languages.

Item 14: Minimize Duplicate Initialization Logic

Writing constructors is often a repetitive task. Many developers write the first constructor and then copy and paste the code into other constructors, to satisfy the multiple overrides defined in the class interface. Hopefully, you're not one of those. If you are, stop it. Veteran C++ programmers would factor the common algorithms into a private helper method. Stop that, too. When you find that multiple constructors contain the same logic, factor that logic into a common constructor instead. You'll get the benefits of avoiding code duplication, and constructor initializers generate much more efficient object code. The C# compiler recognizes the constructor initializer as special syntax and removes the duplicated variable initializers and the duplicated base class constructor calls. The result is that your final object executes the minimum amount of code to properly initialize the object. You also write the least code by delegating responsibilities to a common constructor.

Constructor initializers allow one constructor to call another constructor. This example shows a simple usage:

```
public class MyClass
{
    // collection of data
    private List<ImportantData> coll;
    // Name of the instance:
    private string name;

    public MyClass() :
        this(0, "")
    {
    }

    public MyClass(int initialCount) :
        this(initialCount, string.Empty)
    {
    }

    public MyClass(int initialCount, string name)
    {
        coll = (initialCount > 0) ?
          new List<ImportantData>(initialCount) :
          new List<ImportantData>();
        this.name = name;
    }
}
```

C# 4.0 adds default parameters, which you can use to minimize the duplicated code in constructors. You could replace all the different constructors for MyClass with one constructor that specifies default values for all or many of the values:

```
public class MyClass
{
    // collection of data
    private List<ImportantData> coll;
    // Name of the instance:
    private string name;

    // Needed to satisfy the new() constraint.
    public MyClass() :
        this(0, string.Empty)
    {
    }

    public MyClass(int initialCount = 0, string name = "")
    {
        coll = (initialCount > 0) ?
          new List<ImportantData>(initialCount) :
          new List<ImportantData>();
        this.name = name;
    }
}
```

There are tradeoffs in choosing default parameters over using multiple overloads. (See Item 10.) Default parameters create more options for your users. This version of MyClass specifies the default value for both parameters. Users could specify different values for either or both parameters. Producing all the permutations using overloaded constructors would require four different constructor overloads: a parameterless constructor, one that asked for the initial count, one that asked for the name, and one that asked for both parameters. Add more members to your class, and the number of potential overloads grows as the number of permutations of all the parameters grows. That complexity makes default parameters a very powerful mechanism to minimize the number of potential overloads that you need to create.

Defining default values for all parameters to your type's constructor means that user code will be valid when you call the new MyClass(). When you intend to support this concept, you should create an explicit parameterless constructor in that type, as shown in the example code above. While most code would default all parameters, generic classes that use the new() constraint will not accept a constructor with parameters that all have default values. To satisfy the new() constraint, a class must have an explicit parameterless constructor. Therefore, you should create one so that clients can use your type in generic classes or methods that enforce the new() constraint. That's not to say that every type needs a parameterless constructor. However, if you support one, make sure to add the code so that the parameterless constructor works in all cases, even when called from a generic class with a new() constraint.

You'll note that the second constructor specifies "" for the default value on the name parameter, rather than the more customary string.Empty. That's because string.Empty is not a compile-time constant. It is a static property defined in the string class. Because it is not a compile-time constant, you cannot use it for the default value for a parameter.

However, using default parameters instead of overloads creates tighter coupling between your class and all the clients that use it (see Item 10). In particular, the formal parameter name becomes part of the public interface, as does the current default value. Changing parameter values requires a recompile of all client code in order to pick up those changes. That makes overloaded constructors more resilient in the face of potential future changes. You can add new constructors, or change the default behavior for those constructors that don't specify values without breaking client code.

C# versions 1 through 3 do not support default parameters, which is the preferred solution to this problem. You must write each constructor that you support as a separate function. With constructors, that can mean a lot of duplicated code. Use constructor chaining, by having one constructor invoke another constructor declared in the same class, instead of creating a common utility routine. Several inefficiencies are present in this alternative method of factoring out common constructor logic:

```
public class MyClass
{
    // collection of data
    private List<ImportantData> coll;
    // Name of the instance:
    private string name;

    public MyClass()
    {
        commonConstructor(0, "");
    }
```

```csharp
    public MyClass(int initialCount)
    {
        commonConstructor(initialCount, "");
    }


    public MyClass(int initialCount, string Name)
    {
        commonConstructor(initialCount, Name);
    }


    private void commonConstructor(int count,
      string name)
    {
        coll = (count > 0) ?
          new List<ImportantData>(count) :
          new List<ImportantData>();
        this.name = name;
    }
}
```

That version looks the same, but it generates far less efficient object code. The compiler adds code to perform several functions on your behalf in constructors. It adds statements for all variable initializers (see Item 12). It calls the base class constructor. When you write your own common utility function, the compiler cannot factor out this duplicated code. The IL for the second version is the same as if you'd written this:

```csharp
public class MyClass
{
    private List<ImportantData> coll;
    private string name;

    public MyClass()
    {
        // Instance Initializers would go here.
        object(); // Not legal, illustrative only.
        commonConstructor(0, "");
    }


    public MyClass(int initialCount)
    {
```

```
        // Instance Initializers would go here.
        object(); // Not legal, illustrative only.
        commonConstructor(initialCount, "");
    }

    public MyClass(int initialCount, string Name)
    {
        // Instance Initializers would go here.
        object(); // Not legal, illustrative only.
        commonConstructor(initialCount, Name);
    }

    private void commonConstructor(int count,
      string name)
    {
        coll = (count > 0) ?
          new List<ImportantData>(count) :
          new List<ImportantData>();
        this.name = name;
    }
}
```

If you could write the construction code for the first version the way the compiler sees it, you'd write this:

```
// Not legal, illustrates IL generated:
public class MyClass
{
    private List<ImportantData> coll;
    private string name;

    public MyClass()
    {
        // No variable initializers here.
        // Call the third constructor, shown below.
        this(0, ""); // Not legal, illustrative only.
    }

    public MyClass(int initialCount)
    {
        // No variable initializers here.
```

```
        // Call the third constructor, shown below.
        this(initialCount, "");
    }

    public MyClass(int initialCount, string Name)
    {
        // Instance Initializers would go here.
        object(); // Not legal, illustrative only.
        coll = (initialCount > 0) ?
          new List<ImportantData>(initialCount) :
          new List<ImportantData>();
        name = Name;

    }
}
```

The difference is that the compiler does not generate multiple calls to the base class constructor, nor does it copy the instance variable initializers into each constructor body. The fact that the base class constructor is called only from the last constructor is also significant: You cannot include more than one constructor initializer in a constructor definition. You can delegate to another constructor in this class using `this()`, or you can call a base class constructor using `base()`. You cannot do both.

Still don't buy the case for constructor initializers? Then think about read-only constants. In this example, the name of the object should not change during its lifetime. This means that you should make it read-only. That causes the common utility function to generate compiler errors:

```
public class MyClass
{
    // collection of data
    private List<ImportantData> coll;
    // Number for this instance
    private int counter;
    // Name of the instance:
    private readonly string name;

    public MyClass()
    {
        commonConstructor(0, string.Empty);
    }
```

```
    public MyClass(int initialCount)
    {
        commonConstructor(initialCount, string.Empty);
    }


    public MyClass(int initialCount, string Name)
    {
        commonConstructor(initialCount, Name);
    }


    private void commonConstructor(int count,
      string name)
    {
        coll = (count > 0) ?
          new List<ImportantData>(count) :
          new List<ImportantData>();
        // ERROR changing the name outside of a constructor.
        this.name = name;
    }
}
```

C++ programmers just live with this and initialize Name in all constructors, or they cast away constness in the utility routine. C#'s constructor initializers provide a better alternative. All but the most trivial classes contain more than one constructor. Their job is to initialize all the members of an object. By their very nature, these functions have similar or, ideally, shared logic. Use the C# constructor initializer to factor out those common algorithms so that you write them once and they execute once.

Both default parameters and overloads have their place. In general, you should prefer default values to overloaded constructors. After all, if you are letting client developers specify parameter values at all, your constructor must be capable of handling any values that users specify. Your original default values should always be reasonable and shouldn't generate exceptions. Therefore, even though changing the default parameter values is technically a breaking change, it shouldn't be observable to your clients. Their code will still use the original values, and those original values should still produce reasonable behavior. That minimizes the potential hazards of using default values.

This is the last item about object initialization in C#. That makes it a good time to review the entire sequence of events for constructing an instance of a type. You should understand both the order of operations and the default initialization of an object. You should strive to initialize every member variable exactly once during construction. The best way for you to accomplish this is to initialize values as early as possible. Here is the order of operations for constructing the first instance of a type:

1. Static variable storage is set to 0.
2. Static variable initializers execute.
3. Static constructors for the base class execute.
4. The static constructor executes.
5. Instance variable storage is set to 0.
6. Instance variable initializers execute.
7. The appropriate base class instance constructor executes.
8. The instance constructor executes.

Subsequent instances of the same type start at step 5 because the class initializers execute only once. Also, steps 6 and 7 are optimized so that constructor initializers cause the compiler to remove duplicate instructions.

The C# language compiler guarantees that everything gets initialized in some way when an object gets created. At a minimum, you are guaranteed that all memory your object uses has been set to 0 when an instance is created. This is true for both static members and instance members. Your goal is to make sure that you initialize all the values the way you want and execute that initialization code only once. Use initializers to initialize simple resources. Use constructors to initialize members that require more sophisticated logic. Also factor calls to other constructors, to minimize duplication.

Item 15: Utilize `using` and `try/finally` for Resource Cleanup

Types that use unmanaged system resources should be explicitly released using the Dispose() method of the IDisposable interface. The rules of the .NET environment make that the responsibility of the code that uses the type, not the responsibility of the type or the system. Therefore, anytime you use types that have a Dispose() method, it's your responsibility to release those resources by calling Dispose(). The best way to ensure that Dispose() always gets called is to utilize the `using` statement or a `try/finally` block.

All types that own unmanaged resources implement the IDisposable interface. In addition, they defensively create a finalizer for those times when you forget to dispose properly. If you forget to dispose of those items, those nonmemory resources are freed later, when finalizers get their chance to execute. All those objects then stay in memory that much longer, and your application becomes a slowly executing resource hog.

Luckily for you, the C# language designers knew that explicitly releasing resources would be a common task. They added keywords to the language that make it easy.

Suppose you wrote this code:

```
public void ExecuteCommand(string connString,
  string commandString)
{
    SqlConnection myConnection = new SqlConnection(
      connString);
    SqlCommand mySqlCommand = new SqlCommand(commandString,
      myConnection);

    myConnection.Open();
    mySqlCommand.ExecuteNonQuery();
}
```

Two disposable objects are not properly cleaned up in this example: SqlConnection and SqlCommand. Both of these objects remain in memory until their finalizers are called. (Both of these classes inherit their finalizer from System.ComponentModel.Component.)

You fix this problem by calling Dispose when you are finished with the command and the connection:

```
public void ExecuteCommand(string connString,
  string commandString)
{
    SqlConnection myConnection = new SqlConnection(
      connString);
    SqlCommand mySqlCommand = new SqlCommand(commandString,
      myConnection);

    myConnection.Open();
    mySqlCommand.ExecuteNonQuery();

    mySqlCommand.Dispose();
    myConnection.Dispose();
}
```

That's fine, unless any exceptions get thrown while the SQL command executes. In that case, your calls to Dispose() never happen. The using statement ensures that Dispose() is called. You allocate an object inside a using statement, and the C# compiler generates a `try/finally` block around each object:

```
public void ExecuteCommand(string connString,
  string commandString)
{
    using (SqlConnection myConnection = new
      SqlConnection(connString))
    {
        using (SqlCommand mySqlCommand = new
          SqlCommand(commandString,
          myConnection))
        {
            myConnection.Open();
            mySqlCommand.ExecuteNonQuery();
        }
    }
}
```

Whenever you use one Disposable object in a function, the using clause is the simplest method to use to ensure that objects get disposed of properly. The using statement generates a `try/finally` block around the object being allocated. These two blocks generate exactly the same IL:

```
SqlConnection myConnection = null;

// Example Using clause:
using (myConnection = new SqlConnection(connString))
{
    myConnection.Open();
}

// example Try / Catch block:
try
{
    myConnection = new SqlConnection(connString);
    myConnection.Open();
}
```

```
finally
{
    myConnection.Dispose();
}
```

If you use the `using` statement with a variable of a type that does not support the IDisposable interface, the C# compiler generates an error. For example:

```
// Does not compile:
// String is sealed, and does not support IDisposable.
using (string msg = "This is a message")
    Console.WriteLine(msg);
```

The `using` statement works only if the compile-time type supports the IDisposable interface. You cannot use it with arbitrary objects:

```
// Does not compile.
// Object does not support IDisposable.
using (object obj = Factory.CreateResource())
    Console.WriteLine(obj.ToString());
```

A quick defensive as clause is all you need to safely dispose of objects that might or might not implement IDisposable:

```
// The correct fix.
// Object may or may not support IDisposable.
object obj = Factory.CreateResource();
using (obj as IDisposable)
    Console.WriteLine(obj.ToString());
```

If `obj` implements `IDisposable`, the `using` statement generates the cleanup code. If not, the `using` statement degenerates to `using(null)`, which is safe but doesn't do anything. If you're not sure whether you should wrap an object in a `using` block, err on the side of safety: Assume that it does and wrap it in the `using` clause shown earlier.

That covers the simple case: Whenever you use one disposable object that is local to a method, wrap that one object in a `using` statement. Now you can look at a few more complicated usages. Two different objects need to be disposed in that first example: the connection and the command. My example creates two different `using` statements, one wrapping each of the two objects that need to be disposed. Each `using` statement generates a different try/finally block. In effect, you have written this construct:

```
public void ExecuteCommand(string connString,
  string commandString)
{
    SqlConnection myConnection = null;
    SqlCommand mySqlCommand = null;
    try
    {
        myConnection = new SqlConnection(connString);
        try
        {
            mySqlCommand = new SqlCommand(commandString,
            myConnection);

            myConnection.Open();
            mySqlCommand.ExecuteNonQuery();
        }
        finally
        {
            if (mySqlCommand != null)
                mySqlCommand.Dispose();
        }
    }
    finally
    {
        if (myConnection != null)
            myConnection.Dispose();
    }
}
```

Every using statement creates a new nested try/finally block. Thankfully, it's rare that you'll allocate two different objects that both implement IDisposable in one method. That being the case, it's fine to leave it as is, because it does work. However, I find that an ugly construct, so when I allocate multiple objects that implement IDisposable, I prefer to write my own try/finally blocks:

```
public void ExecuteCommand(string connString,
  string commandString)
```

```
{
    SqlConnection myConnection = null;
    SqlCommand mySqlCommand = null;
    try
    {
        myConnection = new SqlConnection(connString);
        mySqlCommand = new SqlCommand(commandString,
          myConnection);

        myConnection.Open();
        mySqlCommand.ExecuteNonQuery();
    }
    finally
    {
        if (mySqlCommand != null)
            mySqlCommand.Dispose();
        if (myConnection != null)
            myConnection.Dispose();
    }
}
```

One reason to just leave well enough alone is that you can easily get too cute and try to build one `using` clause with `as` statements:

```
public void ExecuteCommand(string connString,
  string commandString)
{
    // Bad idea. Potential resource leak lurks!
    SqlConnection myConnection =
      new SqlConnection(connString);
    SqlCommand mySqlCommand = new SqlCommand(commandString,
        myConnection);
    using (myConnection as IDisposable)
    using (mySqlCommand as IDisposable)
    {
        myConnection.Open();
        mySqlCommand.ExecuteNonQuery();
    }
}
```

It looks cleaner, but it has a subtle bug. The SqlConnection object never gets disposed if the SqlCommand() constructor throws an exception.

myConnection has already been created, but the code has not entered the using block when the SqlCommand constructor executes. Without the constructor inside the using block, the call to Dispose gets skipped. You must make sure that any objects that implement IDisposable are allocated inside the scope of a using block or a try block. Otherwise, resource leaks can occur.

So far, you've handled the two most obvious cases. Whenever you allocate one disposable object in a method, the using statement is the best way to ensure that the resources you've allocated are freed in all cases. When you allocate multiple objects in the same method, create multiple using blocks or write your own single try/finally block.

There is one more nuance to freeing disposable objects. Some types support both a Dispose method and a Close method to free resources. SqlConnection is one of those classes. You could close SqlConnection like this:

```
public void ExecuteCommand(string connString,
    string commandString)
{
    SqlConnection myConnection = null;
    try
    {
        myConnection = new SqlConnection(connString);
        SqlCommand mySqlCommand = new SqlCommand
            (commandString, myConnection);

        myConnection.Open();
        mySqlCommand.ExecuteNonQuery();
    }
    finally
    {
        if (myConnection != null)
            myConnection.Close();
    }
}
```

This version does close the connection, but that's not exactly the same as disposing of it. The Dispose method does more than free resources: It also notifies the Garbage Collector that the object no longer needs to be finalized. Dispose calls GC.SuppressFinalize(). Close typically does not. As a result, the object remains in the finalization queue, even though finalization is not needed. If you have the choice, Dispose() is better than Close(). You'll learn all the gory details in Item 18.

Dispose() does not remove objects from memory. It is a hook to let objects release unmanaged resources. That means you can get into trouble by disposing of objects that are still in use. The examples above use SQLConnection. The SQLConnection's Dispose() method closes the connection to the database. After you dispose of the connection, the SQLConnection object is still in memory, but it is no longer connected to a database. It's in memory, but it's not useful. Do not dispose of objects that are still being referenced elsewhere in your program.

In some ways, resource management can be more difficult in C# than it was in C++. You can't rely on deterministic finalization to clean up every resource you use. But a garbage-collected environment really is much simpler for you. The vast majority of the types you make use of do not implement IDisposable. Less than 100 classes in the .NET Framework implement IDisposable—that's out of more than 1,500 types. When you use the ones that do implement IDisposable, remember to dispose of them in all cases. You should wrap those objects in `using` clauses or `try/finally` blocks. Whichever you use, make sure that objects get disposed properly all the time, every time.

Item 16: Avoid Creating Unnecessary Objects

The Garbage Collector does an excellent job of managing memory for you, and it removes unused objects in a very efficient manner. But no matter how you look at it, allocating and destroying a heap-based object takes more processor time than not allocating and not destroying a heap-based object. You can introduce serious performance drains on your program by creating an excessive number of reference objects that are local to your methods.

So don't overwork the Garbage Collector. You can follow some simple techniques to minimize the amount of work that the Garbage Collector needs to do on your program's behalf. All reference types, even local variables, are allocated on the heap. Every local variable of a reference type becomes garbage as soon as that function exits. One very common bad practice is to allocate GDI objects in a Windows paint handler:

```
// Sample one
protected override void OnPaint(PaintEventArgs e)
{
    // Bad. Created the same font every paint event.
    using (Font MyFont = new Font("Arial", 10.0f))
    {
        e.Graphics.DrawString(DateTime.Now.ToString(),
          MyFont, Brushes.Black, new PointF(0, 0));
    }
    base.OnPaint(e);
}
```

OnPaint() gets called frequently. Every time it gets called, you create another Font object that contains the exact same settings. The Garbage Collector needs to clean those up for you every time. That's incredibly inefficient.

Instead, promote the Font object from a local variable to a member variable. Reuse the same font each time you paint the window:

```
private readonly Font myFont =
  new Font("Arial", 10.0f);

protected override void OnPaint(PaintEventArgs e)
{
    e.Graphics.DrawString(DateTime.Now.ToString(),
      myFont, Brushes.Black, new PointF(0, 0));
    base.OnPaint(e);
}
```

Your program no longer creates garbage with every paint event. The Garbage Collector does less work. Your program runs just a little faster. When you elevate a local variable, such as a font, that implements IDisposable to a member variable, you need to implement IDisposable in your class. Item 18 explains how to properly do just that.

You should promote local variables to member variables when they are reference types (value types don't matter), and they will be used in routines that are called very frequently. The font in the paint routine makes an excellent example. Only local variables in routines that are frequently accessed are good candidates. Infrequently called routines are not. You're trying to avoid creating the same objects repeatedly, not turn every local variable into a member variable.

The static property Brushes.Black used earlier illustrates another technique that you should use to avoid repeatedly allocating similar objects. Create static member variables for commonly used instances of the reference types you need. Consider the black brush used earlier as an example. Every time you need to draw something in your window using the color black, you need a black brush. If you allocate a new one every time you draw anything, you create and destroy a huge number of black brushes during the course of a program. The first approach of creating a black brush as a member of each of your types helps, but it doesn't go far enough. Programs might create dozens of windows and controls, and would create dozens of black brushes. The .NET Framework designers anticipated this and created a single black brush for you to reuse whenever you need it. The Brushes class contains a number of static Brush objects, each with a different common color. Internally, the Brushes class uses a lazy evaluation algorithm to create only those brushes you request. A simplified implementation looks like this:

```
private static Brush blackBrush;
public static Brush Black
{
    get
    {
        if (blackBrush == null)
            blackBrush = new SolidBrush(Color.Black);
        return blackBrush;
    }
}
```

The first time you request a black brush, the Brushes class creates it. The Brushes class keeps a reference to the single black brush and returns that same handle whenever you request it again. The end result is that you create one black brush and reuse it forever. Furthermore, if your application does not need a particular resource—say, the lime green brush—it never gets created. The framework provides a way to limit the objects created to the minimum set you need to accomplish your goals. Copy that technique in your programs.

You've learned two techniques to minimize the number of allocations your program performs as it goes about its business. You can promote often-used local variables to member variables. You can provide a class that stores singleton objects that represent common instances of a given type. The last technique involves building the final value for immutable types. The System.String class is immutable: After you construct a string, the contents of that string cannot be modified. Whenever you write code that appears to modify the contents of a string, you are actually creating a new string object and leaving the old string object as garbage. This seemingly innocent practice:

```
string msg = "Hello, ";
msg += thisUser.Name;
msg += ". Today is ";
msg += System.DateTime.Now.ToString();
```

is just as inefficient as if you had written this:

```
string msg = "Hello, ";
// Not legal, for illustration only:
string tmp1 = new String(msg + thisUser.Name);
msg = tmp1; // "Hello " is garbage.
string tmp2 = new String(msg + ". Today is ");
msg = tmp2; // "Hello <user>" is garbage.
string tmp3 = new String(msg + DateTime.Now.ToString());
msg = tmp3; // "Hello <user>. Today is " is garbage.
```

The strings tmp1, tmp2, and tmp3, and the originally constructed msg ("Hello"), are all garbage. The += method on the string class creates a new string object and returns that string. It does not modify the existing string by concatenating the characters to the original storage. For simple constructs such as the previous one, you should use the string.Format() method:

```
string msg = string.Format("Hello, {0}. Today is {1}",
    thisUser.Name, DateTime.Now.ToString());
```

For more complicated string operations, you can use the StringBuilder class:

```
StringBuilder msg = new StringBuilder("Hello, ");
msg.Append(thisUser.Name);
msg.Append(". Today is ");
msg.Append(DateTime.Now.ToString());
string finalMsg = msg.ToString();
```

StringBuilder is the mutable string class used to build an immutable string object. It provides facilities for mutable strings that let you create and modify text data before you construct an immutable string object. Use StringBuilder to create the final version of a string object. More importantly, learn from that design idiom. When your designs call for immutable types (see Item 20), consider creating builder objects to facilitate the multiphase construction of the final object. That provides a way for users of your class to construct an object in steps, yet maintain the immutability of your type.

The Garbage Collector does an efficient job of managing the memory that your application uses. But remember that creating and destroying heap objects still takes time. Avoid creating excessive objects; don't create what you don't need. Also avoid creating multiple objects of reference types in local functions. Instead, consider promoting local variables to member variables, or create static objects of the most common instances of your types. Finally, consider creating mutable builder classes for immutable types.

Item 17: Implement the Standard Dispose Pattern

We've discussed the importance of disposing of objects that hold unmanaged resources. Now it's time to cover how to write your own resource-management code when you create types that contain resources other than memory. A standard pattern is used throughout the .NET Framework for disposing of unmanaged resources. The users of your type will expect you to follow this standard pattern. The standard dispose idiom frees your unmanaged resources using the IDisposable interface when clients remember, and it uses the finalizer defensively when clients forget. It works with the Garbage Collector to ensure that your objects pay the performance penalty associated with finalizers only when necessary. This is the right way to handle unmanaged resources, so it pays to understand it thoroughly.

The root base class in the class hierarchy should implement the IDisposable interface to free resources. This type should also add a finalizer as a defensive mechanism. Both of these routines delegate the work of freeing resources to a virtual method that derived classes can override for their own resource-management needs. The derived classes need to override the virtual method only when the derived class must free its own resources and it must remember to call the base class version of the function.

To begin, your class must have a finalizer if it uses unmanaged resources. You should not rely on clients to always call the Dispose() method. You'll leak resources when they forget. It's their fault for not calling Dispose, but you'll get the blame. The only way you can guarantee that unmanaged resources get freed properly is to create a finalizer. So create one.

When the Garbage Collector runs, it immediately removes from memory any garbage objects that do not have finalizers. All objects that have finalizers remain in memory. These objects are added to a finalization queue, and the Garbage Collector spawns a new thread to run the finalizers on those objects. After the finalizer thread has finished its work, the garbage objects can be removed from memory. Objects that need finalization stay in memory for far longer than objects without a finalizer. But you have no choice. If you're going to be defensive, you must write a finalizer when your type holds unmanaged resources. But don't worry about performance just yet. The next steps ensure that it's easier for clients to avoid the performance penalty associated with finalization.

Implementing IDisposable is the standard way to inform users and the runtime system that your objects hold resources that must be released in a timely manner. The IDisposable interface contains just one method:

```
public interface IDisposable
{
    void Dispose();
}
```

The implementation of your IDisposable.Dispose() method is responsible for four tasks:

1. Freeing all unmanaged resources.
2. Freeing all managed resources (this includes unhooking events).
3. Setting a state flag to indicate that the object has been disposed. You need to check this state and throw ObjectDisposed exceptions in your public methods, if any get called after disposing of an object.
4. Suppressing finalization. You call GC.SuppressFinalize(this) to accomplish this task.

You accomplish two things by implementing IDisposable: You provide the mechanism for clients to release all managed resources that you hold in a timely fashion, and you give clients a standard way to release all unmanaged resources. That's quite an improvement. After you've implemented IDisposable in your type, clients can avoid the finalization cost. Your class is a reasonably well-behaved member of the .NET community.

But there are still holes in the mechanism you've created. How does a derived class clean up its resources and still let a base class clean up as well? If derived classes override finalize or add their own implementation of IDisposable, those methods must call the base class; otherwise, the base class doesn't clean up properly. Also, finalize and Dispose share some of the same responsibilities: You have almost certainly duplicated code between the finalize method and the Dispose method. As you'll learn in Item 23, overriding interface functions does not work the way you'd expect. The third method in the standard Dispose pattern, a protected virtual helper function, factors out these common tasks and adds a hook for derived classes to free resources they allocate. The base class contains the code for the core interface. The virtual function provides the hook for derived classes to clean up resources in response to Dispose() or finalization:

```
protected virtual void Dispose(bool isDisposing)
```

This overloaded method does the work necessary to support both finalize and Dispose, and because it is virtual, it provides an entry point for all derived classes. Derived classes can override this method, provide the proper implementation to clean up their resources, and call the base class version. You clean up managed and unmanaged resources when isDisposing is true, and you clean up only unmanaged resources when isDisposing is false. In both cases, call the base class's Dispose(bool) method to let it clean up its own resources.

Here is a short sample that shows the framework of code you supply when you implement this pattern. The MyResourceHog class shows the code to implement IDisposable and create the virtual Dispose method:

```
public class MyResourceHog : IDisposable
{
    // Flag for already disposed
    private bool alreadyDisposed = false;

    // Implementation of IDisposable.
    // Call the virtual Dispose method.
    // Suppress Finalization.
    public void Dispose()
    {
        Dispose(true);
        GC.SuppressFinalize(this);
    }
}
```

```csharp
    // Virtual Dispose method
    protected virtual void Dispose(bool isDisposing)
    {
        // Don't dispose more than once.
        if (alreadyDisposed)
            return;
        if (isDisposing)
        {
            // elided: free managed resources here.
        }
        // elided: free unmanaged resources here.
        // Set disposed flag:
        alreadyDisposed = true;
    }

    public void ExampleMethod()
    {
        if (alreadyDisposed)
            throw new ObjectDisposedException(
                "MyResourceHog",
                "Called Example Method on Disposed object");
        // remainder elided.
    }
}
```

If a derived class needs to perform additional cleanup, it implements the protected Dispose method:

```csharp
public class DerivedResourceHog : MyResourceHog
{
    // Have its own disposed flag.
    private bool disposed = false;

    protected override void Dispose(bool isDisposing)
    {
        // Don't dispose more than once.
        if (disposed)
            return;
        if (isDisposing)
        {
            // TODO: free managed resources here.
```

```
        }
        // TODO: free unmanaged resources here.

        // Let the base class free its resources.
        // Base class is responsible for calling
        // GC.SuppressFinalize( )
        base.Dispose(isDisposing);

        // Set derived class disposed flag:
        disposed = true;
    }
}
```

Notice that both the base class and the derived class contain a flag for the disposed state of the object. This is purely defensive. Duplicating the flag encapsulates any possible mistakes made while disposing of an object to only the one type, not all types that make up an object.

You need to write Dispose and finalize defensively. Disposing of objects can happen in any order. You will encounter cases in which one of the member objects in your type is already disposed of before your Dispose() method gets called. You should not view that as a problem because the Dispose() method can be called multiple times. If it's called on an object that has already been disposed of, it does nothing. Finalizers have similar rules. Any object that you reference is still in memory, so you don't need to check null references. However, any object that you reference might be disposed of. It might also have already been finalized.

You'll notice that neither MyResourceHog nor DerivedResourceHog contain a finalizer. The example code I wrote does not directly contain any unmanaged resources. Therefore, a finalizer is not needed. That means the example code never calls Dispose(false). That's the correct pattern. Unless your class directly contains unmanaged resources, you should not implement a finalizer. Only those classes that directly contain an unmanaged resource should implement the finalizer and add that overhead. Even if it's never called, the presence of a finalizer does introduce a rather large performance penalty for your types. Unless your type needs the finalizer, don't add it. However, you should still implement the pattern correctly so that if any derived classes do add unmanaged resources, they can add the finalizer, and implement Dispose(bool) in such a way that unmanaged resources are handled correctly.

This brings me to the most important recommendation for any method associated with disposal or cleanup: You should be releasing resources only. Do not perform any other processing during a dispose method. You can introduce serious complications to object lifetimes by performing other processing in your Dispose or finalize methods. Objects are born when you construct them, and they die when the Garbage Collector reclaims them. You can consider them comatose when your program can no longer access them. If you can't reach an object, you can't call any of its methods. For all intents and purposes, it is dead. But objects that have finalizers get to breathe a last breath before they are declared dead. Finalizers should do nothing but clean up unmanaged resources. If a finalizer somehow makes an object reachable again, it has been resurrected. It's alive and not well, even though it has awoken from a comatose state. Here's an obvious example:

```
public class BadClass
{
    // Store a reference to a global object:
    private static readonly List<BadClass> finalizedList =
        new List<BadClass>();
    private string msg;

    public BadClass(string msg)
    {
        // cache the reference:
        msg = (string)msg.Clone();
    }

    ~BadClass()
    {
        // Add this object to the list.
        // This object is reachable, no
        // longer garbage. It's Back!
        finalizedList.Add(this);
    }
}
```

When a BadClass object executes its finalizer, it puts a reference to itself on a global list. It has just made itself reachable. It's alive again! The number of problems you've just introduced would make anyone cringe. The object has been finalized, so the Garbage Collector now believes there is no need to call its finalizer again. If you actually need to finalize a resurrected object, it won't happen. Second, some of your resources might not be available. The GC will not remove from memory any objects that are reachable only by objects in the finalizer queue, but it might have already finalized them. If so, they are almost certainly no longer usable. Although the members that BadClass owns are still in memory, they will have likely been disposed of or finalized. There is no way in the language that you can control the order of finalization. You cannot make this kind of construct work reliably. Don't try.

I've never seen code that has resurrected objects in such an obvious fashion, except as an academic exercise. But I have seen code in which the finalizer attempts to do some real work and ends up bringing itself back to life when some function that the finalizer calls saves a reference to the object. The moral is to look very carefully at any code in a finalizer and, by extension, both Dispose methods. If that code is doing anything other than releasing resources, look again. Those actions likely will cause bugs in your program in the future. Remove those actions, and make sure that finalizers and Dispose() methods release resources and do nothing else.

In a managed environment, you do not need to write a finalizer for every type you create; you do it only for types that store unmanaged types or when your type contains members that implement IDisposable. Even if you need only the Disposable interface, not a finalizer, implement the entire pattern. Otherwise, you limit your derived classes by complicating their implementation of the standard Dispose idiom. Follow the standard Dispose idiom I've described. That will make life easier for you, for the users of your class, and for those who create derived classes from your types.

Item 18: Distinguish Between Value Types and Reference Types

Value types or reference types? Structs or classes? When should you use each? This isn't C++, in which you define all types as value types and can create references to them. This isn't Java, in which everything is a reference type (unless you are one of the language designers). You must decide how all instances of your type will behave when you create it. It's an important decision to get right the first time. You must live with the consequences of your decision because changing later can cause quite a bit of code to break in subtle ways. It's a simple matter of choosing the `struct` or `class` keyword when you create the type, but it's much more work to update all the clients using your type if you change it later.

It's not as simple as preferring one over the other. The right choice depends on how you expect to use the new type. Value types are not polymorphic. They are better suited to storing the data that your application manipulates. Reference types can be polymorphic and should be used to define the behavior of your application. Consider the expected responsibilities of your new type, and from those responsibilities, decide which type to create. Structs store data. Classes define behavior.

The distinction between value types and reference types was added to .NET and C# because of common problems that occurred in C++ and Java. In C++, all parameters and return values were passed by value. Passing by value is very efficient, but it suffers from one problem: partial copying (sometimes called slicing the object). If you use a derived object where a base object is expected, only the base portion of the object gets copied. You have effectively lost all knowledge that a derived object was ever there. Even calls to virtual functions are sent to the base class version.

The Java language responded by more or less removing value types from the language. All user-defined types are reference types. In the Java language, all parameters and return values are passed by reference. This strategy has the advantage of being consistent, but it's a drain on performance. Let's face it, some types are not polymorphic—they were not intended to be. Java programmers pay a heap allocation and an eventual garbage collection for every variable. They also pay an extra time cost to dereference every variable. All variables are references. In C#, you declare whether a new type should be a value type or a reference type using the `struct` or `class` keywords. Value types should be small, lightweight types. Reference types form your class hierarchy. This section examines different uses for a type so that you understand all the distinctions between value types and reference types.

To start, this type is used as the return value from a method:

```
private MyData myData;
public MyData Foo()
{
    return myData;
}
```

```
// call it:
MyData v = Foo();
TotalSum += v.Value;
```

If MyData is a value type, the return value gets copied into the storage for v. However, if MyData is a reference type, you've exported a reference to an internal variable. You've violated the principle of encapsulation (see Item 26).

Or, consider this variant:

```
public MyData Foo2()
{
    return myData.CreateCopy();
}
```

```
// call it:
MyData v = Foo();
TotalSum += v.Value;
```

Now, v is a copy of the original myData. As a reference type, two objects are created on the heap. You don't have the problem of exposing internal data. Instead, you've created an extra object on the heap. If v is a local variable, it quickly becomes garbage and Clone forces you to use runtime type checking. All in all, it's inefficient.

Types that are used to export data through public methods and properties should be value types. But that's not to say that every type returned from a public member should be a value type. There was an assumption in the earlier code snippet that MyData stores values. Its responsibility is to store those values.

But, consider this alternative code snippet:

```
private MyType myType;
public IMyInterface Foo3()
{
    return myType as IMyInterface;
}
```

```
// call it:
IMyInterface iMe = Foo3();
iMe.DoWork();
```

The myType variable is still returned from the Foo3 method. But this time, instead of accessing the data inside the returned value, the object is accessed to invoke a method through a defined interface. You're accessing the MyType object not for its data contents, but for its behavior. That behavior is expressed through the IMyInterface, which can be implemented by multiple different types. For this example, MyType should be a reference type, not a value type. MyType's responsibilities revolve around its behavior, not its data members.

That simple code snippet starts to show you the distinction: Value types store values, and reference types define behavior. Now look a little deeper at how those types are stored in memory and the performance considerations related to the storage models. Consider this class:

```
public class C
{
    private MyType a = new MyType();
    private MyType b = new MyType();

    // Remaining implementation removed.
}


C cThing = new C();
```

How many objects are created? How big are they? It depends. If MyType is a value type, you've made one allocation. The size of that allocation is twice the size of MyType. However, if MyType is a reference type, you've made three allocations: one for the C object, which is 8 bytes (assuming 32-bit pointers), and two more for each of the MyType objects that are contained in a C object. The difference results because value types are stored inline in an object, whereas reference types are not. Each variable of a reference type holds a reference, and the storage requires extra allocation.

To drive this point home, consider this allocation:

```
MyType[] arrayOfTypes = new MyType[100];
```

If MyType is a value type, one allocation of 100 times the size of a MyType object occurs. However, if MyType is a reference type, one allocation just occurred. Every element of the array is null. When you initialize each element in the array, you will have performed 101 allocations—and 101 allocations take more time than 1 allocation. Allocating a large number of reference types fragments the heap and slows you down. If you are creating types that are meant to store data values, value types are the way to go.

The decision to make a value type or a reference type is an important one. It is a far-reaching change to turn a value type into a class type. Consider this type:

```
public struct Employee
{
    // Properties elided
    public string Position
    {
        get;
        set;
    }

    public decimal CurrentPayAmount
    {
        get;
        set;
    }

    public void Pay(BankAccount b)
    {
        b.Balance += CurrentPayAmount;
    }
}
```

This fairly simple type contains one method to let you pay your employees. Time passes, and the system runs fairly well. Then you decide that there are different classes of Employees: Salespeople get commissions, and managers get bonuses. You decide to change the Employee type into a class:

```
public class Employee2
{
    // Properties elided
    public string Position
    {
        get;
        set;
    }
```

```
public decimal CurrentPayAmount
{
    get;
    set;
}


public virtual void Pay(BankAccount b)
{
    b.Balance += CurrentPayAmount;
}
}
```

That breaks much of the existing code that uses your customer struct. Return by value becomes return by reference. Parameters that were passed by value are now passed by reference. The behavior of this little snippet changed drastically:

```
Employee e1 = Employees.Find(e => e.Position == "CEO");
BankAccount CEOBankAccount = new BankAccount();
decimal Bonus = 10000;
e1.CurrentPayAmount += Bonus; // Add one time bonus.
e1.Pay(CEOBankAccount);
```

What was a one-time bump in pay to add a bonus just became a permanent raise. Where a copy by value had been used, a reference is now in place. The compiler happily makes the changes for you. The CEO is probably happy, too. The CFO, on the other hand, will report the bug. You just can't change your mind about value and reference types after the fact: It changes behavior.

This problem occurred because the Employee type no longer follows the guidelines for a value type. In addition to storing the data elements that define an employee, you've added responsibilities—in this example, paying the employee. Responsibilities are the domain of class types. Classes can define polymorphic implementations of common responsibilities easily; structs cannot and should be limited to storing values.

The documentation for .NET recommends that you consider the size of a type as a determining factor between value types and reference types. In reality, a much better factor is the use of the type. Types that are simple structures or data carriers are excellent candidates for value types. It's true that value types are more efficient in terms of memory management:

There is less heap fragmentation, less garbage, and less indirection. More important, value types are copied when they are returned from methods or properties. There is no danger of exposing references to internal structures. But you pay in terms of features. Value types have very limited support for common object-oriented techniques. You cannot create object hierarchies of value types. You should consider all value types as though they were sealed. You can create value types that implement interfaces but require boxing, which Item 17 shows causes performance degradation. Think of value types as storage containers, not objects in the OO sense.

You'll create more reference types than value types. If you answer yes to all these questions, you should create a value type. Compare these to the previous Employee example:

1. Is this type's principal responsibility data storage?
2. Is its public interface defined entirely by properties that access its data members?
3. Am I confident that this type will never have subclasses?
4. Am I confident that this type will never be treated polymorphically?

Build low-level data storage types as value types. Build the behavior of your application using reference types. You get the safety of copying data that gets exported from your class objects. You get the memory usage benefits that come with stack-based and inline value storage, and you can utilize standard object-oriented techniques to create the logic of your application. When in doubt about the expected use, use a reference type.

Item 19: Ensure That 0 Is a Valid State for Value Types

The default .NET system initialization sets all objects to all 0s. There is no way for you to prevent other programmers from creating an instance of a value type that is initialized to all 0s. Make that the default value for your type.

One special case is enums. Never create an enum that does not include 0 as a valid choice. All enums are derived from System.ValueType. The values for the enumeration start at 0, but you can modify that behavior:

```
public enum Planet
{
    // Explicitly assign values.
```

```
    // Default starts at 0 otherwise.
    Mercury = 1,
    Venus = 2,
    Earth = 3,
    Mars = 4,
    Jupiter = 5,
    Saturn = 6,
    Neptune = 7,
    Uranus = 8
    // First edition included Pluto.
}
```

```
Planet sphere = new Planet();
```

sphere is 0, which is not a valid value. Any code that relies on the (normal) fact that enums are restricted to the defined set of enumerated values won't work. When you create your own values for an enum, make sure that 0 is one of them. If you use bit patterns in your enum, define 0 to be the absence of all the other properties.

As it stands now, you force all users to explicitly initialize the value:

```
Planet sphere2 = Planet.Mars;
```

That makes it harder to build other value types that contain this type:

```
public struct ObservationData
{
    private Planet whichPlanet; //what am I looking at?
    private double magnitude; // perceived brightness.
}
```

Users who create a new ObservationData object will create an invalid Planet field:

```
ObservationData d = new ObservationData();
```

The newly created ObservationData has a 0 magnitude, which is reasonable. But the planet is invalid. You need to make 0 a valid state. If possible, pick the best default as the value 0. The Planet enum does not have an obvious default. It doesn't make any sense to pick some arbitrary planet whenever the user does not. If you run into that situation, use the 0 case for an uninitialized value that can be updated later:

```
public enum Planet2
{
    None = 0,
    Mercury = 1,
    Venus = 2,
    Earth = 3,
    Mars = 4,
    Jupiter = 5,
    Saturn = 6,
    Neptune = 7,
    Uranus = 8
}
```

```
Planet sphere = new Planet();
```

sphere now contains a value for None. Adding this uninitialized default to the Planet enum ripples up to the ObservationData structure. Newly created ObservationData objects have a 0 magnitude and None for the target. Add an explicit constructor to let users of your type initialize all the fields explicitly:

```
public struct ObservationData
{
    Planet whichPlanet; //what am I looking at?
    double magnitude; // perceived brightness.

    ObservationData(Planet target,
      double mag)
    {
        whichPlanet = target;
        magnitude = mag;
    }
}
```

But remember that the default constructor is still visible and part of the structure. Users can still create the system-initialized variant, and you can't stop them.

This is still somewhat faulty, because observing nothing doesn't really make sense. You could solve this specific case by changing Observation-Data to a class, which means that the parameterless constructor does not need to be accessible. But, when you are creating an enum, you cannot force other developers to abide by those rules. The best you can do is to create enum types where the 0 bit pattern is valid, even if that isn't a perfect abstraction.

Before leaving enums to discuss other value types, you need to understand a few special rules for enums used as flags. enums that use the Flags attribute should always set the None value to 0:

```
[Flags]
public enum Styles
{
    None = 0,
    Flat = 1,
    Sunken = 2,
    Raised = 4,
}
```

Many developers use flags enumerations with the bitwise AND operator. 0 values cause serious problems with bitflags. The following test will never work if Flat has the value of 0:

```
if ((flag & Styles.Flat) != 0) // Never true if Flat == 0.
    DoFlatThings();
```

If you use Flags, ensure that 0 is valid and that it means "the absence of all flags."

Another common initialization problem involves value types that contain references. Strings are a common example:

```
public struct LogMessage
{
    private int ErrLevel;
    private string msg;
}


LogMessage MyMessage = new LogMessage();
```

MyMessage contains a null reference in its msg field. There is no way to force a different initialization, but you can localize the problem using properties. You created a property to export the value of msg to all your clients. Add logic to that property to return the empty string instead of null:

```
public struct LogMessage2
{
    private int ErrLevel;
    private string msg;

    public string Message
    {
        get
        {
            return (msg != null) ?
              msg : string.Empty;
        }
        set
        {
            msg = value;
        }
    }
}
```

You should use this property inside your own type. Doing so localizes the null reference check to one location. The Message accessor is almost certainly inlined as well, when called from inside your assembly. You'll get efficient code and minimize errors.

The system initializes all instances of value types to 0. There is no way to prevent users from creating instances of value types that are all 0s. If possible, make the all 0 case the natural default. As a special case, enums used as flags should ensure that 0 is the absence of all flags.

Item 20: Prefer Immutable Atomic Value Types

Immutable types are simple: After they are created, they are constant. If you validate the parameters used to construct the object, you know that it is in a valid state from that point forward. You cannot change the object's internal state to make it invalid. You save yourself a lot of otherwise necessary error checking by disallowing any state changes after an object has been constructed. Immutable types are inherently thread safe: Multiple readers can access the same contents. If the internal state cannot change, there is no chance for different threads to see inconsistent views of the data. Immutable types can be exported from your objects safely. The caller cannot modify the internal state of your objects. Immutable types work better in hash-based collections. The value returned by Object.GetHashCode() must be an instance invariant (see Item 7); that's always true for immutable types.

In practice, it is very difficult to make every type immutable. You would need to clone objects to modify any program state. That's why this recommendation is for both atomic and immutable value types. Decompose your types to the structures that naturally form a single entity. An Address type does. An address is a single thing, composed of multiple related fields. A change in one field likely means changes to other fields. A customer type is not an atomic type. A customer type will likely contain many pieces of information: an address, a name, and one or more phone numbers. Any of these independent pieces of information might change. A customer might change phone numbers without moving. A customer might move, yet still keep the same phone number. A customer might change his or her name without moving or changing phone numbers. A customer object is not atomic; it is built from many different immutable types using composition: an address, a name, or a collection of phone number/type pairs. Atomic types are single entities: You would naturally replace the entire contents of an atomic type. The exception would be to change one of its component fields.

Here is a typical implementation of an address that is mutable:

```
// Mutable Address structure.
public struct Address
{
    private string state;
    private int zipCode;

    // Rely on the default system-generated
    // constructor.

    public string Line1
    {
        get;
        set;
    }
    public string Line2
    {
```

```
            get;
            set;
        }
    public string City
    {
            get;
            set;
    }
    public string State
    {
            get { return state; }
            set
            {
                ValidateState(value);
                state = value;
            }
    }

    public int ZipCode
    {
            get { return zipCode; }
            set
            {
                ValidateZip(value);
                zipCode = value;
            }
    }
    // other details omitted.
}


// Example usage:
Address a1 = new Address();
a1.Line1 = "111 S. Main";
a1.City = "Anytown";
a1.State = "IL";
a1.ZipCode = 61111;
// Modify:
a1.City = "Ann Arbor"; // Zip, State invalid now.
a1.ZipCode = 48103; // State still invalid now.
a1.State = "MI"; // Now fine.
```

Internal state changes mean that it's possible to violate object invariants, at least temporarily. After you have replaced the City field, you have placed a1 in an invalid state. The city has changed and no longer matches the state or ZIP code fields. The code looks harmless enough, but suppose that this fragment is part of a multithreaded program. Any context switch after the city changes and before the state changes would leave the potential for another thread to see an inconsistent view of the data.

Okay, so you think you're not writing a multithreaded program. You can still get into trouble. Imagine that the ZIP code was invalid and the set threw an exception. You've made only some of the changes you intended, and you've left the system in an invalid state. To fix this problem, you would need to add considerable internal validation code to the address structure. That validation code would add considerable size and complexity. To fully implement exception safety, you would need to create defensive copies around any code block in which you change more than one field. Thread safety would require adding significant thread-synchronization checks on each property accessor, both sets and gets. All in all, it would be a significant undertaking—and one that would likely be extended over time as you add new features.

Instead, if you need Address to be a `struct`, make it immutable. Start by changing all instance fields to read-only for outside uses.

```
public struct Address2
{
    // remaining details elided
    public string Line1
    {
        get;
        private set;
    }
    public string Line2
    {
        get;
        private set;
    }
    public string City
    {
        get;
```

```
        private set;
    }
    public string State
    {
        get;
        private set;
    }
    public int ZipCode
    {
        get;
        private set;
    }
}
```

Now you have an immutable type, based on the public interface. To make it useful, you need to add all necessary constructors to initialize the Address structure completely. The Address structure needs only one additional constructor, specifying each field. A copy constructor is not needed because the assignment operator is just as efficient. Remember that the default constructor is still accessible. There is a default address where all the strings are null, and the ZIP code is 0:

```
public Address2(string line1,
    string line2,
    string city,
    string state,
    int zipCode) :
    this()
{
    Line1 = line1;
    Line2 = line2;
    City = city;
    ValidateState(state);
    State = state;
    ValidateZip(zipCode);
    ZipCode = zipCode;
}
```

Using the immutable type requires a slightly different calling sequence to modify its state. You create a new object rather than modify the existing instance:

```
// Create an address:
Address2 a2 = new Address2("111 S. Main",
    "", "Anytown", "IL", 61111);

// To change, re-initialize:
a2 = new Address2(a1.Line1,
    a1.Line2, "Ann Arbor", "MI", 48103);
```

The value of a1 is in one of two states: its original location in Anytown, or its updated location in Ann Arbor. You do not modify the existing address to create any of the invalid temporary states from the previous example. Those interim states exist only during the execution of the Address constructor and are not visible outside that constructor. As soon as a new Address object is constructed, its value is fixed for all time. It's exception safe: a1 has either its original value or its new value. If an exception is thrown during the construction of the new Address object, the original value of a1 is unchanged.

This second Address type is not strictly immutable. Implicit Properties with private setters can still contain methods that change the internal state. If you want a truly immutable type, you would need to make further changes. You need to change the implicit properties to explicit properties, and change the backing field to a `readonly` field of the type:

```
public struct Address3
{
    // remaining details elided
    public string Line1
    {
        get { return Line1; }
    }
    private readonly string line1;

    public string Line2
    {
        get { return line2; }
    }
    private readonly string line2;

    public string City
    {
```

```
        get { return city; }
    }
    private readonly string city;

    public string State
    {
        get { return state; }
    }
    private readonly string state;

    public int ZipCode
    {
        get { return zip; }
    }
    private readonly int zip;

    public Address3(string line1,
        string line2,
        string city,
        string state,
        int zipCode) :
        this()
    {
        this.line1 = line1;
        this.line2 = line2;
        this.city = city;
        ValidateState(state);
        this.state = state;
        ValidateZip(zipCode);
        this.zip = zipCode;
    }
}
```

To create an immutable type, you need to ensure that there are no holes that would allow clients to change your internal state. Value types do not support derived types, so you do not need to defend against derived types modifying fields. But you do need to watch for any fields in an immutable type that are mutable reference types. When you implement your constructors for these types, you need to make a defensive copy of that mutable type. All these examples assume that Phone is an immutable value type because we're concerned only with immutability in value types:

```
// Almost immutable: there are holes that would
// allow state changes.
public struct PhoneList
{
    private readonly Phone[] phones;

    public PhoneList(Phone[] ph)
    {
        phones = ph;
    }

    public IEnumerable<Phone> Phones
    {
        get
        {
            return phones;
        }
    }
}

Phone[] phones = new Phone[10];
// initialize phones
PhoneList pl = new PhoneList(phones);

// Modify the phone list:
// also modifies the internals of the (supposedly)
// immutable object.
phones[5] = Phone.GeneratePhoneNumber();
```

The array class is a reference type. The array referenced inside the PhoneList structure refers to the same array storage (phones) allocated outside the object. Developers can modify your immutable structure through another variable that refers to the same storage. To remove this possibility, you need to make a defensive copy of the array. The previous example shows the pitfalls of a mutable collection. Even more possibilities for mischief exist if the Phone type is a mutable reference type. Clients could modify the values in the collection, even if the collection is protected against any modification. This defensive copy should be made in all constructors whenever your immutable type contains a mutable reference type:

```
// Immutable: A copy is made at construction.
public struct PhoneList2
{
    private readonly Phone[] phones;

    public PhoneList2(Phone[] ph)
    {
        phones = new Phone[ph.Length];
        // Copies values because Phone is a value type.
        ph.CopyTo(phones, 0);
    }

    public IEnumerable<Phone> Phones
    {
        get
        {
            return phones;
        }
    }
}


Phone[] phones2 = new Phone[10];
// initialize phones
PhoneList p2 = new PhoneList(phones);

// Modify the phone list:
// Does not modify the copy in p1.
phones2[5] = Phone.GeneratePhoneNumber();
```

You need to follow the same rules when you return a mutable reference type. If you add a property to retrieve the entire array from the PhoneList struct, that accessor would also need to create a defensive copy. See Item 27 for more details.

The complexity of a type dictates which of three strategies you will use to initialize your immutable type. The Address structure defined one constructor to allow clients to initialize an address. Defining the reasonable set of constructors is often the simplest approach.

You can also create factory methods to initialize the structure. Factories make it easier to create common values. The .NET Framework Color type follows this strategy to initialize system colors. The static methods Color.FromKnownColor() and Color.FromName() return a copy of a color value that represents the current value for a given system color.

Third, you can create a mutable companion class for those instances in which multistep operations are necessary to fully construct an immutable type. The .NET string class follows this strategy with the System.Text .StringBuilder class. You use the StringBuilder class to create a string using multiple operations. After performing all the operations necessary to build the string, you retrieve the immutable string from the StringBuilder.

Immutable types are simpler to code and easier to maintain. Don't blindly create `get` and `set` accessors for every property in your type. Your first choice for types that store data should be immutable, atomic value types. You easily can build more complicated structures from these entities.

3 | Expressing Designs in C#

Beginners using a foreign (human) language can manage to communicate. They know the words, and they can piece them together to get their point across. As beginners transition to experts in a language, they begin to use the proper idioms in this foreign language. The language becomes less foreign, and the person begins speaking more efficiently and more clearly. Programming languages are no different. The techniques you choose communicate your design intent to the developers who maintain, extend, or use the software you develop. C# types all live inside the .NET environment. The environment makes some assumptions about the capabilities of all types as well. If you violate those assumptions, you increase the likelihood that your types won't function correctly.

The items in this chapter are not a compendium of software design techniques—entire volumes have been written about software design. Instead, these items highlight how different C# language features can best express the intent of your software design. The C# language designers added language features to more clearly express modern design idioms. The distinctions among certain language features are subtle, and you often have many alternatives to choose from. More than one alternative might seem "best" at first; the distinctions show up only later, when you find that you must enhance an existing program. Make sure you understand these items well, and apply them carefully with an eye toward the most likely enhancements to the systems you are building.

Some syntax changes give you new vocabulary to describe the idioms you use every day. Properties, indexers, events, and delegates are examples, as is the difference between classes and interfaces: Classes define types. Interfaces declare behavior. Base classes declare types and define common behavior for a related set of types. Other design idioms have changed because of the Garbage Collector. Still others have changed because most variables are reference types.

The recommendations in this chapter will help you pick the most natural expression for your designs. This will enable you to create software that is easier to maintain, easier to extend, and easier to use.

Item 21: Limit Visibility of Your Types

Not everybody needs to see everything. Not every type you create needs to be public. You should give each type the least visibility necessary to accomplish your purpose. That's often less visibility than you think. Internal or private classes can implement public interfaces. All clients can access the functionality defined in the public interfaces declared in a private type.

It's just too easy to create public types. And, it's often expedient to do just that. Many standalone classes that you create should be internal. You can further limit visibility by creating protected or private classes nested inside your original class. The less visibility there is, the less the entire system changes when you make updates later. The fewer places that can access a piece of code, the fewer places you must change when you modify it.

Expose only what needs to be exposed. Try implementing public interfaces with less visible classes. You'll find examples using the Enumerator pattern throughout the .NET Framework library. System.Collections.Generic .List<T> contains a private class, Enumerator<T>, that implements the IEnumerator<T> interface:

```
// For illustration, not complete source
public class List<T> : IEnumerable<T>
{
    private class Enumerator<T> : IEnumerator<T>
    {
        // Contains specific implementation of
        // MoveNext(), Reset(), and Current.

        public Enumerator(List<T> storage)
        {
            // elided
        }
    }

    public IEnumerator<T> GetEnumerator()
    {
        return new Enumerator<T>(this);
    }

    // other List members.
}
```

Client code, written by you, never needs to know about the class Enumerator<T>. All you need to know is that you get an object that implements the IEnumerator<T> interface when you call the GetEnumerator function on a List<T> object. The specific type is an implementation detail. The .NET Framework designers followed this same pattern with the other collection classes: Dictionary<T> contains a private DictionaryEnumerator<T>, Queue<T> contains a QueueEnumerator<T>, and so on. The enumerator class being private gives many advantages. First, the List<T> class can completely replace the type implementing IEnumerator<T>, and you'd be none the wiser. Nothing breaks. Also, the enumerator class need not be Common Language Specification (CLS) compliant. It's not public (see Item 49). Its public interface is compliant. You can use the enumerator without detailed knowledge about the class that implements it.

Creating internal classes is an often-overlooked method of limiting the scope of types. By default, most programmers create public classes all the time, without any thought to the alternatives. It's that VS .NET wizard thing. Instead of unthinkingly accepting the default, you should give careful thought to where your new type will be used. Is it useful to all clients, or is it primarily used internally in this one assembly?

Exposing your functionality using interfaces enables you to more easily create internal classes without limiting their usefulness outside the assembly (see Item 26). Does the type need to be public, or is an aggregation of interfaces a better way to describe its functionality? Internal classes allow you to replace the class with a different version, as long as it implements the same interfaces. As an example, consider a class that validates phone numbers:

```
public class PhoneValidator
{
    public bool ValidateNumber(PhoneNumber ph)
    {
        // perform validation.
        // Check for valid area code, exchange.
        return true;
    }
}
```

Months pass, and this class works fine. Then you get a request to handle international phone numbers. The previous PhoneValidator fails. It was coded to handle only U.S. phone numbers. You still need the U.S. Phone

Validator, but now you need to use an international version in one installation. Rather than stick the extra functionality in this one class, you're better off reducing the coupling between the different items. You create an interface to validate any phone number:

```
public interface IPhoneValidator
{
    bool ValidateNumber(PhoneNumber ph);
}
```

Next, change the existing phone validator to implement that interface, and make it an internal class:

```
internal class USPhoneValidator : IPhoneValidator
{
    public bool ValidateNumber(PhoneNumber ph)
    {
        // perform validation.
        // Check for valid area code, exchange.
        return true;
    }
}
```

Finally, you can create a class for international phone validators:

```
internal class InternationalPhoneValidator : IPhoneValidator
{
    public bool ValidateNumber(PhoneNumber ph)
    {
        // perform validation.
        // Check international code.
        // Check specific phone number rules.
        return true;
    }
}
```

To finish this implementation, you need to create the proper class based on the type of the phone number. You can use the factory pattern for this purpose. Outside the assembly, only the interface is visible. The classes, which are specific for different regions in the world, are visible only inside the assembly. You can add different validation classes for different regions without disturbing any other assemblies in the system. By limiting the scope of the classes, you have limited the code you need to change to update and extend the entire system.

You could also create a public abstract base class for PhoneValidator, which could contain common implementation algorithms. The consumers could access the public functionality through the accessible base class. In this example, I prefer the implementation using public interfaces because there is little, if any, shared functionality. Other uses would be better served with public abstract base classes. Either way you implement it, fewer classes are publicly accessible.

In addition, fewer public types will create a smaller public surface area that will facilitate unit testing coverage. If there are fewer public types, there are fewer publicly accessible methods for which you need to create tests. Also, if more of the public APIs are exposed through interfaces, you have automatically created a system whereby you can replace those types using some kind of stubs for unit test purposes.

Those classes and interfaces that you expose publicly to the outside world are your contract: You must live up to them. The more cluttered that interface is, the more constrained your future direction is. The fewer public types you expose, the more options you have to extend and modify any implementation in the future.

Item 22: Prefer Defining and Implementing Interfaces to Inheritance

Abstract base classes provide a common ancestor for a class hierarchy. An interface describes one atomic piece of functionality that can be implemented by a type. Each has its place, but it is a different place. Interfaces are a way to design by contract: A type that implements an interface must supply an implementation for expected methods. Abstract base classes provide a common abstraction for a set of related types. It's a cliché, but it's one that works: Inheritance means "is a," and interfaces means "behaves like." These clichés have lived so long because they provide a means to describe the differences in both constructs: Base classes describe what an object is; interfaces describe one way in which it behaves.

Interfaces describe a set of functionality, or a contract. You can create placeholders for anything in an interface: methods, properties, indexers, and events. Any type that implements the interface must supply concrete implementations of all elements defined in the interface. You must implement all methods, supply any and all property accessors and indexers, and define all events defined in the interface. You identify and factor reusable behavior into interfaces. You use interfaces as parameters and return values. You also have more chances to reuse code because unrelated types can implement interfaces. What's more, it's easier for other developers to implement an interface than it is to derive from a base class you've created.

What you can't do in an interface is provide implementation for any of these members. Interfaces contain no implementation whatsoever, and they cannot contain any concrete data members. You are declaring the binary contract that must be supported by all types that implement an interface. However, you can create extension methods on those interfaces to give the illusion of an implementation for interfaces. The System .Linq.Enumerable class contains more than 30 extension methods declared on IEnumerable<T>. Those methods appear to be part of any type that implements IEnumerable<T> by virtue of being extension methods. You saw this in Item 8:

```
public static class Extensions
{
    public static void ForAll<T>(
        this IEnumerable<T> sequence,
        Action<T> action)
    {
        foreach (T item in sequence)
            action(item);
    }
}
// usage
foo.ForAll((n) => Console.WriteLine(n.ToString()));
```

Abstract base classes can supply some implementation for derived types, in addition to describing the common behavior. You can specify data members, concrete methods, implementation for virtual methods, properties, events, and indexers. A base class can provide implementation for some of the methods, thereby providing common implementation reuse. Any of the elements can be virtual, abstract, or nonvirtual. An abstract base class can provide an implementation for any concrete behavior; interfaces cannot.

This implementation reuse provides another benefit: If you add a method to the base class, all derived classes are automatically and implicitly enhanced. In that sense, base classes provide a way to extend the behavior of several types efficiently over time: By adding and implementing functionality in the base class, all derived classes immediately incorporate that behavior. Adding a member to an interface breaks all the classes that implement that interface. They will not contain the new method and will no longer compile. Each implementer must update that type to include the new member.

Choosing between an abstract base class and an interface is a question of how best to support your abstractions over time. Interfaces are fixed: You release an interface as a contract for a set of functionality that any type can implement. Base classes can be extended over time. Those extensions become part of every derived class.

The two models can be mixed to reuse implementation code while supporting multiple interfaces. One obvious example in the .NET Framework is the IEnumerable<T> interface and the System.Linq.Enumerable class. The System.Linq.Enumerable class contains a large number of extension methods defined on the System.Collections.Generic.IEnumerable<T> interface. That separation enables very important benefits. Any class that implements IEnumerable<T> appears to include all those extension methods. However, those additional methods are not formally defined in the IEnumerable<T> interface. That means class developers do not need to create their own implementation of all those methods.

Examine this class that implements IEnumerable<T> for weather observations.

```
public enum Direction
{
    North,
    NorthEast,
    East,
    SouthEast,
    South,
    SouthWest,
    West,
    NorthWest
}
```

```csharp
public class WeatherData
{
    public double Temperature { get; set; }
    public int WindSpeed { get; set; }
    public Direction WindDirection { get; set; }
    public override string ToString()
    {
        return string.Format(
        "Temperature = {0}, Wind is {1} mph from the {2}",
            Temperature, WindSpeed, WindDirection);
    }
}


public class WeatherDataStream : IEnumerable<WeatherData>
{
    private Random generator = new Random();

    public WeatherDataStream(string location)
    {
        // elided
    }

    private IEnumerator<WeatherData> getElements()
    {
        // Real implementation would read from
        // a weather station.
        for (int i = 0; i < 100; i++)
            yield return new WeatherData
            {
                Temperature = generator.NextDouble() * 90,
                WindSpeed = generator.Next(70),
                WindDirection = (Direction)generator.Next(7)
            };
    }

    #region IEnumerable<WeatherData> Members
    public IEnumerator<WeatherData> GetEnumerator()
    {
        return getElements();
    }
    #endregion
```

```
    #region IEnumerable Members
    System.Collections.IEnumerator
        System.Collections.IEnumerable.GetEnumerator()
    {
        return getElements();
    }
    #endregion
}
```

The WeatherStream class models a sequence of weather observations. To do that it implements IEnumerable<WeatherData>. That means creating two methods: the GetEnumerator<T> method and the classic GetEnumerator method. The latter interface is explicitly implemented so that client code would naturally be drawn to the generic interface over the version typed as System.Object.

Implementing those two methods means that the WeatherStream class supports all the extension methods defined in System.Linq.Enumerable. That means WeatherStream can be a source for LINQ queries:

```
var warmDays = from item in
               new WeatherDataStream("Ann Arbor")
               where item.Temperature > 80
               select item;
```

LINQ query syntax compiles to method calls. The query above translates to the following calls:

```
var warmDays2 = new WeatherDataStream("Ann Arbor").
                Where(item => item.Temperature > 80).
                Select(item => item);
```

In the code above, the Where and Select calls look like they belong to IEnumerable<WeatherData>. They do not. Those methods appear to belong to IEnumerable<WeatherData> because they are extension methods. They are actually static methods in System.Linq.Enumerable. The compiler translates those calls into the following static calls:

```
// Don't write this, for explanatory purposes
var warmDays3 = Enumerable.Select(
                Enumerable.Where(
                new WeatherDataStream("Ann Arbor"),
                item => item.Temperature > 80),
                item => item);
```

I wrote that last version to show you that interfaces really can't contain implementation. You can emulate that by using extension methods. LINQ does that by creating several extension methods on IEnumerable<T> in the System.Linq.Enumerable class.

That brings me to the topic of using interfaces as parameters and return values. An interface can be implemented by any number of unrelated types. Coding to interfaces provides greater flexibility to other developers than coding to base class types. That's important because of the single inheritance hierarchy that the .NET environment enforces.

These three methods perform the same task:

```
public static void PrintCollection<T>(
    IEnumerable<T> collection)
{
    foreach (T o in collection)
        Console.WriteLine("Collection contains {0}",
            o.ToString());
}


public static void PrintCollection(
    System.Collections.IEnumerable collection)
{
    foreach (object o in collection)
        Console.WriteLine("Collection contains {0}",
            o.ToString());
}


public static void PrintCollection(
    WeatherDataStream collection)
{
    foreach (object o in collection)
        Console.WriteLine("Collection contains {0}",
            o.ToString());
}
```

The first method is most reusable. Any type that supports IEnumerable<T> can use that method. In addition to WeatherDataStream, you can use List<T>, SortedList<T>, any Array, and the results of any LINQ query. The second method will also work with many types, but uses the less preferable nongeneric IEnumerable. The final method is far less reusable. It cannot be used with Arrays, ArrayLists, DataTables, Hashtables, ImageLists, or many other collection classes. Coding the method using interfaces as its parameter types is far more generic and far easier to reuse.

Using interfaces to define the APIs for a class also provides greater flexibility. The WeatherDataStream class could implement a method that returned a collection of WeatherData objects. That would look something like this:

```
public List<WeatherData> DataSequence
{
    get { return sequence; }
}
private List<WeatherData> sequence = new List<WeatherData>();
```

That leaves you vulnerable to future problems. At some point, you might change from using a List<WeatherData> to exposing an array, a SortedList<T>. Any of those changes will break the code. Sure, you can change the parameter type, but that's changing the public interface to your class. Changing the public interface to a class causes you to make many more changes to a large system; you would need to change all the locations where the public property was accessed.

The second problem is more immediate and more troubling: The List<T> class provides numerous methods to change the data it contains. Users of your class could delete, modify, or even replace every object in the sequence. That's almost certainly not your intent. Luckily, you can limit the capabilities of the users of your class. Instead of returning a reference to some internal object, you should return the interface you intend clients to use. That would mean returning an IEnumerable<WeatherData>.

When your type exposes properties as class types, it exposes the entire interface to that class. Using interfaces, you can choose to expose only the methods and properties you want clients to use. The class used to implement the interface is an implementation detail that can change over time (see Item 26).

Furthermore, unrelated types can implement the same interface. Suppose you're building an application that manages employees, customers, and vendors. Those are unrelated, at least in terms of the class hierarchy. But they share some common functionality. They all have names, and you will likely display those names in controls in your applications.

```csharp
public class Employee
{
    public string FirstName { get; set; }
    public string LastName { get; set; }

    public string Name
    {
        get
        {
            return string.Format("{0}, {1}",
                LastName, FirstName);
        }
    }

    // other details elided.
}

public class Customer
{
    public string Name
    {
        get
        {
            return customerName;
        }
    }

    // other details elided
    private string customerName;
}

public class Vendor
{
    public string Name
    {
        get
        {
            return vendorName;
        }
    }
}
```

```
    // other details elided
    private string vendorName;
}
```

The Employee, Customer, and Vendor classes should not share a common base class. But they do share some properties: names (as shown earlier), addresses, and contact phone numbers. You could factor out those properties into an interface:

```
public interface IContactInfo
{
    string Name { get; }
    PhoneNumber PrimaryContact { get; }
    PhoneNumber Fax { get; }
    Address PrimaryAddress { get; }
}


public class Employee : IContactInfo
{
    // implementation elided.
}
```

This new interface can simplify your programming tasks by letting you build common routines for unrelated types:

```
public void PrintMailingLabel(IContactInfo ic)
{
    // implementation deleted.
}
```

This one routine works for all entities that implement the IContactInfo interface. Customer, Employee, and Vendor all use the same routine—but only because you factored them into interfaces.

Using interfaces also means that you can occasionally save an unboxing penalty for structs. When you place a struct in a box, the box supports all interfaces that the struct supports. When you access the struct through the interface pointer, you don't have to unbox the struct to access that object. To illustrate, imagine this struct that defines a link and a description:

```
public struct URLInfo : IComparable<URLInfo>, IComparable
{
```

```
    private string URL;
    private string description;

    #region IComparable<URLInfo> Members
    public int CompareTo(URLInfo other)
    {
        return URL.CompareTo(other.URL);
    }
    #endregion

    #region IComparable Members
    int IComparable.CompareTo(object obj)
    {
        if (obj is URLInfo)
        {
            URLInfo other = (URLInfo)obj;
            return CompareTo(other);
        }
        else
            throw new ArgumentException(
                "Compared object is not URLInfo");
    }
    #endregion
}
```

You can create a sorted list of URLInfo objects easily because URLInfo implements IComparable<T> and IComparable. Even code that relies on the classic IComparable will have fewer times when boxing and unboxing is necessary because the client can call IComparable.CompareTo() without unboxing the object.

Base classes describe and implement common behaviors across related concrete types. Interfaces describe atomic pieces of functionality that unrelated concrete types can implement. Both have their place. Classes define the types you create. Interfaces describe the behavior of those types as pieces of functionality. If you understand the differences, you will create more expressive designs that are more resilient in the face of change. Use class hierarchies to define related types. Expose functionality using interfaces implemented across those types.

Item 23: Understand How Interface Methods Differ from Virtual Methods

At first glance, implementing an interface seems to be the same as over-riding a virtual function. You provide a definition for a member that has been declared in another type. That first glance is very deceiving. Implementing an interface is very different from overriding a virtual function. Members declared in interfaces are not virtual—at least, not by default. Derived classes cannot override an interface member implemented in a base class. Interfaces can be explicitly implemented, which hides them from a class's public interface. They are different concepts with different uses.

But you can implement interfaces in such a manner that derived classes can modify your implementation. You just have to create hooks for derived classes.

To illustrate the differences, examine a simple interface and implementation of it in one class:

```
interface IMsg
{
    void Message();
}


public class MyClass : IMsg
{
    public void Message()
    {
        Console.WriteLine("MyClass");
    }
}
```

The Message() method is part of MyClass's public interface. Message can also be accessed through the IMsg point that is part of the MyClass type. Now let's complicate the situation a little by adding a derived class:

```
public class MyDerivedClass : MyClass
{
    public void Message()
    {
        Console.WriteLine("MyDerivedClass");
    }
}
```

Notice that I had to add the new keyword to the definition of the previous Message method (see Item 33). MyClass.Message() is not virtual. Derived classes cannot provide an overridden version of Message. The MyDerived class creates a new Message method, but that method does not override MyClass.Message: It hides it. Furthermore, MyClass.Message is still available through the IMsg reference:

```
MyDerivedClass d = new MyDerivedClass();
d.Message(); // prints "MyDerivedClass".
IMsg m = d as IMsg;
m.Message(); // prints "MyClass"
```

Interface methods are not virtual. When you implement an interface, you are declaring a concrete implementation of a particular contract in that type.

But you often want to create interfaces, implement them in base classes, and modify the behavior in derived classes. You can. You've got two options. If you do not have access to the base class, you can reimplement the interface in the derived class:

```
public class MyDerivedClass : MyClass
{
    public new void Message()
    {
        Console.WriteLine("MyDerivedClass");
    }
}
```

The addition of the IMsg keyword changes the behavior of your derived class so that IMsg.Message() now uses the derived class version:

```
MyDerivedClass d = new MyDerivedClass();
d.Message(); // prints "MyDerivedClass".
IMsg m = d as IMsg;
m.Message(); // prints " MyDerivedClass "
```

You still need the new keyword on the MyDerivedClass.Message() method. That's your clue that there are still problems (see Item 33). The base class version is still accessible through a reference to the base class:

```
MyDerivedClass d = new MyDerivedClass();
d.Message(); // prints "MyDerivedClass".
```

```
IMsg m = d as IMsg;
m.Message(); // prints "MyDerivedClass"
MyClass b = d;
b.Message(); // prints "MyClass"
```

One way to fix this problem is to modify the base class, declaring that the interface methods should be virtual:

```
public class MyClass : IMsg
{
    public virtual void Message()
    {
        Console.WriteLine("MyClass");
    }
}


public class MyDerivedClass : MyClass
{
    public override void Message()
    {
        Console.WriteLine("MyDerivedClass");
    }
}
```

MyDerivedClass—and all classes derived from MyClass—can declare their own methods for Message(). The overridden version will be called every time: through the MyDerivedClass reference, through the IMsg reference, and through the MyClass reference.

If you dislike the concept of impure virtual functions, just make one small change to the definition of MyClass:

```
public abstract class MyClass : IMsg
{
    public abstract void Message();
}
```

Yes, you can implement an interface without actually implementing the methods in that interface. By declaring abstract versions of the methods in the interface, you declare that all types derived from your type must implement that interface. The IMsg interface is part of the declaration of MyClass, but defining the methods is deferred to each derived class.

Derived classes can also prevent further overrides by sealing the method:

```
public class MyDerivedClass2 : MyClass
{
    public sealed override void Message()
    {
        Console.WriteLine("MyDerivedClass");
    }
}
```

Another solution is to implement the interface, and include a call to a virtual method that enables derived classes to participate in the interface contract. You would do that in MyClass this way:

```
public class MyClass2 : IMsg
{
    protected virtual void OnMessage()
    {
    }

    public void Message()
    {
        OnMessage();
        Console.WriteLine("MyClass");
    }
}
```

Any derived class can override OnMessage() and add their own work to the Message() method declared in MyClass2. It's a pattern you've seen before when classes implement IDisposable (see Item 17).

Explicit interface implementation (see Item 31) enables you to implement an interface, yet hide its members from the public interface of your type. Its use throws a few other twists into the relationships between implementing interfaces and overriding virtual functions. You use explicit interface implementation to limit client code from using the interface methods when a more appropriate version is available. The IComparable idiom in Item 31 shows this in detail.

There is also one last wrinkle to add to working with interfaces and base classes. A base class can provide a default implementation for methods in an interface. Then, a derived class can declare that it implements an interface and inherit the implementation from that base class, as this example shows.

```
public class DefaultMessageGenerator
{
    public void Message()
    {
        Console.WriteLine("This is a default message");
    }
}


public class AnotherMessageGenerator :
    DefaultMessageGenerator, IMsg
{
    // No explicit Message() method needed.
}
```

Notice that the derived class can declare the interface as part of its contract, even though it does not provide any implementation of the IMsg methods. As long as it has a publicly accessible method with the proper signature, the interface contract is satisfied. Using this method, you cannot use explicit interface implementation.

Implementing interfaces allows more options than creating and overriding virtual functions. You can create sealed implementations, virtual implementations, or abstract contracts for class hierarchies. You can also create a sealed implementation and provide virtual method calls in the methods that implement interfaces. You can decide exactly how and when derived classes can modify the default behavior for members of any interface your class implements. Interface methods are not virtual methods but a separate contract.

Item 24: Express Callbacks with Delegates

> Me: "Son, go mow the yard. I'm going to read for a while."
> Scott: "Dad, I cleaned up the yard."
> Scott: "Dad, I put gas in the mower."
> Scott: "Dad, the mower won't start."
> Me: "I'll start it."
> Scott: "Dad, I'm done."

This little exchange illustrates callbacks. I gave my son a task, and he (repeatedly) interrupted me with the status. I did not block my own progress while I waited for him to finish each part of the task. He was able to interrupt me periodically when he had an important (or even unimportant) status to report or needed my assistance. Callbacks are used to provide feedback from a server to a client asynchronously. They might involve multithreading, or they might simply provide an entry point for synchronous updates. Callbacks are expressed using delegates in the C# language.

Delegates provide type-safe callback definitions. Although the most common use of delegates is events, that should not be the only time you use this language feature. Anytime you need to configure the communication between classes and you desire less coupling than you get from interfaces, a delegate is the right choice. Delegates let you configure the target at runtime and notify multiple clients. A delegate is an object that contains a reference to a method. That method can be either a static method or an instance method. Using the delegate, you can communicate with one or many client objects, configured at runtime.

Callbacks and delegates are such a common idiom that the C# language provides compact syntax in the form of lambda expressions to express delegates. In addition, the .NET Framework library defines many common delegate forms using Predicate<T>, Action<>, and Func<>. A predicate is a Boolean function that tests a condition. A Func<> takes a number of parameters and produces a single result. Yes, that means a Func<T, bool> has the same form as a Predicate<T>. The compiler will not view Predicate<T> and Func<T, bool> as the same though. Finally, Action<> takes any number of parameters and has the void return type.

LINQ was built using these concepts. The List<T> class also contains many methods that make use of callbacks. Examine this code snippet:

```
List<int> numbers = Enumerable.Range(1, 200).ToList();

var oddNumbers = numbers.Find(n => n % 2 == 1);
var test = numbers.TrueForAll(n => n < 50);

numbers.RemoveAll(n => n % 2 == 0);

numbers.ForEach(item => Console.WriteLine(item));
```

The Find() method takes a delegate, in the form of a Predicate<int> to perform a test on each element in the list. It's a simple callback. The Find() method tests each item, using the callback, and returns the elements that pass the test embodied in the predicate. The compiler takes the lambda expression, converts that to a delegate, and uses the delegate to express the callback.

TrueForAll() is similar in that it applies the test to each of the elements, and determines if the predicate is true for all items. RemoveAll() modifies the list container by removing all items for which the predicate is true.

Finally, the List.ForEach() method performs the specified action on each of the elements in the list. As before, the compiler converts the lambda expression into a method and creates a delegate referring to that method.

You'll find numerous examples of this concept in the .NET Framework. All of LINQ is built on delegates. Callbacks are used to handle cross-thread marshalling in WPF and Windows Forms. Everywhere that the .NET Framework needs a single method, it will use a delegate that callers can express in the form of a lambda expression. You should follow the same example when you need a callback idiom in any of your APIs.

For historical reasons, all delegates are multicast delegates. Multicast delegates wrap all the target functions that have been added to the delegate in a single call. Two caveats apply to this construct: It is not safe in the face of exceptions, and the return value will be the return value of the last target function invoked by the multicast delegate.

Inside a multicast delegate invocation, each target is called in succession. The delegate does not catch any exceptions. Therefore, any exception that the target throws ends the delegate invocation chain.

A similar problem exists with return values. You can define delegates that have return types other than void. You could write a callback to check for user aborts:

```
public void LengthyOperation(Func<bool> pred)
{
    foreach (ComplicatedClass cl in container)
    {
        cl.DoLengthyOperation();
        // Check for user abort:
        if (false == pred())
            return;
    }
}
```

It works as a single delegate, but using it as a multicast is problematic:

```
Func<bool> cp = () => CheckWithUser();
cp += () => CheckWithSystem();


c.LengthyOperation(cp);
```

The value returned from invoking the delegate is the return value from the last function in the multicast chain. All other return values are ignored. The return from the CheckWithUser() predicate is ignored.

You address both issues by invoking each delegate target yourself. Each delegate you create contains a list of delegates. To examine the chain yourself and call each one, iterate the invocation list yourself:

```
public void LengthyOperation2(Func<bool> pred)
{
    bool bContinue = true;
    foreach (ComplicatedClass cl in container)
    {
        cl.DoLengthyOperation();
        foreach (Func<bool> pr in pred.GetInvocationList())
            bContinue &= pr();

        if (!bContinue)
            return;
    }
}
```

In this case, I've defined the semantics so that each delegate must be true for the iteration to continue.

Delegates provide the best way to utilize callbacks at runtime, with simpler requirements on client classes. You can configure delegate targets at runtime. You can support multiple client targets. Client callbacks should be implemented using delegates in .NET.

Item 25: Implement the Event Pattern for Notifications

The .NET Event Pattern is nothing more than syntax conventions on the Observer Pattern. (See *Design Patterns*, Gamma, Helm, Johnson, and Vlissides pp. 293-303.) Events define the notifications for your type. Events are built on delegates to provide type-safe function signatures for event handlers. Add to this the fact that most examples that use delegates are events, and developers start thinking that events and delegates are the same things. In Item 24, I showed you examples of when you can use delegates without defining events. You should raise events when your type must communicate with multiple clients to inform them of actions in the system. Events are how objects notify observers.

Consider a simple example. You're building a log class that acts as a dispatcher of all messages in an application. It will accept all messages from sources in your application and will dispatch those messages to any interested listeners. These listeners might be attached to the console, a database, the system log, or some other mechanism. You define the class as follows, to raise one event whenever a message arrives:

```
public class LoggerEventArgs : EventArgs
{
    public string Message { get; private set; }
    public int Priority { get; private set; }

    public LoggerEventArgs(int p, string m)
    {
        Priority = p;
        Message = m;
    }
}

public class Logger
{
    static Logger()
    {
        theOnly = new Logger();
    }

    private Logger()
    {
    }

    private static Logger theOnly = null;
    public static Logger Singleton
    {
```

```
        get { return theOnly; }
    }


    // Define the event:
    public event EventHandler<LoggerEventArgs> Log;


    // add a message, and log it.
    public void AddMsg(int priority, string msg)
    {
        // This idiom discussed below.
        EventHandler<LoggerEventArgs> l = Log;
        if (l != null)
            l(this, new LoggerEventArgs(priority, msg));
    }
}
```

The AddMsg method shows the proper way to raise events. The temporary variable to reference the log event handler is an important safeguard against race conditions in multithreaded programs. Without the copy of the reference, clients could remove event handlers between the if statement check and the execution of the event handler. By copying the reference, that can't happen.

I've defined LoggerEventArgs to hold the priority of an event and the message. The delegate defines the signature for the event handler. Inside the Logger class, the event field defines the event handler. The compiler sees the public event field definition and creates the Add and Remove operators for you. The generated code is exactly the same as though you had written the following:

```
public class Logger
{
    private EventHandler<LoggerEventArgs> log;

    public event EventHandler<LoggerEventArgs> Log
    {
        add { log = log + value; }
        remove { log = log - value; }
    }
}
```

```csharp
    public void AddMsg(int priority, string msg)
    {
        EventHandler<LoggerEventArgs> l = log;
        if (l != null)
            l(null, new LoggerEventArgs(priority, msg));
    }
}
```

The C# compiler creates the add and remove accessors for the event. I find the public event declaration language more concise and easier to read and maintain than the add/remove syntax. When you create events in your class, declare public events and let the compiler create the add and remove properties for you. Writing your own add and remove handlers lets you do more work in the add and remove handlers.

Events do not need to have any knowledge about the potential listeners. The following class automatically routes all messages to the Standard Error console:

```csharp
class ConsoleLogger
{
    static ConsoleLogger()
    {
        Logger.Singleton.Log += (sender, msg) =>
            {
                Console.Error.WriteLine("{0}:\t{1}",
                    msg.Priority.ToString(),
                    msg.Message);
            };
    }
}
```

Another class could direct output to the system event log:

```csharp
class EventLogger
{
    private static Logger logger = Logger.Singleton;
    private static string eventSource;
    private static EventLog logDest;

    static EventLogger()
    {
```

```
        logger.Log += (sender, msg) =>
        {
            if (logDest != null)
                logDest.WriteEntry(msg.Message,
                    EventLogEntryType.Information,
                    msg.Priority);
        };
    }

    public static string EventSource
    {
        get { return eventSource; }

        set
        {
            eventSource = value;
            if (!EventLog.SourceExists(eventSource))
                EventLog.CreateEventSource(eventSource,
                    "ApplicationEventLogger");

            if (logDest != null)
                logDest.Dispose();
            logDest = new EventLog();
            logDest.Source = eventSource;
        }
    }
}
```

Events notify any number of interested clients that something happened. The Logger class does not need any prior knowledge of which objects are interested in logging events.

The Logger class contained only one event. There are classes (mostly Windows controls) that have very large numbers of events. In those cases, the idea of using one field per event might be unacceptable. In some cases, only a small number of the defined events is actually used in any one application. If you encounter that situation, you can modify the design to create the event objects only when needed at runtime.

The core framework contains examples of how to do this in the Windows control subsystem. To show you how, add subsystems to the Logger class.

You create an event for each subsystem. Clients register on the event that is pertinent to their subsystems.

The extended Logger class has a System.ComponentModel.EventHandlerList container that stores all the event objects that should be raised for a given system. The updated AddMsg() method now takes a string parameter that specifies the subsystem generating the log message. If the subsystem has any listeners, the event gets raised. Also, if an event listener has registered an interest in all messages, its event gets raised:

```
public sealed class Logger
{
    private static System.ComponentModel.EventHandlerList
      Handlers = new EventHandlerList();

    static public void AddLogger(
      string system, EventHandler<LoggerEventArgs> ev)
    {
        Handlers.AddHandler(system, ev);
    }

    static public void RemoveLogger(string system,
        EventHandler<LoggerEventArgs> ev)
    {
        Handlers.RemoveHandler(system, ev);
    }

    static public void AddMsg(string system,
      int priority, string msg)
    {
        if (!string.IsNullOrEmpty(system))
        {
            EventHandler<LoggerEventArgs> l =
              Handlers[system] as
              EventHandler<LoggerEventArgs>;

            LoggerEventArgs args = new LoggerEventArgs(
              priority, msg);
            if (l != null)
                l(null, args);
```

```
            // The empty string means receive all messages:
            l = Handlers[""] as
                EventHandler<LoggerEventArgs>;
            if (l != null)
                l(null, args);
        }
    }
}
```

This new example stores the individual event handlers in the EventHandlerList collection. Sadly, there is no generic version of EventHandlerList. Therefore, you'll see a lot more casts and conversions in this block of code than you'll see in many of the samples in this book. Client code attaches to a specific subsystem, and a new event object is created. Subsequent requests for the same subsystem retrieve the same event object. If you develop a class that contains a large number of events in its interface, you should consider using this collection of event handlers. You create event members when clients attach to the event handler on their choice. Inside the .NET Framework, the System.Windows.Forms.Control class uses a more complicated variation of this implementation to hide the complexity of all its event fields. Each event field internally accesses a collection of objects to add and remove the particular handlers. You can find more information that shows this idiom in the C# language specification.

The EventHandlerList class is one of the classes that have not been updated with a new generic version. It's not hard to construct your own from the Dictionary class:

```
public sealed class Logger
{
    private static Dictionary<string,
        EventHandler<LoggerEventArgs>>
      Handlers = new Dictionary<string,
        EventHandler<LoggerEventArgs>>();

    static public void AddLogger(
      string system, EventHandler<LoggerEventArgs> ev)
    {
        if (Handlers.ContainsKey(system))
            Handlers[system] += ev;
        else
```

```
                    Handlers.Add(system, ev);
        }

        static public void RemoveLogger(string system,
            EventHandler<LoggerEventArgs> ev)
        {
            // will throw exception if system
            // does not contain a handler.
            Handlers[system] -= ev;
        }

        static public void AddMsg(string system,
          int priority, string msg)
        {
            if (string.IsNullOrEmpty(system))
            {
                EventHandler<LoggerEventArgs> l = null;
                Handlers.TryGetValue(system, out l);

                LoggerEventArgs args = new LoggerEventArgs(
                  priority, msg);
                if (l != null)
                    l(null, args);

                // The empty string means receive all messages:
                l = Handlers[""] as
                    EventHandler<LoggerEventArgs>;
                if (l != null)
                    l(null, args);
            }
        }
    }
}
```

The generic version trades casts and type conversions for increased code to handle event maps. I'd prefer the generic version, but it's a close tradeoff.

Events provide a standard syntax for notifying listeners. The .NET Event Pattern follows the event syntax to implement the Observer Pattern. Any number of clients can attach handlers to the events and process them. Those clients need not be known at compile time. Events don't need subscribers for the system to function properly. Using events in C# decouples the sender and the possible receivers of notifications. The sender can be developed completely independently of any receivers. Events are the standard way to broadcast information about actions that your type has taken.

Item 26: Avoid Returning References to Internal Class Objects

You'd like to think that a read-only property is read-only and that callers can't modify it. Unfortunately, that's not always the way it works. If you create a property that returns a reference type, the caller can access any public member of that object, including those that modify the state of the property. For example:

```
public class MyBusinessObject
{
    // Read Only property providing access to a
    // private data member:
    private BindingList<ImportantData> listOfData =
        new BindingList<ImportantData>();

    public BindingList<ImportantData> Data
    {
        get { return listOfData; }
    }
    // other details elided
}


// Access the collection:
BindingList<ImportantData> stuff = bizObj.Data;
// Not intended, but allowed:
stuff.Clear(); // Deletes all data.
```

Any public client of MyBusinessObject can modify your internal dataset. You created properties to hide your internal data structures. You provided methods to let clients manipulate the data only through known methods, so your class can manage any changes to internal state. And then a read-only property opens a gaping hole in your class encapsulation. It's not a read-write property, where you would consider these issues, but a read-only property.

Welcome to the wonderful world of reference-based systems. Any member that returns a reference type returns a handle to that object. You gave the caller a handle to your internal structures, so the caller no longer needs to go through your object to modify that contained reference.

Clearly, you want to prevent this kind of behavior. You built the interface to your class, and you want users to follow it. You don't want users to access or modify the internal state of your objects without your knowledge. You've got four different strategies for protecting your internal data structures from unintended modifications: value types, immutable types, interfaces, and wrappers.

Value types are copied when clients access them through a property. Any changes to the copy retrieved by the clients of your class do not affect your object's internal state. Clients can change the copy as much as necessary to achieve their purposes. This does not affect your internal state.

Immutable types, such as System.String, are also safe (see Item 20). You can return strings, or any immutable type, safely knowing that no client of your class can modify the string. Your internal state is safe.

The third option is to define interfaces that allow clients to access a subset of your internal member's functionality (see Item 22). When you create your own classes, you can create sets of interfaces that support subsets of the functionality of your class. By exposing the functionality through those interfaces, you minimize the possibility that your internal data changes in ways you did not intend. Clients can access the internal object through the interface you supplied, which will not include the full functionality of the class. Exposing the IEnumerable<T> interface pointer in the List<T> is one example of this strategy. The Machiavellian programmers out there can defeat that by guessing the type of the object that implements the interface and using a cast. But programmers who go to that much work to create bugs get what they deserve.

There is one strange twist in the BindingList class that may cause some problems. There isn't a generic version of IBindingList, so you may want to create two different API methods for accessing the data: one that supports DataBinding via the IBindingList interface, and one that supports programming through the ICollection<T>, or similar interface.

```
public class MyBusinessObject
{
    // Read Only property providing access to a
    // private data member:
```

```
private BindingList<ImportantData> listOfData = new
    BindingList<ImportantData>();
public IBindingList BindingData
{
    get { return listOfData; }
}
public ICollection<ImportantData> CollectionOfData
{
    get { return listOfData; }
}
// other details elided
}
```

Before we talk about how to create a completely read-only view of the data, let's take a brief look at how you can respond to changes in your data when you allow public clients to modify it. This is important because you'll often want to export an IBindingList to UI controls so that the user can edit the data. You've undoubtedly already used Windows forms data binding to provide the means for your users to edit private data in your objects. The BindingList<T> class supports the IBindingList interface so that you can respond to any additions, updates, or deletions of items in the collection being shown to the user.

You can generalize this technique anytime you want to expose internal data elements for modification by public clients, but you need to validate and respond to those changes. Your class subscribes to events generated by your internal data structure. Event handlers validate changes or respond to those changes by updating other internal state. (See Item 25.)

Going back to the original problem, you want to let clients view your data but not make any changes. When your data is stored in a BindingList<T>, you can enforce that by setting various properties on the BindingList object (AddEdit, AllowNew, AllowRemove, etc.). The values of these properties are honored by UI controls. The UI controls enable and disable different actions based on the value of these properties. These are public properties, so that you can modify the behavior of your collection. But that also means you should not expose the BindingList<T> object as a public property. Clients could modify those properties and circumvent your intent to make a read-only binding collection. Once again, exposing the internal storage through an interface type rather than the class type will limit what client code can do with that object.

The final choice is to provide a wrapper object and export an instance of the wrapper, which minimizes access to the contained object. The System .Collections.ObjectModel.ReadOnlyCollection<T> type is the standard way to wrap a collection and export a read-only version of that data:

```
public class MyBusinessObject
{
    // Read Only property providing access to a
    // private data member:
    private BindingList<ImportantData> listOfData = new
        BindingList<ImportantData>();
    public IBindingList BindingData
    {
        get { return listOfData; }
    }
    public ReadOnlyCollection<ImportantData> CollectionOfData
    {
        get
        {
            return new ReadOnlyCollection<ImportantData>
                (listOfData);
        }
    }
    // other details elided
}
```

Exposing reference types through your public interface allows users of your object to modify its internals without going through the methods and properties you've defined. That seems counterintuitive, which makes it a common mistake. You need to modify your class's interfaces to take into account that you are exporting references rather than values. If you simply return internal data, you've given access to those contained members. Your clients can call any method that is available in your members. You limit that access by exposing private internal data using interfaces, wrapper objects, or value types.

Item 27: Prefer Making Your Types Serializable

Persistence is a core feature of a type. It's one of those basic elements that no one notices until you neglect to support it. If your type does not support serialization properly, you create more work for all developers who intend to use your types as a member or base class. When your type does not support serialization, they must work around it, adding their own implementation of a standard feature. It's unlikely that clients could properly implement serialization for your types without access to private details in your types. If you don't supply serialization, it's difficult or impossible for users of your class to add it.

Instead, prefer adding serialization to your types when practical. It should be practical for all types that do not represent UI widgets, windows, or forms. The extra perceived work is no excuse. .NET serialization support is so simple that you don't have any reasonable excuse not to support it. In many cases, adding the Serializable attribute is enough:

```
[Serializable]
public class MyType
{
    private string label;
    private int value;
}
```

Adding the Serializable attribute works because all the members of this type are serializable: `string` and `int` both support .NET serialization. The reason it's important for you to support serialization wherever possible becomes obvious when you add another field of a custom type:

```
 [Serializable]
public class MyType
{
    private string label;
    private int value;
    private OtherClass otherThing;
}
```

The Serializable attribute works here only if the OtherClass type supports .NET serialization. If OtherClass is not serializable, you get a runtime error and you have to write your own code to serialize MyType and the OtherClass object inside it. That's just not possible without extensive knowledge of the internals defined in OtherClass.

.NET serialization saves all member variables in your object to the output stream. In addition, the .NET serialization code supports arbitrary object graphs: Even if you have circular references in your objects, the serialize and deserialize methods will save and restore each actual object only once. The .NET Serialization Framework also will re-create the web of references when the web of objects is deserialized. Any web of related objects that you have created is restored correctly when the object graph is deserialized. A last important note is that the Serializable attribute supports both binary and SOAP serialization. All the techniques in this item will support both serialization formats. But remember that this works only if all the types in an object graph support serialization. That's why it's important to support serialization in all your types. As soon as you leave out one class, you create a hole in the object graph that makes it harder for anyone using your types to support serialization easily. Before long, everyone is writing their own serialization code again.

Adding the Serializable attribute is the simplest technique to support serializable objects. But the simplest solution is not always the right solution. Sometimes, you do not want to serialize all the members of an object: Some members might exist only to cache the result of a lengthy operation. Other members might hold on to runtime resources that are needed only for in-memory operations. You can manage these possibilities using attributes as well. Attach the [NonSerialized] attribute to any of the data members that should not be saved as part of the object state. This marks them as nonserializable attributes:

```
[Serializable]
public class MyType
{
    private string label;

    [NonSerialized]
    private int cachedValue;

    private OtherClass otherThing;
}
```

Nonserialized members add a little more work for you, the class designer. The serialization APIs do not initialize nonserialized members for you during the deserialization process. None of your types' constructors is called, so the member initializers are not executed, either. When you use the serializable attributes, nonserialized members get the default system-initialized value: 0 or null. When the default 0 initialization is not right, you need to implement the IDeserializationCallback interface to initialize these non-serializable members. IDeserializationCallback contains one method: OnDeserialization. The framework calls this method after the entire object graph has been deserialized. You use this method to initialize any non-serialized members in your object. Because the entire object graph has been read, you know that any function you might want to call on your object or any of its serialized members is safe. Unfortunately, it's not foolproof. After the entire object graph has been read, the framework calls OnDeserialization on every object in the graph that supports the IDeserializationCallback interface. Any other objects in the object graph can call your object's public members when processing OnDeserialization. If they go first, your object's nonserialized members are null, or 0. Order is not guaranteed, so you must ensure that all your public methods handle the case in which nonserialized members have not been initialized.

So far, you've learned about why you should add serialization to all your types: Nonserializable types cause more work when used in types that should be serialized. You've learned about the simplest serialization methods using attributes, including how to initialize nonserialized members.

Serialized data has a way of living on between versions of your program. Adding serialization to your types means that one day you will need to read an older version. The code generated by the Serializable attribute throws exceptions when it finds fields that have been added or removed from the object graph. When you find yourself ready to support multiple versions and you need more control over the serialization process, use the ISerializable interface. This interface defines the hooks for you to customize the serialization of your types. The methods and storage that the ISerializable interface uses are consistent with the methods and storage that the default serialization methods use. That means you can use the serialization attributes when you create a class. If it ever becomes necessary to provide your own extensions, you then add support for the ISerializable interface.

As an example, consider how you would support MyType, version 2, when you add another field to your type. Simply adding a new field produces a new format that is incompatible with the previously stored versions on disk:

```
[Serializable]
public class MyType
{
```

```
private MyType(SerializationInfo info,
  StreamingContext cntxt)
{
}

private string label;

[NonSerialized]
private int value;

private OtherClass otherThing;

// Added in version 2
// The runtime throws Exceptions
// with it finds this field missing in version 1.0
// files.
private int value2;
}
```

You add support for ISerializable to address this behavior. The ISerializable interface defines one method, but you have to implement two. ISerializable defines the GetObjectData() method that is used to write data to a stream. In addition, you must provide a serialization constructor to initialize the object from the stream:

```
private MyType(SerializationInfo info,
    StreamingContext cntxt)
```

The serialization constructor in the following class shows how to read a previous version of the type and read the current version consistently with the default implementation generated by adding the Serializable attribute:

```
using global::System.Runtime.Serialization;
using global::System.Security.Permissions;
[Serializable]
public sealed class MyType : ISerializable
{
    private string label;

    [NonSerialized]
    private int value;
```

```
    private OtherClass otherThing;

    private const int DEFAULT_VALUE = 5;
    private int value2;

    // public constructors elided.

    // Private constructor used only
    // by the Serialization framework.
    private MyType(SerializationInfo info,
      StreamingContext cntxt)
    {
        label = info.GetString("label");
        otherThing = (OtherClass)info.GetValue("otherThing",
            typeof(OtherClass));
        try
        {
            value2 = info.GetInt32("value2");
        }
        catch (SerializationException)
        {
            // Found version 1.
            value2 = DEFAULT_VALUE;
        }
    }


    [SecurityPermissionAttribute(SecurityAction.Demand,
      SerializationFormatter = true)]
    void ISerializable.GetObjectData(SerializationInfo inf,
      StreamingContext cxt)
    {
        inf.AddValue("label", label);
        inf.AddValue("otherThing", otherThing);
        inf.AddValue("value2", value2);
    }
}
```

The serialization stream stores each item as a key/value pair. The code generated from the attributes uses the variable name as the key for each value. When you add the ISerializable interface, you must match the key name and the order of the variables. The order is the order declared in the class. (By the way, this fact means that rearranging the order of variables in a class or renaming variables breaks the compatibility with files already created.)

Also, I have demanded the SerializationFormatter security permission. GetObjectData could be a security hole into your class if it is not properly protected. Malicious code could create a StreamingContext, get the values from an object using GetObjectData, serialize modified versions to another SerializationInfo, and reconstitute a modified object. It would allow a malicious developer to access the internal state of your object, modify it in the stream, and send the changes back to you. Demanding the SerializationFormatter permission seals this potential hole. It ensures that only properly trusted code can access this routine to get at the internal state of the object.

But there's a downside to implementing the ISerializable interface. You can see that I made MyType sealed earlier. That forces it to be a leaf class. Implementing the ISerializable interface in a base class complicates serialization for all derived classes. Implementing ISerializable means that every derived class must create the protected constructor for deserialization. In addition, to support nonsealed classes, you need to create hooks in the GetObjectData method for derived classes to add their own data to the stream. The compiler does not catch either of these errors. The lack of a proper constructor causes the runtime to throw an exception when reading a derived object from a stream. The lack of a hook for GetObjectData() means that the data from the derived portion of the object never gets saved to the file. No errors are thrown. I'd like the recommendation to be "implement Serializable in leaf classes." I did not say that because that won't work. Your base classes must be serializable for the derived classes to be serializable. To modify MyType so that it can be a serializable base class, you change the serializable constructor to protected and create a virtual method that derived classes can override to store their data:

```
using global::System.Runtime.Serialization;
using global::System.Security.Permissions;

[Serializable]
public class MyType : ISerializable
{
    private string label;
```

```csharp
[NonSerialized]
private int value;

private OtherClass otherThing;

private const int DEFAULT_VALUE = 5;
private int value2;

// public constructors elided.

// Protected constructor used only by the
// Serialization framework.
protected MyType(SerializationInfo info,
  StreamingContext cntxt)
{
    label = info.GetString("label");
    otherThing = (OtherClass)info.GetValue("otherThing",
      typeof(OtherClass));
    try
    {
        value2 = info.GetInt32("value2");
    }
    catch (SerializationException e)
    {
        // Found version 1.
        value2 = DEFAULT_VALUE;
    }
}


[SecurityPermissionAttribute(SecurityAction.Demand,
 SerializationFormatter = true)]
void ISerializable.GetObjectData(
  SerializationInfo inf,
  StreamingContext cxt)
{
    inf.AddValue("label", label);
    inf.AddValue("otherThing", otherThing);
    inf.AddValue("value2", value2);

    WriteObjectData(inf, cxt);
}
```

```
// Overridden in derived classes to write
// derived class data:
protected virtual void
    WriteObjectData(
    SerializationInfo inf,
    StreamingContext cxt)
{
    // Should be an abstract method,
    // if MyType should be an abstract class.
}
}
```

A derived class would provide its own serialization constructor and override the WriteObjectData method:

```
public class DerivedType : MyType
{
    private int derivedVal;

    private DerivedType(SerializationInfo info,
        StreamingContext cntxt) :
        base(info, cntxt)
    {
        derivedVal = info.GetInt32("_DerivedVal");
    }

    protected override void WriteObjectData(
        SerializationInfo inf,
        StreamingContext cxt)
    {
        inf.AddValue("_DerivedVal", derivedVal);
    }
}
```

The order of writing and retrieving values from the serialization stream must be consistent. I've chosen to read and write the base class values first because I believe it is simpler. If your read and write code does not serialize the entire hierarchy in the exact same order, your serialization code won't work.

None of the code samples in this item use automatic properties. That's by design. Automatic properties use a compiler-generated backing field for their storage. You can't access that backing field, because the field name is an invalid C# token (it is a valid CLR symbol). That makes binary serialization very brittle for types that use automatic properties. You cannot write your own serialization constructor, or GetObjectData methods to access those backing fields. Serialization will work for the simplest types, but any derived classes, or future additional fields will break code. And, by the time you discover the problem, you'll have persisted the original version in the field, and you won't be able to fix the issue. Anytime you add the Serializable attribute to a class, you must concretely implement the properties with your own backing store.

The .NET Framework provides a simple, standard algorithm for serializing your objects. If your type should be persisted, you should follow the standard implementation. If you don't support serialization in your types, other classes that use your type can't support serialization, either. Make it as easy as possible for clients of your class. Use the default methods when you can, and implement the ISerializable interface when the default attributes don't suffice.

Item 28: Create Large-Grain Internet Service APIs

The cost and inconvenience of a communication protocol dictates how you should use the medium. You communicate differently using the phone, fax, letters, and email. Think back on the last time you ordered from a catalog. When you order by phone, you engage in a question-and-answer session with the sales staff:

> "Can I have your first item?"
> "Item number 123-456."
> "How many would you like?"
> "Three."

This conversation continues until the sales staff has your entire order, your billing address, your credit card information, your shipping address, and any other information necessary to complete the transaction. It's comforting on the phone to have this back-and-forth discussion. You never give long soliloquies with no feedback. You never endure long periods of silence wondering if the salesperson is still there.

Contrast that with ordering by fax. You fill out the entire document and fax the completed document to the company. One document, one transaction. You do not fill out one product line, fax it, add your address, fax again, add your credit card number, and fax again.

This illustrates the common pitfalls of a poorly defined service interface. Whether you use a Web service, .NET Remoting, or Azure-based programming, you must remember that the most expensive part of the operation comes when you transfer objects between distant machines. You must stop creating remote APIs that are simply a repackaging of the same local interfaces that you use. It works, but it reeks of inefficiency. It's using the phone call metaphor to process your catalog request via fax. Your application waits for the network each time you make a round-trip to pass a new piece of information through the pipe. The more granular the API is, the higher percentage of time your application spends waiting for data to return from the server.

Instead, create Web-based interfaces based on serializing documents or sets of objects between client and server. Your remote communications should work like the order form you fax to the catalog company: The client machine should be capable of working for extended periods of time without contacting the server. Then, when all the information to complete the transaction is filled in, the client can send the entire document to the server. The server's responses work the same way: When information gets sent from the server to the client, the client receives all the information necessary to complete all the tasks at hand.

Sticking with the customer order metaphor, we'll design a customer order-processing system that consists of a central server and desktop clients accessing information via Web services. One class in the system is the customer class. If you ignore the transport issues, the customer class might look something like this, which allows client code to retrieve or modify the name, shipping address, and account information:

```
public class Customer
{
    public Customer()
    {
    }

    // Properties to access and modify customer fields:
    public string Name { get; set; }

    public Address ShippingAddr { get; set; }
```

```
    public Account CreditCardInfo { get; set; }
}
```

The customer class does not contain the kind of API that should be called remotely. Calling a remote customer results in excessive traffic between the client and the server:

```
// create customer on the server.
Customer c = Server.NewCustomer();
// round trip to set the name.
c.Name = dlg.Name;
// round trip to set the addr.
c.ShippingAddr = dlg.ShippingAddr;
// round trip to set the cc card.
c.CreditCardInfo = dlg.CreditCardInfo;
```

Instead, you would create a local Customer object and transfer the Customer to the server after all the fields have been set:

```
// create customer on the client.
Customer c2 = new Customer();
// Set local copy
c2.Name = dlg.Name;
// set the local addr.
c2.ShippingAddr = dlg.ShippingAddr;
// set the local cc card.
c2.CreditCardInfo = dlg.CreditCardInfo;
// send the finished object to the server. (one trip)
Server.AddCustomer(c2);
```

The customer example illustrates an obvious and simple example: Transfer entire objects back and forth between client and server. But to write efficient programs, you need to extend that simple example to include the right set of related objects. Making remote invocations to set a single property of an object is too small of a granularity. But one customer might not be the right granularity for transactions between the client and server, either.

To extend this example into the real-world design issues you'll encounter in your programs, we'll make a few assumptions about the system. This software system supports a major online vendor with more than 1 million customers. Imagine that it is a major catalog ordering house and that each customer has, on average, 15 orders in the last year. Each telephone operator uses one machine during the shift and must look up or create customer records whenever he or she answers the phone. Your design task is to determine the most efficient set of objects to transfer between client machines and the server.

You can begin by eliminating some obvious choices. Retrieving every customer and every order is clearly prohibitive: 1 million customers and 15 million order records are just too much data to bring to each client. You've simply traded one bottleneck for another. Instead of constantly bombarding your server with every possible data update, you send the server a request for more than 15 million objects. Sure, it's only one transaction, but it's a very inefficient transaction.

Instead, consider how you can best retrieve a set of objects that can constitute a good approximation of the set of data that an operator must use for the next several minutes. An operator will answer the phone and be interacting with one customer. During the course of the phone call, that operator might add or remove orders, change orders, or modify a customer's account information. The obvious choice is to retrieve one customer, with all orders that have been placed by that customer. The server method would be something like this:

```
public OrderDataCollection FindOrders(string customerName)
{
    // Search for the customer by name.
    // Find all orders by that customer.
}
```

Or is that right? Orders that have been shipped and received by the customer are almost certainly not needed at the client machine. A better answer is to retrieve only the open orders for the requested customer. The server method would change to something like this:

```
public OrderData FindOpenOrders(string customerName)
{
    // Search for the customer by name.
    // Find all orders by that customer.
    // Filter out those that have already
    // been received.
}
```

You are still making the client machine request data at the start of each customer phone call. Are there ways to optimize this communication channel more than including orders in the customer download? We'll add a few more assumptions on the business processes to give you some more ideas. Suppose that the call center is partitioned so that each working team receives calls from only one area code. Now you can modify your design to optimize the communication quite a bit more.

Each operator would retrieve the updated customer and order information for that one area code at the start of the shift. After each call, the client application would push the modified data back to the server, and the server would respond with all changes since the last time this client machine asked for data. The end result is that after every phone call, the operator sends any changes made and retrieves all changes made by any other operator in the same work group. This design means that there is one transaction per phone call, and each operator should always have the right set of data available when he or she answers a call. It has saved one round-trip per call. Now the server contains two methods that would look something like this:

```csharp
public CustomerSet RetrieveCustomerData(
    AreaCode theAreaCode)
{
    // Find all customers for a given area code.
    // Foreach customer in that area code:
    // Find all orders by that customer.
    // Filter out those that have already
    // been received.
    // Return the result.
}


public CustomerSet UpdateCustomer(CustomerData
  updates, DateTime lastUpdate, AreaCode theAreaCode)
{
    // First, save any updates.

    // Next, get the updates:
    // Find all customers for a given area code.
    // Foreach customer in that area code:
    // Find all orders by that customer that have been
    // updated since the last time. Add those to the result.
    // Return the result.
}
```

But you might still be wasting some bandwidth. Your last design works best when every known customer calls every day. That's probably not true. If it is, your company has customer service problems that are far outside the scope of a software program.

How can we further limit the size of each transaction without increasing the number of transactions or the latency of the service rep's responsiveness to a customer? You can make some assumptions about which customers in the database are going to place calls. You track some statistics and find that if customers go six months without ordering, they are very unlikely to order again. So you stop retrieving those customers and their orders at the beginning of the day. That shrinks the size of the initial transaction. You also find that any customer who calls shortly after placing an order is usually inquiring about the last order. So you modify the list of orders sent down to the client to include only the last order rather than all orders. This would not change the signatures of the server methods, but it would shrink the size of the packets sent back to the client.

This hypothetical discussion focused on getting you to think about the communication between remote machines: You want to minimize both the frequency and the size of the transactions sent between machines. Those two goals are at odds, and you need to make tradeoffs between them. You should end up close to the center of the two extremes, but err toward the side of fewer, larger transactions.

Item 29: Support Generic Covariance and Contravariance

Type variance, and specifically, covariance and contravariance define the conditions under which one type can be substituted for another type. Whenever possible, you should decorate generic interfaces and delegate definitions to support generic covariance and contravariance. Doing so will enable your APIs to be used in more different ways, and safely. If you cannot substitute one type for another, it is called invariant.

Type variance is one of those topics that many developers have encountered but not really understood. Covariance and contravariance are two different forms of type substitution. A return type is covariant if you can substitute a more derived type than the type declared. A parameter type is contravariant if you can substitute a more base parameter type than the type declared. Object-oriented languages generally support covariance of parameter types. You can pass an object of a derived type to any method that expects a more base type. For example, Console.WriteLine() has an overload that takes a System.Object parameter. You can pass an instance of any type that derives from object. When you override an instance of a method that returns a System.Object, you can return anything that is derived from System.Object.

That common behavior led many developers to believe that generics would follow the same rules. You should be able to use an IEnumerable<MyDerived Type> with a method that has a parameter of IEnumerable<Object>. You would expect that if a method returns an IEnumerable<MyDerivedType>, you could assign that to a variable of type IEnumerable<object>. No so. Prior to C# 4.0, all generic types were invariant. That meant there were many times when you would reasonably expect covariance or contravariance with generics only to be told by the compiler that your code was invalid. Arrays were treated covariantly. However, Arrays do not support safe covariance. As of C# 4.0, new keywords are available to enable you to use generics covariantly and contravariantly. That makes generics much more useful, especially if you remember to include the in and out parameters where possible on generic interfaces and delegates.

Let's begin by understanding the problems with array covariance. Consider this small class hierarchy:

```
abstract public class CelestialBody
{
    public double Mass { get; set; }
    public string Name { get; set; }
    // elided
}


public class Planet : CelestialBody
{
    // elided
}


public class Moon : CelestialBody
{
    // elided
}
```

```
public class Asteroid : CelestialBody
{
    // elided
}
```

This method treats arrays of CelestialBody objects covariantly, and does so safely:

```
public static void CoVariantArray(CelestialBody[] baseItems)
{
    foreach (var thing in baseItems)
        Console.WriteLine("{0} has a mass of {1} Kg",
        thing.Name, thing.Mass);
}
```

This method also treats arrays of CelestialBody objects covariantly, but it is not safe. The assignment statement will throw an exception.

```
public static void UnsafeVariantArray(
    CelestialBody[] baseItems)
{
    baseItems[0] = new Asteroid
        { Name = "Hygiea", Mass = 8.85e19 };
}
```

You can have the same problem simply by assigning an array of a derived class to a variable that is an array of a base type:

```
CelestialBody[] spaceJunk = new Asteroid[5];
spaceJunk[0] = new Planet();
```

Treating collections as covariant means that when there is an inheritance relationship between two types, you can imagine there is a similar inheritance relationship between arrays of those two types. This isn't a strict definition, but it's a useful picture to keep in your mind. A Planet can be passed to any method that expects CelestialBody. That's because Planet is derived from CelestialBody. Similarly, you can pass a Planet[] to any method that expects a CelestialBody[]. But, as the above example shows, that doesn't always work the way you'd expect.

When generics were first introduced, this issue was dealt with in a rather draconian fashion. Generics were always treated invariantly. Generic types had to have an exact match. However, in C# 4.0, you can now decorate

generic interfaces such that they can be treated covariantly, or contravariantly. Let's discuss generic covariance first, and then we'll move on to
contravariance.

This method can be called with a List<Planet>:

```
public static void CoVariantGeneric(
    IEnumerable<CelestialBody> baseItems)


{

    foreach (var thing in baseItems)
        Console.WriteLine("{0} has a mass of {1} Kg",
        thing.Name, thing.Mass);
}
```

That's because IEnumerable<T> has been augmented to limit T to only
output positions in its interface:

```
public interface IEnumerable<out T> : IEnumerable
{
    IEnumerator<T> GetEnumerator();
}
public interface IEnumerator<out T> :
    IDisposable, IEnumerator
{
    T Current { get; }
    // MoveNext(), Reset() inherited from IEnumerator
}
```

I included both the IEnumerable<T> and IEnumerator<T> definition
here, because the IEnumerator<T> has the important restrictions. Notice
that IEnumerator<T> now decorates the type parameter T with the out
modifier. That forces the compiler to limit T to output positions. Output
positions are limited to function return values, property get accessors, and
certain delegate positions.

Therefore, using IEnumerable<out T>, the compiler knows that you will
look at every T in the sequence, but never modify the contents of the source
sequence. Treating every Planet as a CelestialBody in this case works.

IEnumerable<T> can be covariant only because IEnumerator<T> is also
covariant. If IEnumerable<T> returned an interface that was not declared
as covariant, the compiler would generate an error. Covariant types must

return either the type parameter, or an interface on the type parameter that is also covariant.

However, the method that replaces the first item in the list will be invariant when using generics:

```
public static void InvariantGeneric(
    IList<CelestialBody> baseItems)
{
    baseItems[0] = new Asteroid
        { Name = "Hygiea", Mass = 8.85e19 };
}
```

Because IList<T> is neither decorated with the in or out modifier on T, you must use the exact type match.

Of course, you can create Contravariant generic interfaces and delegates as well. Substitute the in modifier for the out modifier. That instructs the compiler that the type parameter may only appear in input positions. The .NET Framework has added the in modifier to the IComparable<T> interface:

```
public interface IComparable<in T>
{
    int CompareTo(T other);
}
```

That means you could make CelestialBody implement IComparable<T>, using an object's mass. It would compare two Planets, a Planet and a Moon, a Moon and an Asteroid, or any other combination. By comparing the mass of the objects, that's a valid comparison.

You'll notice that IEquatable<T> is invariant. By definition, a Planet cannot be equal to a Moon. They are different types, so it makes no sense. It is necessary, if not sufficient, for two objects to be of the same type if they are equal (see Item 6).

Type parameters that are contravariant can only appear as method parameters, and some locations in delegate parameters.

By now, you've probably noticed that I've used the phrase "some locations in delegate parameters" twice. Delegate definitions can be covariant or contravariant as well. It's usually pretty simple: Method parameters are contravariant (`in`), and method return types are covariant (`out`). The BCL updated many of their delegate definitions to include variance:

```
public delegate TResult Func<out TResult>();
public delegate TResult Func<in T, out TResult>(T arg);
public delegate TResult Func<in T1, T2, out TResult>(T1 arg1,
    T2 arg2);
public delegate void Action<in T>(T arg);
public delegate void Action<in T1, in T2>(T1 arg1, T2 arg2);
public delegate void Action<in T1, in T2, T3>(T1 arg1,
    T2 arg2, T3 arg3);
```

Again, this probably isn't too hard. But, when you mix them, things start to get to be mind benders. You already saw that you cannot return invariant interfaces from covariant interfaces. You can't use delegates to get around the covariant and contravariant restrictions, either.

Delegates have a tendency to "flip" the covariance and contravariance in an interface if you're not careful. Here are a couple examples:

```
public interface ICovariantDelegates<out T>
{
    T GetAnItem();
    Func<T> GetAnItemLater();
    void GiveAnItemLater(Action<T> whatToDo);
}


public interface IContravariantDelegates<in T>
{
    void ActOnAnItem(T item);
    void GetAnItemLater(Func<T> item);
    Action<T> ActOnAnItemLater();
}
```

I've named the methods in these interfaces specifically to show why it works the way it does. Look closely at the ICovariantDelegate interface definition. GetAnItemLater() is just a way to retrieve an item lazily. The caller can invoke the Func<T> returned by the method later to retrieve a value. T still exists in the output position. That probably still makes sense. The GetAnItemLater() method probably is a bit more confusing. Here, you're method takes an delegate that will accept a T object whenever you call it. So, even though Action<in T> is covariant, its position in the

ICovariantDelegate interface means that it is actually a means by which T objects are returned from an ICovariantDelegate<T> implementing object. It may look like it should be contravariant, but it is covariant with respect to the interface.

IContravariantDelegate<T> is similar but shows how you can use delegates in a contravariant interface. Again, the ActOnAnItem method should be obvious. The ActOnAnItemLater() method is just a little more complicated. You're returning a method that will accept a T object sometime later. That last method, once again, may cause some confusion. It's the same concept as with the other interface. The GetAnItemLater() method accepts a method that will return a T object sometime later. Even though Func<out T> is declared covariant, its use is to bring an input to the object implementing IContravariantDelegate. Its use is contravariant with respect to the IContravariantDelegate.

It certainly can get complicated describing exactly how covariance and contravariance work. Thankfully, now the language supports decorating generic interfaces and delegates with in (contravariant) and out (covariant) modifiers. You should decorate any interfaces and delegates you define with the in or out modifiers wherever possible. Then, the compiler can correct any possible misuses of the variance you've defined. The compiler will catch it both in your interface and delegate definitions, and it will detect any misuse of the types you've created.

4 | Working with the Framework

My friend and colleague Martin Shoemaker crated a roundtable called "Do I Have to Write That .NET Code?" shortly after .NET was first released in 2002. It was a great roundtable back then, and it's much more relevant now. The .NET Framework has grown and now includes many more new classes and features than it did back then. It's important that you don't create features that already exist.

The .NET Framework is a rich class library. The more you learn about the framework, the less code you need to write yourself. The framework library will do more of the work for you. Sadly, the Base Class Library must now contend with the problems associated with release 4. There are better ways to solve problems than existed in release 1. But the framework team can't just delete those old APIs and classes. It may not even make sense to mark those older APIs as deprecated. They still work, and it is not in your best interest to rewrite working code. But when you're creating new code, you should reach for the best tool that exists now. This chapter shows you techniques to get the most out of the .NET Framework now, in version 4.0. Other items help you choose the best option when multiple choices are available in the framework. Still other items explain some of the techniques you should use if you want your classes to operate well with the classes created by the framework designers.

Item 30: Prefer Overrides to Event Handlers

Many .NET classes provide two different ways to handle events from the system. You can attach an event handler, or you can override a `virtual` function in the `base` class. Why provide two ways of doing the same thing? Because different situations call for different methods, that's why. Inside derived classes, you should always override the `virtual` function. Limit your use of the event handlers to responding to events in unrelated objects.

You write a nifty Windows Presentation Foundation (WPF) application that needs to respond to mouse down events. In your form class, you can choose to override the OnMouseDown() method:

```
public partial class Window1 : Window
{
    // other code elided

    public Window1()
    {
        InitializeComponent();
    }

    protected override void OnMouseDown(
        MouseButtonEventArgs e)
    {
        DoMouseThings(e);
        base.OnMouseDown(e);
    }
}
```

Or, you could attach an event handler (which requires both C# and XAML):

```
<!-- XAML File -->
<Window x:Class="Item36_OverridesAndEvent.Window1"
        xmlns=
    "http://schemas.microsoft.com/winfx/2006/xaml/presentation"
    xmlns:x="http://schemas.microsoft.com/winfx/2006/xaml"
        Title="Window1" Height="300" Width="300"
MouseDown="OnMouseDown">
    <Grid>

    </Grid>
</Window>


// C Sharp file:
public partial class Window1 : Window
{
    // other code elided
```

```
public Window1()
{
    InitializeComponent();
}


private void OnMouseDown(object sender,
    MouseButtonEventArgs e)
{
    DoMouseThings(e);
}


private void DoMouseThings(MouseButtonEventArgs e)
{
    throw new NotImplementedException();
}
}
```

The first solution is preferred. This may seem surprising given the emphasis on declarative code in WPF applications. Even so, if the logic must be implemented in code, you should use the virtual method. If an event handler throws an exception, no other handlers in the chain for that event are called (see Items 24 and 25). Some other ill-formed code prevents the system from calling your event handler. By overriding the protected `virtual` function, your handler gets called first. The `base` class version of the `virtual` function is responsible for calling any event handlers attached to the particular event. That means that if you want the event handlers called (and you almost always do), you must call the `base` class. In some rare cases, you will want to replace the default behavior instead of calling the `base` class version so that none of the event handlers gets called. You can't guarantee that all the event handlers will be called because some ill-formed event handler might throw an exception, but you can guarantee that your derived class's behavior is correct.

Using the override is more efficient than attaching the event handler. You will remember from Item 25 that events are built on top of multicast delegates. That enables any event source to have multiple observers. The event-handling mechanism takes more work for the processor because it must examine the event to see if any event handlers have been attached. If so, it must iterate the entire invocation list, which may contain any number of target methods. Each method in the event invocation list must be called. Determining whether there are event handlers and iterating each at runtime takes more execution time than invoking one virtual function.

If that's not enough for you, examine the first listing in this item again. Which is clearer? Overriding a virtual function has one function to examine and modify if you need to maintain the form. The event mechanism has two points to maintain: the event handler function and the code that wires up the event. Either of these could be the point of failure. One function is simpler.

Okay, I've been giving all these reasons to use the overrides and not use the event handlers. The .NET Framework designers must have added events for a reason, right? Of course they did. Like the rest of us, they're too busy to write code nobody uses. The overrides are for derived classes. Every other class must use the event mechanism. That also means declarative actions defined in the XAML file will be accessed through the event handlers. In this example, your designer may have actions that are supposed to occur on a MouseDown event. The designer will create XAML declarations for those behaviors. Those behaviors will be accessed using events on the form. You could redefine all that behavior in your code, but that's way too much work to handle one event. It only moves the problem from the designer's hands to yours. You clearly want designers doing design work instead of you. The obvious way to handle that is to create an event and access the XAML declarations created by a design tool. So, in the end, you have created a new class to send an event to the form class. It would be simpler to just attach the form's event handler to the form in the first place. After all, that's why the .NET Framework designers put those events in the forms.

Another reason for the event mechanism is that events are wired up at runtime. You have more flexibility using events. You can wire up different event handlers, depending on the circumstances of the program. Suppose that you write a drawing program. Depending on the state of the program, a mouse down might start drawing a line, or it might select an object. When the user switches modes, you can switch event handlers. Different classes, with different event handlers, handle the event depending on the state of the application.

Finally, with events, you can hook up multiple event handlers to the same event. Imagine the same drawing program again. You might have multiple event handlers hooked up on the MouseDown event. The first would perform the particular action. The second might update the status bar or update the accessibility of different commands. Multiple actions can take place in response to the same event.

When you have one function that handles one event in a derived class, the override is the better approach. It is easier to maintain, more likely to be correct over time, and more efficient. Reserve the event handlers for other uses. Prefer overriding the base class implementation to attaching an event handler.

Item 31: Implement Ordering Relations with IComparable<T> and IComparer<T>

Your types need ordering relationships to describe how collections should be sorted and searched. The .NET Framework defines two interfaces that describe ordering relationships in your types: IComparable<T> and IComparer<T>. IComparable defines the natural order for your types. A type implements IComparer to describe alternative orderings. You can define your own implementations of the relational operators (<, >, <=, >=) to provide type-specific comparisons, to avoid some runtime inefficiencies in the interface implementations. This item discusses how to implement ordering relations so that the core .NET Framework orders your types through the defined interfaces and so that other users get the best performance from these operations.

The IComparable interface contains one method: CompareTo(). This method follows the long-standing tradition started with the C library function strcmp: Its return value is less than 0 if the current object is less than the comparison object, 0 if they are equal, and greater than 0 if the current object is greater than the comparison object. IComparable<T> will be used by most newer APIs in the .NET landscape. However, some older APIs will use the classic IComparable interface. Therefore, when you implement IComparable<T>, you should also implement IComparable. IComparable takes parameters of type System.Object. You need to perform runtime type checking on the argument to this function. Every time comparisons are performed, you must reinterpret the type of the argument:

```
public struct Customer : IComparable<Customer>, IComparable
{
    private readonly string name;
```

```
    public Customer(string name)
    {
        this.name = name;
    }


    #region IComparable<Customer> Members
    public int CompareTo(Customer other)
    {
        return name.CompareTo(other.name);
    }
    #endregion


    #region IComparable Members
    int IComparable.CompareTo(object obj)
    {
        if (!(obj is Customer))
            throw new ArgumentException(
                "Argument is not a Customer", "obj");
        Customer otherCustomer = (Customer)obj;
        return this.CompareTo(otherCustomer);
    }
    #endregion
}
```

Notice that IComparable is explicitly implemented in this structure. That ensures that the only code that will call the object-typed version of CompareTo() is code that was written for the previous interface. There's just too much to dislike about the classic version of IComparable. You've got to check the runtime type of the argument. Incorrect code could legally call this method with anything as the argument to the CompareTo method. More so, proper arguments must be boxed and unboxed to provide the actual comparison. That's an extra runtime expense for each compare. Sorting a collection will make, on average n lg(n) comparisons of your object using the IComparable.Compare method. Each of those will cause three boxing and unboxing operations. For an array with 1,000 points, that will be more than 20,000 boxing and unboxing operations, on average: n lg(n) is almost 7,000, and there are 3 box and unbox operations per comparison.

You may be wondering why you should implement the nongeneric IComparable interface at all. There are two reasons. First, there's simple backward compatibility. Your types will interact with code created before

.NET 2.0. That means supporting the pregeneric interface. Second, even more modern code will avoid generics when it's based on reflection. Reflection using generics is possible, but it's much more difficult than reflection using nongeneric type definitions. Supporting the nongeneric version of the IComparable interface makes your type easier to use for algorithms making use of reflection.

Because the classic IComparable.CompareTo() is now an explicit interface implementation, it can be called only through an IComparable reference. Users of your customer `struct` will get the type-safe comparison, and the unsafe comparison is inaccessible. The following innocent mistake no longer compiles:

```
Customer c1;
Employee e1;
if (c1.CompareTo(e1) > 0)
    Console.WriteLine("Customer one is greater");
```

It does not compile because the arguments are wrong for the public Customer.CompareTo(Customer right) method. The IComparable .CompareTo(object right) method is not accessible. You can access the IComparable method only by explicitly casting the reference:

```
Customer c1 = new Customer();
Employee e1 = new Employee();
if ((c1 as IComparable).CompareTo(e1) > 0)
    Console.WriteLine("Customer one is greater");
```

When you implement IComparable, use explicit interface implementation and provide a strongly typed public overload. The strongly typed overload improves performance and decreases the likelihood that someone will misuse the CompareTo method. You won't see all the benefits in the Sort function that the .NET Framework uses because it will still access CompareTo() through the interface pointer (see Item 22), but code that knows the type of both objects being compared will get better performance.

We'll make one last small change to the Customer `struct`. The C# language lets you overload the standard relational operators. Those should make use of the type-safe CompareTo() method:

```
public struct Customer : IComparable<Customer>, IComparable
{
    private readonly string name;
```

```csharp
    public Customer(string name)
    {
        this.name = name;
    }


    #region IComparable<Customer> Members
    public int CompareTo(Customer other)
    {
        return name.CompareTo(other.name);
    }
    #endregion


    #region IComparable Members
    int IComparable.CompareTo(object obj)
    {
        if (!(obj is Customer))
            throw new ArgumentException(
                "Argument is not a Customer", "obj");
        Customer otherCustomer = (Customer)obj;
        return this.CompareTo(otherCustomer);
    }
    #endregion


    // Relational Operators.
    public static bool operator <(Customer left,
      Customer right)
    {
        return left.CompareTo(right) < 0;
    }
    public static bool operator <=(Customer left,
      Customer right)
    {
        return left.CompareTo(right) <= 0;
    }
    public static bool operator >(Customer left,
      Customer right)
    {
        return left.CompareTo(right) > 0;
    }
```

```
    public static bool operator >=(Customer left,
       Customer right)
    {
       return left.CompareTo(right) >= 0;
    }
}
```

That's all for the standard order of customers: by name. Later, you must create a report sorting all customers by revenue. You still need the normal comparison functionality defined by the Customer `struct`, sorting them by name. Most APIs developed after generics became part of the .NET Framework will ask for a Comparison<T> delegate to perform some other sort. It's simple to create static properties in the Customer type that provide other comparison orders. For example, this delegate compares the revenue generated by two customers:

```
public static Comparison<Customer> CompareByReview
{
    get
    {
        return (left,right) =>
            left.revenue.CompareTo(right.revenue);
    }
}
```

Older libraries will ask for this kind of functionality using the IComparer interface. IComparer provides the standard way to provide alternative orders for a type without using generics. Any of the methods delivered in the 1.x .NET FCL that work on IComparable types provide overloads that order objects through IComparer. Because you authored the Customer `struct`, you can create this new class (RevenueComparer) as a private nested class inside the Customer `struct`. It gets exposed through a static property in the Customer `struct`:

```
public struct Customer : IComparable<Customer>, IComparable
{
    private readonly string name;
    private double revenue;

    public Customer(string name, double revenue)
    {
        this.name = name;
```

```csharp
        this.revenue = revenue;
    }

    #region IComparable<Customer> Members
    public int CompareTo(Customer other)
    {
        return name.CompareTo(other.name);
    }
    #endregion

    #region IComparable Members
    int IComparable.CompareTo(object obj)
    {
        if (!(obj is Customer))
            throw new ArgumentException(
                "Argument is not a Customer", "obj");
        Customer otherCustomer = (Customer)obj;
        return this.CompareTo(otherCustomer);
    }
    #endregion

    // Relational Operators.
    public static bool operator <(Customer left,
      Customer right)
    {
        return left.CompareTo(right) < 0;
    }
    public static bool operator <=(Customer left,
      Customer right)
    {
        return left.CompareTo(right) <= 0;
    }
    public static bool operator >(Customer left,
      Customer right)
    {
        return left.CompareTo(right) > 0;
    }
    public static bool operator >=(Customer left,
      Customer right)
    {
```

```
        return left.CompareTo(right) >= 0;
}

private static RevenueComparer revComp = null;

// return an object that implements IComparer
// use lazy evaluation to create just one.
public static IComparer<Customer> RevenueCompare
{
    get
    {
        if (revComp == null)
            revComp = new RevenueComparer();
        return revComp;
    }
}

public static Comparison<Customer> CompareByReview
{
    get
    {
        return (left,right) =>
            left.revenue.CompareTo(right.revenue);
    }
}

// Class to compare customers by revenue.
// This is always used via the interface pointer,
// so only provide the interface override.
private class RevenueComparer : IComparer<Customer>
{
    #region IComparer<Customer> Members
    int IComparer<Customer>.Compare(Customer left,
        Customer right)
    {
        return left.revenue.CompareTo(
            right.revenue);
    }
    #endregion
}
}
```

The last version of the Customer struct, with the embedded Revenue-Comparer, lets you order a collection of customers by name, the natural order for customers, and provides an alternative order by exposing a class that implements the IComparer interface to order customers by revenue. If you don't have access to the source for the Customer class, you can still provide an IComparer that orders customers using any of its public properties. You should use that idiom only when you do not have access to the source for the class, as when you need a different ordering for one of the classes in the .NET Framework.

Nowhere in this item did I mention Equals() or the == operator (see Item 6). Ordering relations and equality are distinct operations. You do not need to implement an equality comparison to have an ordering relation. In fact, reference types commonly implement ordering based on the object contents, yet implement equality based on object identity. CompareTo() returns 0, even though Equals() returns false. That's perfectly legal. Equality and ordering relations are not necessarily the same.

IComparable and IComparer are the standard mechanisms for providing ordering relations for your types. IComparable should be used for the most natural ordering. When you implement IComparable, you should overload the comparison operators (<, >, <=, >=) consistently with our IComparable ordering. IComparable.CompareTo() uses System.Object parameters, so you should also provide a type-specific overload of the CompareTo() method. IComparer can be used to provide alternative orderings or can be used when you need to provide ordering for a type that does not provide it for you.

Item 32: Avoid ICloneable

ICloneable sounds like a good idea: You implement the ICloneable interface for types that support copies. If you don't want to support copies, don't implement it. But your type does not live in a vacuum. Your decision to support ICloneable affects derived types as well. Once a type supports ICloneable, all its derived types must do the same. All its member types must also support ICloneable or have some other mechanism to create a copy. Finally, supporting deep copies is very problematic when you create designs that contain webs of objects. ICloneable finesses this problem in its official definition: It supports either a deep or a shallow copy. A shallow copy creates a new object that contains copies of all member variables. If those member variables are reference types, the new object refers to the same object that the original does. A deep copy creates a new object that copies all member variables as well. All reference types are cloned recursively in the copy. In built-in types, such as integers, the deep and shallow copies produce the same results. Which one does a type support? That depends on the type. But mixing shallow and deep copies in the same object causes quite a few inconsistencies. When you go wading into the ICloneable waters, it can be hard to escape. Most often, avoiding ICloneable altogether makes a simpler class. It's easier to use, and it's easier to implement.

Any value type that contains only built-in types as members does not need to support ICloneable; a simple assignment copies all the values of the `struct` more efficiently than Clone(). Clone() must box its return so that it can be coerced into a System.Object reference. The caller must perform another cast to extract the value from the box. You've got enough to do. Don't write a Clone() function that replicates an assignment.

What about value types that contain reference types? The most obvious case is a value type that contains a `string`:

```
public struct ErrorMessage
{
    private int errCode;
    private int details;
    private string msg;

    // details elided
}
```

`string` is a special case because this class is immutable. If you assign an error message object, both error message objects refer to the same `string`. This does not cause any of the problems that might happen with a general reference type. If you change the msg variable through either reference, you create a new `string` object (see Item 16).

The general case of creating a `struct` that contains arbitrary reference variables is more complicated. It's also far rarer. The built-in assignment for the `struct` creates a shallow copy, with both `structs` referring to the same object. To create a deep copy, you need to clone the contained reference type, and you need to know that the reference type supported a deep copy with its Clone() method. Even then, that will only work if the contained reference type also supports ICloneable, and its Clone() method creates a deep copy.

Now let's move on to reference types. Reference types could support the ICloneable interface to indicate that they support either shallow or deep copying. You could add support for ICloneable judiciously because doing so mandates that all classes derived from your type must also support ICloneable. Consider this small hierarchy:

```
class BaseType : ICloneable
{
    private string label = "class name";
    private int[] values = new int[10];

    public object Clone()
    {
        BaseType rVal = new BaseType();
        rVal.label = label;
        for (int i = 0; i < values.Length; i++)
            rVal.values[i] = values[i];
        return rVal;
    }
}


class Derived : BaseType
{
    private double[] dValues = new double[10];

    static void Main(string[] args)
    {
        Derived d = new Derived();
        Derived d2 = d.Clone() as Derived;

        if (d2 == null)
            Console.WriteLine("null");
    }
}
```

If you run this program, you will find that the value of d2 is null. The Derived class does inherit ICloneable.Clone() from BaseType, but that implementation is not correct for the Derived type: It only clones the base type. BaseType.Clone() creates a BaseType object, not a Derived object. That is why d2 is null in the test program—it's not a Derived object. However, even if you could overcome this problem, BaseType.Clone() could not properly copy the dValues array that was defined in Derived. When you implement ICloneable, you force all derived classes to implement it as well. In fact, you should provide a hook function to let all derived classes use your implementation (see Item 23). To support cloning, derived classes can add only member variables that are value types or reference types that implement ICloneable. That is a very stringent limitation on all derived classes. Adding ICloneable support to base classes usually creates such a burden on derived types that you should avoid implementing ICloneable in nonsealed classes.

When an entire hierarchy must implement ICloneable, you can create an abstract Clone() method and force all derived classes to implement it. In those cases, you need to define a way for the derived classes to create copies of the base members. That's done by defining a protected copy constructor:

```csharp
class BaseType
{
    private string label;
    private int[] values;

    protected BaseType()
    {
        label = "class name";
        values = new int[10];
    }

    // Used by devived values to clone
    protected BaseType(BaseType right)
    {
        label = right.label;
        values = right.values.Clone() as int[];
    }
}

sealed class Derived : BaseType, ICloneable
{
    private double[] dValues = new double[10];

    public Derived()
    {
        dValues = new double[10];
    }
```

```
// Construct a copy
// using the base class copy ctor
private Derived(Derived right) :
    base(right)
{
    dValues = right.dValues.Clone()
        as double[];
}

public object Clone()
{
    Derived rVal = new Derived(this);
    return rVal;
}
}
```

Base classes do not implement ICloneable; they provide a protected copy constructor that enables derived classes to copy the base class parts. Leaf classes, which should all be sealed, implement ICloneable when necessary. The base class does not force all derived classes to implement ICloneable, but it provides the necessary methods for any derived classes that want ICloneable support.

ICloneable does have its use, but it is the exception rather than rule. It's significant that the .NET Framework did not add an ICloneable<T> when it was updated with generic support. You should never add support for ICloneable to value types; use the assignment operation instead. You should add support for ICloneable to leaf classes when a copy operation is truly necessary for the type. Base classes that are likely to be used where ICloneable will be supported should create a protected copy constructor. In all other cases, avoid ICloneable.

Item 33: Use the new Modifier Only to React to Base Class Updates

You use the new modifier on a class member to redefine a nonvirtual member inherited from a base class. Just because you can do something doesn't mean you should, though. Redefining nonvirtual methods creates ambiguous behavior. Most developers would look at these two blocks of code and immediately assume that they did exactly the same thing, if the two classes were related by inheritance:

```
object c = MakeObject();

// Call through MyClass reference:
MyClass cl = c as MyClass;
cl.MagicMethod();

// Call through MyOtherClass reference:
MyOtherClass cl2 = c as MyOtherClass;
cl2.MagicMethod();
```

When the new modifier is involved, that just isn't the case:

```
public class MyClass
{
    public void MagicMethod()
    {
        // details elided.
    }
}


public class MyOtherClass : MyClass
{
    // Redefine MagicMethod for this class.
    public new void MagicMethod()
    {
        // details elided
    }
}
```

This kind of practice leads to a lot of developer confusion. If you call the same function on the same object, you expect the same code to execute. The fact that changing the reference, the label, that you use to call the function changes the behavior feels very wrong. It's inconsistent. A MyOtherClass object behaves differently in response to how you refer to it. The new modifier does not make a nonvirtual method into a virtual method after the fact. Instead, it lets you add a different method in your class's naming scope.

Nonvirtual methods are statically bound. Any source code anywhere that references MyClass.MagicMethod() calls exactly that function. Nothing in the runtime looks for a different version defined in any derived classes. Virtual functions, on the other hand, are dynamically bound. The runtime invokes the proper function based on the runtime type of the object.

The recommendation to avoid using the new modifier to redefine nonvirtual functions should not be interpreted as a recommendation to make everything virtual when you define base classes. A library designer makes a contract when making a function virtual. You indicate that any derived class is expected to change the implementation of virtual functions. The set of virtual functions defines all behaviors that derived classes are expected to change. The "virtual by default" design says that derived classes can modify all the behavior of your class. It really says that you didn't think through all the ramifications of which behaviors derived classes might want to modify. Instead, spend the time to think through what methods and properties are intended as polymorphic. Make those—and only those—virtual. Don't think of it as restricting the users of your class. Instead, think of it as providing guidance for the entry points you provided for customizing the behavior of your types.

There is one time, and one time only, when you want to use the new modifier. You add the new modifier to incorporate a new version of a base class that contains a method name that you already use. You've already got code that depends on the name of the method in your class. You might already have other assemblies in the field that use this method. You've created the following class in your library, using BaseWidget that is defined in another library:

```
public class MyWidget : BaseWidget
{
    public void NormalizeValues()
    {
        // details elided.
    }
}
```

You finish your widget, and customers are using it. Then you find that the BaseWidget company has released a new version. Eagerly awaiting new features, you immediately purchase it and try to build your MyWidget class. It fails because the BaseWidget folks have added their own NormalizeValues method:

```
public class BaseWidget
{
    public void Normalizevalues()
    {
```

```
        // details elided.
    }
}
```

This is a problem. Your base class snuck a method underneath your class's naming scope. There are two ways to fix this. You could change that name of your NormalizeValues method. Note that I've implied that BaseWidget.NormalizeValues() is semantically the same operation as MyWidget.NormalizeAllValues. If not, you should not call the base class implementation.

```
public class MyWidget : BaseWidget
{
    public void NormalizeAllValues()
    {
        // details elided.
        // Call the base class only if (by luck)
        // the new method does the same operation.
        base.NormalizeValues();
    }
}
```

Or, you could use the new modifier:

```
public class MyWidget : BaseWidget
{
    public void new NormalizeValues()
    {
        // details elided.
        // Call the base class only if (by luck)
        // the new method does the same operation.
        base.NormalizeValues();
    }
}
```

If you have access to the source for all clients of the MyWidget class, you should change the method name because it's easier in the long run. However, if you have released your MyWidget class to the world, that would force all your users to make numerous changes. That's where the new modifier comes in handy. Your clients will continue to use your NormalizeValues() method without changing. None of them would be calling BaseWidget .NormalizeValues () because it did not exist. The new modifier handles the case in which an upgrade to a base class now collides with a member that you previously declared in your class.

Of course, over time, your users might begin wanting to use the BaseWidget .NormalizeValues() method. Then you are back to the original problem: two methods that look the same but are different. Think through all the long-term ramifications of the new modifier. Sometimes, the short-term inconvenience of changing your method is still better.

The new modifier must be used with caution. If you apply it indiscriminately, you create ambiguous method calls in your objects. It's for the special case in which upgrades in your base class cause collisions in your class. Even in that situation, think carefully before using it. Most importantly, don't use it in any other situations.

Item 34: Avoid Overloading Methods Defined in Base Classes

When a base class chooses the name of a member, it assigns the semantics to that name. Under no circumstances may the derived class use the same name for different purposes. And yet, there are many other reasons why a derived class may want to use the same name. It may want to implement the same semantics in a different way, or with different parameters. Sometimes that's naturally supported by the language: Class designers declare virtual functions so that derived classes can implement semantics differently. Item 33 covered why using the new modifier could lead to hard-to-find bugs in your code. In this item, you'll learn why creating overloads of methods that are defined in a base class leads to similar issues. You should not overload methods declared in a base class.

The rules for overload resolution in the C# language are necessarily complicated. Possible candidate methods might be declared in the target class, any of its base classes, any extension method using the class, and interfaces it implements. Add generic methods and generic extension methods, and it gets very complicated. Throw in optional parameters, and I'm not sure anyone could know exactly what the results will be. Do you really want to add more complexity to this situation? Creating overloads for methods declared in your base class adds more possibilities to the best overload match. That increases the chance of ambiguity. It increases the chance that your interpretation of the spec is different than the compilers, and it will certainly confuse your users. The solution is simple: Pick a different method name. It's your class, and you certainly have enough brilliance to come up with a different name for a method, especially if the alternative is confusion for everyone using your types.

The guidance here is straightforward, and yet people always question if it really should be so strict. Maybe that's because overloading sounds very much like overriding. Overriding virtual methods is such a core principle of object-oriented languages; that's obviously not what I mean. Overloading means creating multiple methods with the same name and different parameter lists. Does overloading base class methods really have that much of an effect on overload resolution? Let's look at the different ways where overloading methods in the base class can cause issues.

There are a lot of permutations to this problem. Let's start simple. The interplay between overloads in base classes has a lot to do with base and derived classes used for parameters. For all the following examples, any class that begins with "B" is the base class, and any class that begins with "D" is the derived class. The samples use this class hierarchy for parameters:

```
public class B2 { }
public class D2 : B2 {}
```

Here's a class with one method, using the derived parameter (D2):

```
public class B
{
    public void Foo(D2 parm)
    {
        Console.WriteLine("In B.Foo");
    }
}
```

Obviously, this snippet of code writes "In B.Foo":

```
var obj1 = new D();
obj1.Bar(new D2());
```

Now, let's add a new derived class with an overloaded method:

```
public class D : B
{
    public void Foo(B2 parm)
    {
        Console.WriteLine("In D.Foo");
    }
}
```

Now, what happens when you execute this code?

```
var obj2 = new D();
obj2.Foo(new D2());
obj2.Foo(new B2());
```

Both lines print "in D.Foo". You always call the method in the derived class. Any number of developers would figure that the first call would print "in B.Foo". However, even the simple overload rules can be surprising. The reason both calls resolve to D.Foo is that when there is a candidate method in the most derived compile-time type, that method is the better method. That's still true when there is even a better match in a base class. Of course, this is very fragile. What do you suppose this does:

```
B obj3 = new D();
obj3.Foo(new D2());
```

I chose the words above very carefully because obj3 has the compile-time type of B (your Base class), even though the runtime type is D (your Derived class). Foo isn't virtual; therefore, obj3.Foo() must resolve to B.Foo.

If your poor users actually want to get the resolution rules they might expect, they need to use casts:

```
var obj4 = new D();
((B)obj4).Foo(new D2());
obj4.Foo(new B2());
```

If your API forces this kind of construct on your users, you've failed. You can easily add a bit more confusion. Add one method to your base class, B:

```
public class B
{
    public void Foo(D2 parm)
    {
        Console.WriteLine("In B.Foo");
    }

    public void Bar(B2 parm)
    {
        Console.WriteLine("In B.Bar");
    }
}
```

Clearly, the following code prints "In B.Bar":

```
var obj1 = new D();
obj1.Bar(new D2());
```

Now, add a different overload, and include an optional parameter:

```
public class D : B
{
    public void Foo(B2 parm)
    {
        Console.WriteLine("In D.Foo");
    }

    public void Bar(B2 parm1, B2 parm2 = null)
    {
        Console.WriteLine("In D.Bar");
    }
}
```

Hopefully, you've already seen what will happen here. This same snippet of code now prints "In D.Bar" (you're calling your derived class again):

```
var obj1 = new D();
obj1.Bar(new D2());
```

The only way to get at the method in the base class (again) is to provide a cast in the calling code.

These examples show the kinds of problems you can get into with one parameter method. The issues become more and more confusing as you add parameters based on generics. Suppose you add this method:

```
public class B
{
    public void Foo(D2 parm)
    {
        Console.WriteLine("In B.Foo");
    }

    public void Bar(B2 parm)
    {
        Console.WriteLine("In B.Bar");
    }
```

```
    public void Foo2(IEnumerable<D2> parm)
    {
        Console.WriteLine("In B.Foo2");
    }
}
```

Then, provide a different overload in the derived class:

```
public class D : B
{
    public void Foo(B2 parm)
    {
        Console.WriteLine("In D.Foo");
    }

    public void Bar(B2 parm1, B2 parm2 = null)
    {
        Console.WriteLine("In D.Bar");
    }
    public void Foo2(IEnumerable<B2> parm)
    {
        Console.WriteLine("In D.Foo2");
    }
}
```

Call Foo2 in a manner similar to before:

```
var sequence = new List<D2> { new D2(), new D2() };
var obj2 = new D();

obj2.Foo2(sequence);
```

What do you suppose gets printed this time? If you've been paying attention, you'd figure that "In D.Foo2" gets printed. That answer gets you partial
credit. That is what happens in C# 4.0. Starting in C# 4.0, generic interfaces
support covariance and contravariance, which means D.Foo2 is a candidate
method for an IEnumerable<D2> when its formal parameter type is an
IEnumerable<B2>. However, earlier versions of C# do not support generic
variance. Generic parameters are invariant. In those versions, D.Foo2 is
not a candidate method when the parameter is an IEnumerable<D2>. The
only candidate method is B.Foo2, which is the correct answer in those
versions.

The code samples above showed that you sometimes need casts to help the compiler pick the method you want in many complicated situations. In the real world, you'll undoubtedly run into situations where you need to use casts because class hierarchies, implemented interfaces, and extension methods have conspired to make the method you want, not the method the compiler picks as the "best" method. But the fact that real-world situations are occasionally ugly does not mean you should add to the problem by creating more overloads yourself.

Now you can amaze your friends at programmer cocktail parties with a more in-depth knowledge of overload resolution in C#. It can be useful information to have, and the more you know about your chosen language the better you'll be as a developer. But don't expect your users to have the same level of knowledge. More importantly, don't rely on everyone having that kind of detailed knowledge of how overload resolution works to be able to use your API. Instead, don't overload methods declared in a base class. It doesn't provide any value, and it will only lead to confusion among your users.

Item 35: Learn How PLINQ Implements Parallel Algorithms

This is the item where I wish I could say that parallel programming is now as simple as adding AsParallel() to all your loops. It's not, but PLINQ does make it much easier than it was to leverage multiple cores in your programs and still have programs that are correct. It's by no means trivial to create programs that make use of multiple cores, but PLINQ makes it easier.

You still have to understand when data access must be synchronized. You still need to measure the effects of parallel and sequential versions of the methods declared in ParallelEnumerable. Some of the methods involved in LINQ queries can execute in parallel very easily. Others force more sequential access to the sequence of elements—or, at least, require the complete sequence (like Sort). Let's walk through a few samples using PLINQ and learn what works well, and where some of the pitfalls still exist. All the samples and discussions for this item use LINQ to Objects. The title even calls out "Enumerable," not "Queryable". PLINQ really won't help you parallelize LINQ to SQL, or Entity Framework algorithms. That's not really a limiting feature, because those implementations leverage the parallel database engines to execute queries in parallel.

Here's a simple query using method call syntax that calculates n! for the first 150 numbers:

```
var nums = data.Where(m => m < 150).
    Select(n => Factorial(n));
```

You can make this a parallel query by simply adding AsParallel() as the first method on the query:

```
var numsParallel = data.AsParallel().
    Where(m => m < 150).Select(n => Factorial(n));
```

Of course, you can do the same kind of work with query syntax.

```
var nums = from n in data
           where n < 150
           select Factorial(n);
```

The Parallel version relies on putting AsParallel() on the data sequence:

```
var numsParallel = from n in data.AsParallel()
                   where n < 150
                   select Factorial(n);
```

The results are the same as with the method call version.

This first sample is very simple yet it does illustrate a few important concepts used throughout PLINQ. AsParallel() is the method you call to opt in to parallel execution of any query expression. Once you call AsParallel(), subsequent operations will occur on multiple cores using multiple threads. AsParallel() returns an IParallelEnumerable() rather than an IEnumerable(). PLINQ is implemented as a set of extension methods on IParallelEnumerable. They have almost exactly the same signatures as the methods found in the Enumerable class that extends IEnumerable. Simply substitute IParallelEnumerable for IEnumerable in both parameters and return values. The advantage of this choice is that PLINQ follows the same patterns that all LINQ providers follow. That makes PLINQ very easy to learn. Everything you know about LINQ, in general, will apply to PLINQ.

Of course, it's not quite that simple. This initial query is very easy to use with PLINQ. It does not have any shared data. The order of the results doesn't matter. That's why it is possible to get a speedup that's in direct proportion to the number of cores in the machine upon which this code is running. To help you get the best performance out of PLINQ, there are several methods that control how the parallel task library functions are accessible using IParallelEnumerable.

Every parallel query begins with a partitioning step. PLINQ needs to partition the input elements and distribute those over the number of tasks created to perform the query. Partitioning is one of the most important aspects of PLINQ, so it is important to understand the different approaches, how PLINQ decides which to use, and how each one works. First, partitioning can't take much time. That would cause the PLINQ library to spend too much time partitioning, and too little time actually processing your data. PLINQ uses four different partitioning algorithms, based on the input source and the type of query you are creating. The simplest algorithm is range partitioning. Range partitioning divides the input sequence by the number of tasks and gives each task one set of items. For example, an input sequence with 1,000 items running on a quad core machine would create four ranges of 250 items each. Range partitioning is used only when the query source supports indexing the sequence and reports how many items are in the sequence. That means range partitioning is limited to query sources that are like List<T>, arrays, and other sequences that support the IList<T> interface. Range partitioning is usually used when the source of the query supports those operations.

The second choice for partitioning is chunk partitioning. This algorithm gives each task a "chunk" of input items anytime it requests more work. The internals of the chunking algorithm will continue to change over time, so I won't cover the current implementation in depth. You can expect that the size of chunks will start small, because an input sequence may be small. That prevents the situation where one task must process an entire small sequence. You can also expect that as work continues, chunks may grow in size. That minimizes the threading overhead and helps to maximize throughput. Chunks may also change in size depending on the time cost for delegates in the query and the number of elements rejected by where clauses. The goal is to have all tasks finish at close to the same time to maximize the overall throughput.

The other two partitioning schemes optimize for certain query operations. First is a striped partition. A striped partition is a special case of range partitioning that optimizes processing the beginning elements of a sequence. Each of the worker threads processes items by skipping N items and then processing the next M. After processing M items, the worker thread will skip the next N items again. The stripe algorithm is easiest to understand if you imagine a stripe of 1 item. In the case of four worker tasks, one task gets the items at indices 0, 4, 8, 12, and so on. The second task gets items at indices 1, 5, 9, 13, and so on. Striped partitions avoid any interthread synchronization to implement TakeWhile() and SkipWhile() for the entire query. Also, it lets each worker thread move to the next items it should process using simple arithmetic.

The final algorithm is a Hash Partitioning. Hash Partitioning is a special-purpose algorithm designed for queries with the Join, GroupJoin, GroupBy, Distinct, Except, Union, and Intersect operations. Those are more expensive operations, and a specific partitioning algorithm can enable greater parallelism on those queries. Hash Partitioning ensures that all items generating the same hash code are processed by the same task. That minimizes the intertask communications for those operations.

Independent of the partitioning algorithm, there are three different algorithms used by PLINQ to parallelize tasks in your code: Pipelining, Stop & Go, and Inverted Enumeration. Pipelining is the default, so I'll explain that one first. In pipelining, one thread handles the enumeration (the `foreach`, or query sequence). Multiple threads are used to process the query on each of the elements in the sequence. As each new item in the sequence is requested, it will be processed by a different thread. The number of threads used by PLINQ in pipelining mode will usually be the number of cores (for most CPU bound queries). In my factorial example, it would work with two threads on my dual core machine. The first item would be retrieved from the sequence and processed by one thread. Immediately the second item would be requested and processed by a second thread. Then, when one of those items finished, the third item would be requested, and the query expression would be processed by that thread. Throughout the execution of the query for the entire sequence, both threads would be busy with query items. On a machine with more cores, more items would be processed in parallel.

For example, on a 16 core machine, the first 16 items would be processed immediately by 16 different threads (presumably running on 16 different cores). I've simplified a little. There is a thread that handles the enumeration, and that often means Pipelining creates (Number of Cores + 1) threads. In most scenarios, the enumeration thread is waiting most of the time, so it makes sense to create one extra.

Stop and Go means that the thread starting the enumeration will join on all the threads running the query expression. That method is used when you request that immediate execution of a query by using ToList() or ToArray(), or anytime PLINQ needs the full result set before continuing such as ordering and sorting. Both of the following queries use Stop and Go:

```
var stopAndGoArray = (from n in data.AsParallel()
                      where n < 150
                      select Factorial(n)).ToArray();


var stopAndGoList = (from n in data.AsParallel()
                     where n < 150
                     select Factorial(n)).ToList();
```

Using Stop and Go processing you'll often get slightly better performance at a cost of a higher memory footprint. However, notice that I've still constructed the entire query before executing any of the query expressions. You'll still want to compose the entire query, rather than processing each portion using Stop and Go and then composing the final results using another query. That will often cause the threading overhead to overwhelm performance gains. Processing the entire query expression as one composed operation is almost always preferable.

The final algorithm used by the parallel task library is Inverted Enumeration. Inverted Enumeration doesn't produce a result. Instead, it performs some action on the result of every query expression. In my earlier samples, I printed the results of the Factorial computation to the console:

```
var numsParallel = from n in data.AsParallel()
                   where n < 150
                   select Factorial(n);
foreach (var item in numsParallel)
   Console.WriteLine(item);
```

LINQ to Objects (nonparallel) queries are evaluated lazily. That means each value is produced only when it is requested. You can opt into the parallel execution model (which is a bit different) while processing the result of the query. That's how you ask for the Inverted Enumeration model:

```
var nums2 = from n in data.AsParallel()
            where n < 150
            select Factorial(n);
nums2.ForAll(item => Console.WriteLine(item));
```

Inverted enumeration uses less memory than the Stop and Go method. Also, it enables parallel actions on your results. Notice that you still need to use AsParallel() in your query in order to use ForAll(). ForAll() has a lower memory footprint than the Stop and Go model. In some situations, depending on the amount of work being done by the action on the result of the query expression, inverted enumeration may often be the fastest enumeration method.

All LINQ queries are executed lazily. You create queries, and those queries are only executed when you ask for the items produced by the query. LINQ to Objects goes a step further. LINQ to Objects executes the query on each item as you ask for that item. PLINQ works differently. Its model is closer to LINQ to SQL, or the Entity Framework. In those models, when you ask for the first item, the entire result sequence is generated. PLINQ is closer to that model, but it's not exactly right. If you misunderstand how PLINQ executes queries, then you'll use more resources than necessary, and you can actually make parallel queries run more slowly than LINQ to Objects queries on multicore machines.

To demonstrate some of the differences, I'll walk through a reasonably simple query. I'll show you how adding AsParallel() changes the execution model. Both models are valid. The rules for LINQ focus on what the results are, not how they are generated. You'll see that both models will generate the exact same results. Differences in how would only manifest themselves if your algorithm has side effects in the query clauses.

Here's the query I used to demonstrate the differences:

```
var answers = from n in Enumerable.Range(0, 300)
              where n.SomeTest()
              select n.SomeProjection();
```

I instrumented the SomeTest() and SomeProjection() methods to show when each gets called:

```
public static bool SomeTest(this int inputValue)
{
    Console.WriteLine("testing element: {0}", inputValue);
    return inputValue % 10 == 0;
}


public static string SomeProjection(this int input)
{
```

```
Console.WriteLine("projecting an element: {0}", input);
return string.Format("Delivered {0} at {1}",
    input.ToString(),
    DateTime.Now.ToLongTimeString());
}
```

Finally, instead of a simple `foreach` loop, I iterated the results using the IEnumerator<string> members so that you can see when different actions take place. This is so that I can more clearly show exactly how the sequence is generated (in parallel) and enumerated (in this enumeration loop). In production code, I prefer a different implementation.

```
var iter = answers.GetEnumerator();

Console.WriteLine("About to start iterating");
while (iter.MoveNext())
{
    Console.WriteLine("called MoveNext");
    Console.WriteLine(iter.Current);
}
```

Using the standard LINQ to Objects implementation, you'll see output that looks like this:

```
About to start iterating
testing element: 0
projecting an element: 0
called MoveNext
Delivered 0 at 1:46:08 PM
testing element: 1
testing element: 2
testing element: 3
testing element: 4
testing element: 5
testing element: 6
testing element: 7
testing element: 8
testing element: 9
testing element: 10
projecting an element: 10
called MoveNext
Delivered 10 at 1:46:08 PM
```

```
testing element: 11
testing element: 12
testing element: 13
testing element: 14
testing element: 15
testing element: 16
testing element: 17
testing element: 18
testing element: 19
testing element: 20
projecting an element: 20
called MoveNext
Delivered 20 at 1:46:08 PM
testing element: 21
testing element: 22
testing element: 23
testing element: 24
testing element: 25
testing element: 26
testing element: 27
testing element: 28
testing element: 29
testing element: 30
projecting an element: 30
```

The query does not begin to execute until the first call to MoveNext() on
the enumerator. The first call to MoveNext() executes the query on enough
elements to retrieve the first element on the result sequence (which happens to be one element for this query). The next call to MoveNext()
processes elements in the input sequence until the next item in the output
sequence has been produced. Using LINQ to Objects, each call to
MoveNext() executes the query on as many elements are necessary to produce the next output element.

The rules change once you change the query to be a parallel query:

```
var answers = from n in ParallelEnumerable.Range(0, 300)
              where n.SomeTest()
              select n.SomeProjection();
```

The output from this query will look very different. Here's a sample from
one run (it will change somewhat for each run):

```
About to start iterating
testing element: 150
projecting an element: 150
testing element: 0
testing element: 151
projecting an element: 0
testing element: 1
testing element: 2
testing element: 3
testing element: 4
testing element: 5
testing element: 6
testing element: 7
testing element: 8
testing element: 9
testing element: 10
projecting an element: 10
testing element: 11
testing element: 12
testing element: 13
testing element: 14
testing element: 15
testing element: 16
testing element: 17
testing element: 18
testing element: 19
testing element: 152
testing element: 153
testing element: 154
testing element: 155
testing element: 156
testing element: 157
testing element: 20
... Lots more here elided ...
testing element: 286
testing element: 287
testing element: 288
testing element: 289
testing element: 290
Delivered 130 at 1:50:39 PM
```

```
called MoveNext
Delivered 140 at 1:50:39 PM
projecting an element: 290
testing element: 291
testing element: 292
testing element: 293
testing element: 294
testing element: 295
testing element: 296
testing element: 297
testing element: 298
testing element: 299
called MoveNext
Delivered 150 at 1:50:39 PM
called MoveNext
Delivered 160 at 1:50:39 PM
called MoveNext
Delivered 170 at 1:50:39 PM
called MoveNext
Delivered 180 at 1:50:39 PM
called MoveNext
Delivered 190 at 1:50:39 PM
called MoveNext
Delivered 200 at 1:50:39 PM
called MoveNext
Delivered 210 at 1:50:39 PM
called MoveNext
Delivered 220 at 1:50:39 PM
called MoveNext
Delivered 230 at 1:50:39 PM
called MoveNext
Delivered 240 at 1:50:39 PM
called MoveNext
Delivered 250 at 1:50:39 PM
called MoveNext
Delivered 260 at 1:50:39 PM
called MoveNext
Delivered 270 at 1:50:39 PM
called MoveNext
Delivered 280 at 1:50:39 PM
```

```
called MoveNext
Delivered 290 at 1:50:39 PM
```

Notice how much it changed. The very first call to MoveNext() causes PLINQ to start all the threads involved in generating the results. That causes quite a few (in this case, almost all) result objects to be produced. Each subsequent call to MoveNext() will grab the next item from those already produced. You can't predict when a particular input element will be processed. All you know is that the query will begin executing (on several threads) as soon as you ask for the first element of the query.

PLINQ's methods that support query syntax understand how this behavior can affect performance on queries. Suppose you modify the query to select the second page of results using Skip() and Take():

```
var answers = (from n in ParallelEnumerable.Range(0, 300)
              where n.SomeTest()
              select n.SomeProjection()).
              Skip(20).Take(20);
```

Executing this query produces output that is identical to that produced by LINQ to Objects. That's because PLINQ knows that it will be faster to produce only 20 elements rather than 300. (I'm simplifying, but PLINQ's implementation of Skip() and Take() do tend to favor a sequential algorithm more than other algorithms.)

You can modify the query a bit more, and get PLINQ to generate all the elements using the parallel execution model. Just add an `orderby` clause:

```
var answers = (from n in ParallelEnumerable.Range(0, 300)
              where n.SomeTest()
              orderby n.ToString().Length
              select n.SomeProjection()).
              Skip(20).Take(20);
```

The lambda argument for `orderby` must not be something that the compiler can optimize away (that's why I used n.ToString().Length rather than just n above). Now, the query engine must generate all the elements of the output sequence before it can order them properly. Only once the elements are ordered properly can the Skip() and Take() methods know which elements should be returned. Of course, it's faster on multicore machines to use multiple threads to generate all the output than it would be to generate the sequence sequentially. PLINQ knows that, too, so it starts multiple threads to create the output.

PLINQ tries to create the best implementation for the queries you write in order to generate the results you need with the least amount of work, and in the least amount of time. Sometimes that means PLINQ queries will execute in a different manner than you would expect. Sometimes it will act more like LINQ to Objects, where asking for the next item in the output sequence executes the code that produces it. Sometimes it will behave more like LINQ to SQL or Entity Framework in that asking for the first item will produce all of them. Sometimes it will behave like a mixture of the two. You should make sure that you don't introduce any side effects in your LINQ queries. Those will be unreliable in a PLINQ execution model. You should construct your queries with some care to ensure that you get the most out of the underlying technology. That requires you to understand how they work differently.

Parallel algorithms are limited by Amdahl's law: The speedup of a program using multiple processors is limited by the sequential fraction of the program. The extension methods in ParallelEnumerable are no exception to this rule. Many of these methods can operate in parallel, but some of them will affect the degree of parallelism due to their nature. Obviously OrderBy and ThenBy require some coordination between tasks. Skip, SkipWhile, Take, and TakeWhile will affect the degree of parallelism. Parallel tasks running on different cores may finish in different orders. You can use the AsOrdered() and AsUnordered() methods to instruct PLINQ as to whether or not order matters in the result sequence.

Sometimes your own algorithm relies on side effects and cannot be parallelized. You can force sequential execution using the ParallelEnumerable .AsSequential() extension method to interpret a parallel sequence as an IEnumerable and force sequential execution.

Finally, ParallelEnumerable contains methods that allow you to control how PLINQ executes parallel queries. You can use WithExecutionMode() to suggest parallel execution, even if that means selecting a high overhead algorithm. By default, PLINQ will parallelize those constructs where it expects parallelism to help. You can use WithDegreeOfParallelism() to suggest the number of threads that may be used in your algorithm. Usually, PLINQ will allocate threads based on the number of processors on the current machine. You can also use the WithMergeOptions() to request a change in how PLINQ controls buffering results during a query. Usually, PLINQ will buffer some results from each thread before making them available to the consumer thread. You can request no buffering to make results available immediately. You can request full buffering, which will increase performance at a cost of higher latency. Auto Buffering, the default, provides a balance between latency and performance. Buffering is a hint, not a demand. PLINQ may ignore your request.

I'm not providing any specific guidance on which of these settings is best for you because they will be highly dependent on your algorithm. However, you have those settings that you can change, and you should experiment on a variety of target machines to see if these will help your algorithms. If you don't have several different target machines to experiment with, I'd recommend using the defaults.

PLINQ makes parallel computing much easier than it previously was. It's an important time for these additions; parallel computing will continue to become more important as more and more cores become commonplace for desktop and laptop computers. It's still not easy. And poorly designed algorithms may not see performance improvements from parallelization. Your task is to look for loops and other tasks that can be parallelized. Take those algorithms and try the parallel versions. Measure the results. Work on the algorithms to get better results on the performance. Realize that some algorithms aren't easily parallelizable, and keep those serial.

Item 36: Understand How to Use PLINQ for I/O Bound Operations

The Parallel Task Library looks like it would be optimized for CPU bound operations. While that is a core mission for the library, it does work well with I/O bound operations as well. In fact, the design of the Parallel Task Library handles I/O bound operations rather well by default. It will update the number of threads allocated to your algorithms based on the how busy those threads are. More blocked threads (waiting for I/O operations) will result in the ThreadPool allocating more threads to the tasks at hand.

As with other parallel extensions, you can use method calls, or LINQ query syntax to opt into a parallel execution model. Parallel execution for I/O bound operations behaves a little differently than CPU bound operations. You'll often want more threads than cores, because the I/O bound threads spend more of their time waiting for some external event. PLINQ provides a framework for these idioms as well.

This snippet of code performs Web downloads from a series of Web sites:

```
foreach (var url in urls)
{
    var result = new WebClient().DownloadData(url);
    UseResult(result);
}
```

The DownloadData() call makes a Web synchronous request and waits until all the data is retrieved. This algorithm will spend a lot of time waiting. You can quickly change to a parallel model by using a parallel `for` loop:

```
Parallel.ForEach(urls, url =>
{
    var result = new WebClient().DownloadData(url);
    UseResult(result);
});
```

Parallel.ForEach() opts into a parallel processing model. This version takes much less time than the serial version. In fact, on my dual core machine, the speedup is roughly proportional to the number of elements in the urls collection. Threads are spending much of their time waiting, so the Parallel Task Library will create more threads.

You can use PLINQ and query syntax to produce the same kind of result:

```
var results = from url in urls.AsParallel()
              select new WebClient().DownloadData(url);
results.ForAll(result => UseResult(result));
```

PLINQ operates a bit differently than the Parallel Task Library's Parallel.ForEach() support. PLINQ will use a fixed number of threads, whereas AsParallel() will ramp the number of threads up or down to increase throughput. You can control the number of threads in PLINQ using ParallelEnumerable.WithDegreeOfParallelism() (see Item 35), but Parallel.ForEach() will manage it for you. Parallel.ForEach() works best when the load is some mixture of I/O bound and CPU bound operation. Parallel.ForEach() will manage the number of active threads based on the current load. When more threads are blocked waiting on I/O operations, it will create more threads to increase throughput. When more threads are working, it will allow the number of active threads to go down to minimize context switching.

The code shown above is not truly asynchronous. It's making use of multiple threads to perform some work in parallel, but the surrounding program will wait for all the Web requests to finish before continuing with other work. The Parallel Task Library provides other primitives to implement the async pattern. One very common pattern is to begin a number of I/O bound tasks and perform some action on those results. Ideally, I'd like to write something like:

```
urls.RunAsync(
    url => startDownload(url),
    task => finishDownload(task.AsyncState.ToString(),
    task.Result));
```

This would use the startDownload() method to begin downloading each URL. As each download finishes, finishDownload() would be called. Once all the downloads have finished, RunAsync() would finish. There is a reasonable amount of work using the Parallel Task Library to accomplish this, so let's examine it closely. The best place to begin is the RunAsync method itself:

```
public static void RunAsync<T, TResult>(
    this IEnumerable<T> taskParms,
    Func<T, Task<TResult>> taskStarter,
    Action<Task<TResult>> taskFinisher)
{
    taskParms.Select(parm => taskStarter(parm)).
        AsParallel().
        ForAll(t => t.ContinueWith(t2 => taskFinisher(t2)));
}
```

This method creates a task per input parameter. The Select() method returns the sequence of tasks. Next, you need to opt into parallel processing of the results, by using AsParallel(). For every single task, you'll want to call the post processing method for every task. The Task<T> class represents a (possibly parallel) task and contains properties to report on the input and output values from the task. One of the methods of Task<T> is ContinueWith(). It will be called as the task finishes and allows you to perform any processing after the task has finished running. In the RunAsync method, it calls the taskFinisher, giving the Task object as the parameter. That enables the caller to perform any processing as the task finishes. ForAll() performs the inverted enumeration, so that it blocks until all tasks have completed.

Let's dig a little deeper into this pattern to examine the methods used for starting and reporting the completion of each download. The finish-Download method is rather simple, and I'll show it only for completeness:

```
private static void finishDownload(string url, byte[] bytes)
{
    Console.WriteLine("Read {0} bytes from {1}",
        bytes.Length, url);
}
```

StartDownload shows a bit more of the interface provided by the Parallel Task Library. The specific types used help to support the Task interface. I'd like to abstract that away, but handling these types will be a bit different for each specific task you want to accomplish. In fact, the Parallel Task Library puts a common interface on top of the many different async patterns that existed in the .NET BCL prior to this version.

```
private static Task<byte[]> startDownload(string url)
{
    var tcs = new TaskCompletionSource<byte[]>(url);
    var wc = new WebClient();
    wc.DownloadDataCompleted += (sender, e) =>
    {
        if (e.UserState == tcs)
        {
            if (e.Cancelled)
                tcs.TrySetCanceled();
            else if (e.Error != null)
                tcs.TrySetException(e.Error);
            else
                tcs.TrySetResult(e.Result);
        }
    };
    wc.DownloadDataAsync(new Uri(url), tcs);
    return tcs.Task;
}
```

This method has a mix of general Task code and code specific to downloading data from a URL, so let's go through it very carefully. First, it creates a TaskCompletionSource object for this task. A TaskCompletionSource object enables you to separate the creation of a task from its completion.

It's important here because you are using the WebClient class's async methods to create the task. The type parameter for the TaskCompletion-Source is the type of result returned from the task.

The WebClient class uses the Event-based Asynchronous Pattern (EAP). That means you register a handler for an event that will be raised when an asynchronous operation completes. startDownload() stores the task completion information in the TaskCompletionSource when that event is raised. The TaskSheduler picks up the task and then the download is started. The method returns the Task object embedded inside the TaskCompletionSource so that the event results can be processed once the task completes.

After this bit of work, the Web download occurs asynchronously on another thread. When the download completes, the DownloadDataCompleted event is raised. The event handler will set the completion status for the TaskCompletionSource. That signals the Task embedded in the TaskCompletionSource that it has finished.

Now, the task will invoke ContinueWith(), which will report the results for that download. It takes a bit of unwinding, but after you've unwound it once, the pattern isn't that hard to understand.

The sample shown above is the correct idiom to use when the underlying source uses the Event-based Asynchronous Pattern. Other areas of the .NET library will use the Asynchronous Programming Model (APM) pattern. In that pattern, for some operation Foo you'll call BeginFoo(), which will return an IAsyncResult. Once the operation has completed, you'll call EndFoo(), passing in the IAsyncResult. You can use the Task<TResult> .Factory.FromAsync() method to implement this pattern using the Parallel Task Library. The underlying idiom will be similar to the version I've shown for downloading Web data. The difference would be where you create the task you'd provide a different set of delegates to match the async method being used.

The Parallel Task Library provides a series of methods that enable working with I/O bound operations as well as CPU bound partitions of work. Using the Task class, you can support a variety of asynchronous patterns that work with I/O bound operations, or those that are a mixture of I/O and CPU bound operations. Parallel tasks are still not easy, but the Parallel Task Library and PLINQ provide better language level support for asynchronous programming than previous libraries had. It will continue to be more important as more of our programs must access data on different machines and more threads are waiting for responses from remote machines.

Item 37: Construct Parallel Algorithms with Exceptions in Mind

The previous two items blissfully ignored the possibility of anything going wrong with any of the child threads doing its work. That's clearly not how the real world works. Exceptions will occur in your child threads, and you'll be left to pick up the pieces somehow. Of course, exceptions in background threads increase the complexity in several ways. Exceptions can't just continue up the call stack across thread boundaries. Instead, if an Exception reaches the thread start method, that thread gets terminated. There's no way for the calling thread to retrieve the error, or do anything about it. Furthermore, if your parallel algorithm must support rollback if there are problems, you'll have to do more work to understand any side effects that have occurred and what you should do to recover from those errors. Every algorithm has different requirements, so there are no universal answers for handling exceptions in a parallel environment. The guidelines I provide here are just that: guidelines that you can use to determine the best strategy for your particular application.

Let's begin with the async download method from the last item. That has a very simple strategy in that there are no side effects, and the downloads from all other Web hosts can continue without concern for the one download that is failing. Parallel operations use the new AggregateException type to handle exceptions in parallel operations. The AggregateException is a container that holds all exceptions generated from any of the parallel operations in an InnerExceptions property. There are a couple different ways to handle the exception in this process. First, I'll show the more general case, how to handle any errors generated by subtasks in the outer processing.

The RunAsync() method shown in the previous Item uses more than one parallel operation. That means you may have AggregateExceptions in the InnerExceptions collection that is part of the AggregateException you actually catch. The more parallel operations you have, the deeper this nesting can go. Because of the way parallel operations compose with each other, you may end up with multiple copies of the original exception in the final collection of exceptions. I modified the call to RunAsync() to process possible errors:

```
try
{
    urls.RunAsync(
        url => startDownload(url),
        task => finishDownload(
            task.AsyncState.ToString(), task.Result));
}
catch (AggregateException problems)
{
    ReportAggregateError(problems);
}

private static void ReportAggregateError(
    AggregateException aggregate)
{
    foreach (var exception in aggregate.InnerExceptions)
        if (exception is AggregateException)
            ReportAggregateError(
            exception as AggregateException);
        else
            Console.WriteLine(exception.Message);
}
```

The ReportAggregateError prints out the messages for all exceptions that are not themselves AggregateExceptions. Of course, this has the nasty side effect of swallowing all exceptions, whether you anticipated them or not. That's rather dangerous. Instead, what you want to do is handle only those exceptions from which you can recover, and rethrow any other exceptions.

There are enough recursive collections here that a utility method makes sense. The generic method must know which exception types you want to handle, and which are not expected and how you'll handle the ones you are handling. You need to send this method a set of exception types, and the code to handle the exception. That's simply a dictionary of types and Action<T> lambda expressions. And, if the handler doesn't process everything in the collection of InnerExceptions, clearly something else went wrong. That means it's time to rethrow the original exception. Here's the updated code that calls RunAsync:

```
try
{
    urls.RunAsync(
```

```
                url => startDownload(url),
                task => finishDownload(task.AsyncState.ToString(),
                task.Result));
    }
    catch (AggregateException problems)
    {
        var handlers = new Dictionary<Type, Action<Exception>>();
        handlers.Add(typeof(WebException),
            ex => Console.WriteLine(ex.Message));

        if (!HandleAggregateError(problems, handlers))
            throw;
    }
```

The HandleAggregateError method recursively looks at every exception. If the exception is expected, the handler is called. Otherwise, HandleAggregateError returns false, indicating that this set of aggregate exceptions cannot be processed correctly.

```
private static bool HandleAggregateError(
    AggregateException aggregate,
    Dictionary<Type, Action<Exception>> exceptionHandlers)
{
    foreach (var exception in aggregate.InnerExceptions)
        if (exception is AggregateException)
            return HandleAggregateError(
                exception as AggregateException,
                exceptionHandlers);
        else if (exceptionHandlers.ContainsKey(
            exception.GetType()))
        {
            exceptionHandlers[exception.GetType()]
                (exception);
        }
        else
            return false;
    return true;
}
```

This code does look a bit dense, but it's not that hard. When it encounters an AggregateException, it evaluates that child list recursively. When it encounters any other kind of exception, it looks into the dictionary. If a handler Action<> has been registered, it calls that handler. If not, then it returns false immediately, having found an exception that it should not be handled.

You may be wondering why the original AggregateException gets thrown rather than the single exception for which there was no handler. The problem is that throwing one exception out of the collection could lose important information. The InnerExceptions may contain any number of exceptions. More than one may be of a type that is not expected. You must return the entire collection or risk losing much of that information. In many cases, there will be only one exception in the AggregateException's InnerExceptions collection. However, you should not code that way because when you do need that extra information, it won't be there.

Of course, this feels a bit ugly. Wouldn't it be better to prevent the exception from leaving the task doing the background work? In almost all cases, that is better. That requires changing the code that runs the background task to ensure that no exceptions can exit the background task. Whenever you use the TaskCompletionSource<> class, that means never calling TrySetException(), but rather ensuring that every task somehow calls TrySetResult() to indicate completeness. That would mean the following changes to startDownload. But, just like I said earlier, you should not be catching every single exception. You should catch only those exceptions from which you can recover. In this example, you can reasonably recover from a WebException, indicating that the remote host isn't available. Other exception types would indicate more serious problems. Those should continue to generate exceptions and stop all processing. That causes the following changes to the startDownload method:

```
private static Task<byte[]> startDownload(string url)
{
    var tcs = new TaskCompletionSource<byte[]>(url);
    var wc = new WebClient();
    wc.DownloadDataCompleted += (sender, e) =>
    {
        if (e.UserState == tcs)
        {
            if (e.Cancelled)
                tcs.TrySetCanceled();
            else if (e.Error != null)
```

```
        {
            if (e.Error is WebException)
                tcs.TrySetResult(new byte[0]);
            else
                tcs.TrySetException(e.Error);
        }
        else
            tcs.TrySetResult(e.Result);
    }
};
wc.DownloadDataAsync(new Uri(url), tcs);
return tcs.Task;
}
```

A WebException causes a return indicating 0 bytes read, and all other exceptions are thrown through the normal channels. Yes, this does mean that you still need to handle what happens when AggregateExceptions are thrown. It's possible that you merely need to treat those as fatal errors, and your background tasks can handle all other errors. But you do need to understand that it's a different kind of exception.

Of course, errors in background tasks create other issues when you use LINQ syntax. Remember from Item 35 that I described three different parallel algorithms. In all cases, using PLINQ makes some changes to the normal lazy evaluation, and these changes are important for how you must handle exceptions in your PLINQ algorithms. Remember that usually, a query executes only as other code requests the items produced by the query. That isn't quite how it works with PLINQ. Background threads generate results as they run, and another task constructs the final result sequence. It's not exactly an eager evaluation. The query results are not produced immediately. However, the background threads that produce the results will start as soon as the scheduler allows. Not immediately, but very soon. Processing any of those items may throw an exception. Now, that means you must change your exception handling code. In a typical LINQ query, you can put try/catch blocks around the code that uses the query results. It's not needed around the code that defines the LINQ query expression:

```
var nums = from n in data
           where n < 150
           select Factorial(n);
```

```
try
{
    foreach (var item in nums)
        Console.WriteLine(item);
}
catch (InvalidOperationException inv)
{
    // elided
}
```

Once PLINQ is involved, you must enclose the definition of the query in the `try`/`catch` block as well. And, of course, remember that once you use PLINQ, you must catch AggregateException instead of whatever exception you had been originally expecting. This is true whether you use Pipelining, Stop and Go, or Inverted Enumeration.

Exceptions are complicated in any algorithm. Parallel tasks create more complications. The Parallel Task Library uses the AggregateException class to hold any and all exceptions thrown somewhere in the depths of your parallel algorithms. Once any of the background threads throws an exception, any other background operations are also stopped. Your best plan is to try to ensure that no exceptions can be thrown from the code executing in your parallel tasks. Even so, other exceptions that you don't expect may be thrown elsewhere. That means you must handle any AggregateException in the controlling thread that initiated all the background work.

5 | Dynamic Programming in C#

There are advantages to both static typing and dynamic typing. Dynamic typing can enable quicker development times and easier interoperability with dissimilar systems. Static typing enables the compiler to find classes of errors. Because the compiler can make those checks, runtime checks can be streamlined, which results in better performance. C# is a statically typed language and will remain one. However, for those times when dynamic languages provide more efficient solutions, C# now contains dynamic features. Those features enable you to switch between static typing and dynamic typing when the needs arise. The wealth of features that you have in static typing means that most of your C# code will be statically typed. This chapter shows you the problems suited for dynamic programming and the techniques you will use to solve those problems most efficiently.

Item 38: Understand the Pros and Cons of Dynamic

C#'s support for dynamic typing is meant to provide a bridge to other locations. It's not meant to encourage general dynamic language programming, but rather to provide a smoother transition between the strong, static typing associated with C# and those environments that use a dynamic typing model.

However, that doesn't mean you should restrict your use of dynamic to interoperating with other environments. C# types can be coerced into dynamic objects and treated as dynamic objects. Like everything else in this world, there's good and bad in treating C# objects as dynamic objects. Let's look at one example and go over what happens, both good and bad.

One of the limitations of C# generics is that in order to access methods beyond those defined in System.Object, you need to specify constraints. Furthermore, constraints must be in the form of a base class, a set of interfaces, or the special constraints for reference type, value type, and the existence of a public parameterless constructor. You can't specify that some known method is available. This can be especially limiting when you want to create a general method that relies on some operator, like +. Dynamic invocation can fix that. As long as a member is available at runtime, it can be used. Here's a method that adds two dynamic objects, as long as there is an available operator + at runtime:

```
public static dynamic Add(dynamic left,
    dynamic right)
{
    return left + right;
}
```

This is my first discussion of dynamic, so let's look into what it's doing. Dynamic can be thought of as "System.Object with runtime binding." At compile time, dynamic variables have only those methods defined in System.Object. However, the compiler adds code so that every member access is implemented as a dynamic call site. At runtime, code executes to examine the object and determine if the requested method is available. (See Item 41 on implementing dynamic objects.) This is often referred to as "duck typing": If it walks like a duck and talks like a duck, it may as well be a duck. You don't need to declare a particular interface, or provide any compile-time type operations. As long as the members needed are available at runtime, it will work.

For this method above, the dynamic call site will determine if there is an accessible + operator for the actual runtime types of the two objects listed. All of these calls will provide a correct answer:

```
dynamic answer = Add(5, 5);
answer = Add(5.5, 7.3);
answer = Add(5, 12.3);
```

Notice that the answer must be declared as a dynamic object. Because the call is dynamic, the compiler can't know the type of the return value. That must be resolved at runtime. The only way to resolve the type of the return code at runtime is to make it a dynamic object. The static type of the return value is dynamic. Its runtime type is resolved at runtime.

Of course, this dynamic Add method is not limited to numeric type. You can add strings (because string does have an operator + defined):

```
dynamic label = Add("Here is ", "a label");
```

You can add a timespan to a date:

```
dynamic tomorrow = Add(DateTime.Now, TimeSpan.FromDays(1));
```

As long as there is an accessible operator +, the dynamic version of Add will work.

This opening explanation of dynamic might lead you to overuse dynamic programming. I've only discussed the pros of dynamic programming. It's time to consider the cons as well. You've left the safety of the type system behind, and with that, you've limited how the compiler can help you. Any mistakes in interpreting the type will only be discovered at runtime.

The result of any operation where one of the operands (including a possible `this` reference) is dynamic is itself dynamic. At some point, you'll want to bring those dynamic objects back into the static type system used by most of your C# code. That's going to require either a cast or a conversion operation:

```
answer = Add(5, 12.3);
int value = (int)answer;
string stringLabel = System.Convert.ToString(answer);
```

The cast operation will work when the actual type of the dynamic object is the target type, or can be cast to the target type. You'll need to know the correct type of the result of any dynamic operation to give it a strong type. Otherwise, the conversion will fail at runtime, throwing an exception.

Using dynamic typing is the right tool when you have to resolve methods at runtime without knowledge of the types involved. When you do have compile-time knowledge, you should use lambda expressions and functional programming constructs to create the solution you need. You could rewrite the Add method using lambdas like this:

```
public static TResult Add<T1, T2, TResult>(T1 left, T2 right,
    Func<T1, T2, TResult> AddMethod)
{
    return AddMethod(left, right);
}
```

Every caller would be required to supply the specific method. All the previous examples could be implemented using this strategy:

```
var lambdaAnswer = Add(5, 5, (a, b) => a + b);
var lambdaAnswer2 = Add(5.5, 7.3, (a, b) => a + b);
```

```
var lambdaAnswer3 = Add(5, 12.3, (a, b) => a + b);
var lambdaLabel = Add("Here is ", "a label",
    (a, b) => a + b);
dynamic tomorrow = Add(DateTime.Now, TimeSpan.FromDays(1));
var finalLabel = Add("something", 3,
    (a,b) => a + b.ToString());
```

You can see that the last method requires you to specify the conversion from int to string. It also has a slightly ugly feel in that all those lambdas look like they could be turned into a common method. Unfortunately, that's just how this solution works. You have to supply the lambda at a location where the types can be inferred. That means a fair amount of code that looks the same to humans must be repeated because the code isn't the same to the compiler. Of course, defining the Add method to implement Add seems silly. In practice, you'd use this technique for methods that used the lambda but weren't simply executing it. It's the technique used in the .NET library Enumerable.Aggregate(). Aggregate() enumerates an entire sequence and produces a single result by adding (or performing some other operation):

```
var accumulatedTotal = Enumerable.Aggregate(sequence,
    (a, b) => a + b);
```

It still feels like you are repeating code. One way to avoid this repeated code is to use Expression Trees. It's another way to build code at runtime. The System.Linq.Expression class and its derived classes provide APIs for you to build expression trees. Once you've built the expression tree, you convert it to a lambda expression and compile the resulting lambda expression into a delegate. For example, this code builds and executes Add on three values of the same type:

```
// Naive Implementation. Read on for a better version
public static T AddExpression<T>(T left, T right)
{
    ParameterExpression leftOperand = Expression.Parameter(
        typeof(T), "left");
    ParameterExpression rightOperand = Expression.Parameter(
        typeof(T), "right");
    BinaryExpression body = Expression.Add(
        leftOperand, rightOperand);
    Expression<Func<T, T, T>> adder =
        Expression.Lambda<Func<T, T, T>>(
```

```
    body, leftOperand, rightOperand);
  Func<T, T, T> theDelegate = adder.Compile();
  return theDelegate(left, right);
}
```

Most of the interesting work involves type information, so rather than using var as I would in production code for clarity, I've specifically named all the types.

The first two lines create parameter expressions for variables named "left" and "right," both of type T. The next line creates an Add expression using those two parameters. The Add expression is derived from BinaryExpression. You should be able to create similar expressions for other binary operators.

Next, you need to build a lambda expression from the expression body and the two parameters. Finally, you create the Func<T,T,T> delegate by compiling the expression. Once compiled, you can execute it and return the result. Of course, you can call it just like any other generic method:

```
int sum = AddExpression(5, 7);
```

I added the comment above the last example indicating that this was a naïve implementation. DO NOT copy this code into your working application. This version has two problems. First, there are a lot of situations where it doesn't work but Add() should work. There are several examples of valid Add() methods that take dissimilar parameters: int and double, DateTime and TimeSpan, etc. Those won't work with this method. Let's fix that. You must add two more generic parameters to the method. Then, you can specify different operands on the left and the right side of the operation. While at it, I replaced some of the local variable names with var declarations. This obscures the type information, but it does help make the logic of the method a little more clear.

```
// A little better.
public static TResult AddExpression<T1, T2, TResult>
    (T1 left, T2 right)
{
    var leftOperand = Expression.Parameter(typeof(T1),
        "left");
    var rightOperand = Expression.Parameter(typeof(T2),
        "right");
    var body = Expression.Add(leftOperand, rightOperand);
```

```
    var adder = Expression.Lambda<Func<T1, T2, TResult>>(
        body, leftOperand, rightOperand);
    return adder.Compile()(left, right);
}
```

This method looks very similar to the previous version; it just enables you to call it with different types for the left and the right operand. The only downside is that you need to specify all three parameter types whenever you call this version:

```
int sum2 = AddExpression<int, int, int>(5, 7);
```

However, because you specify all three parameters, expressions with dissimilar parameters work:

```
DateTime nextWeek= AddExpression<DateTime, TimeSpan,
    DateTime>(
    DateTime.Now, TimeSpan.FromDays(7));
```

It's time to address the other nagging issue. The code, as I have shown so far, compiles the expression into a delegate every time the AddExpression() method is called. That's quite inefficient, especially if you end up executing the same expression repeatedly. Compiling the expression is expensive, so you should cache the compiled delegate for future invocations. Here's a first pass at that class:

```
// dangerous but working version
public static class BinaryOperator<T1, T2, TResult>
{
    static Func<T1, T2, TResult> compiledExpression;

    public static TResult Add(T1 left, T2 right)
    {
        if (compiledExpression == null)
            createFunc();

        return compiledExpression(left, right);
    }

    private static void createFunc()
    {
        var leftOperand = Expression.Parameter(typeof(T1),
            "left");
```

```
        var rightOperand = Expression.Parameter(typeof(T2),
            "right");
        var body = Expression.Add(leftOperand, rightOperand);
        var adder = Expression.Lambda<Func<T1, T2, TResult>>(
            body, leftOperand, rightOperand);
        compiledExpression = adder.Compile();
    }
}
```

At this point, you're probably wondering which technique to use: dynamic or Expressions. That decision depends on the situation. The Expression version uses a slightly simpler set of runtime computations. That might make it faster in many circumstances. However, expressions are a little less dynamic than dynamic invocation. Remember that with dynamic invocation, you could add many different types successfully: `int` and `double`, `short` and `float`, whatever. As long as it was legal in C# code, it was legal in the compiled version. You could even add a string and number. If you try those same scenarios using the expression version, any of those legal dynamic versions will throw an InvalidOperationException. Even though there are conversion operations that work, the Expressions you've built don't build those conversions into the lambda expression. Dynamic invocation does more work and therefore supports more different types of operations. For instance, suppose you want to update the AddExpression to add different types and perform the proper conversions. Well, you just have to update the code that builds the expression to include the conversions from the parameter types to the result type yourself. Here's what it looks like:

```
// A fix for one problem causes another
public static TResult AddExpressionWithConversion
    <T1, T2, TResult>(T1 left, T2 right)
{
    var leftOperand = Expression.Parameter(typeof(T1),
        "left");
    Expression convertedLeft = leftOperand;
    if (typeof(T1) != typeof(TResult))
    {
        convertedLeft = Expression.Convert(leftOperand,
            typeof(TResult));
    }
    var rightOperand = Expression.Parameter(typeof(T2),
        "right");
```

```
    Expression convertedRight = rightOperand;
    if (typeof(T2) != typeof(TResult))
    {
        convertedRight = Expression.Convert(rightOperand,
        typeof(TResult));
    }
    var body = Expression.Add(convertedLeft, convertedRight);
    var adder = Expression.Lambda<Func<T1, T2, TResult>>(
        body, leftOperand, rightOperand);
    return adder.Compile()(left, right);
}
```

That will fix all the problems with any addition that needs a conversion, like adding `doubles` and `ints`, or adding a `double` to `string` with the result being a string. However, it breaks valid usages where the parameters should not be the same as the result. In particular, this version would not work with the example above adding a TimeSpan to a DateTime. With a lot more code, you could solve this. However, at that point, you've pretty much reimplemented the code that handles dynamic dispatch for C# (see Item 41). Instead of all that work, just use dynamic.

You should use the expression version for those times when the operands and the result are the same. That gives you generic type parameter inference and fewer permutations when the code fails at runtime. Here's the version I would recommend to use Expression for implementing runtime dispatch:

```
public static class BinaryOperators<T>
{
    static Func<T, T, T> compiledExpression;

    public static T Add(T left, T right)
    {
        if (compiledExpression == null)
            createFunc();

        return compiledExpression(left, right);
    }

    private static void createFunc()
    {
        var leftOperand = Expression.Parameter(typeof(T),
            "left");
```

```
    var rightOperand = Expression.Parameter(typeof(T),
        "right");
    var body = Expression.Add(leftOperand, rightOperand);
    var adder = Expression.Lambda<Func<T, T, T>>(
        body, leftOperand, rightOperand);
    compiledExpression = adder.Compile();
    }
}
```

You still need to specify the one type parameter when you call Add. Doing so does give you the advantage of being able to leverage the compiler to create any conversions at the callsite. The compiler can promote ints to doubles and so on.

There are also performance costs with using dynamic and with building expressions at runtime. Just like any dynamic type system, your program has more work to do at runtime because the compiler did not perform any of its usual type checking. The compiler must generate instructions to perform all those checks at runtime. I don't want to overstate this, because the C# compiler does produce efficient code for doing the runtime checking. In most cases, using dynamic will be faster than writing your own code to use reflection and produce your own version of late binding. However, the amount of runtime work is nonzero; the time it takes is also nonzero. If you can solve a problem using static typing, it will undoubtedly be more efficient than using dynamic types.

When you control all the types involved, and you can create an interface instead of using dynamic programming, that's the better solution. You can define the interface, program against the interface, and implement the interface in all your types that should exhibit the behavior defined by the interface. The C# type system will make it harder to introduce type errors in your code, and the compiler will produce more efficient code because it can assume that certain classes of errors are not possible.

In many cases, you can create the generic API using lambdas and force callers to define the code you would execute in the dynamic algorithm.

The next choice would be using expressions. That's the right choice if you have a relatively small number of permutations for different types, and a small number of possible conversions. You can control what expressions get created and therefore how much work happens at runtime.

When you use dynamic, the underlying dynamic infrastructure will work to make any possible legal construct work, no matter how expensive the work is at runtime.

However, for the Add() method I demonstrated at the beginning of this item, that's not possible. Add() should work on a number of types that are already defined in the .NET class library. You can't go back and add an IAdd interface to those types. You also can't guarantee that all third-party libraries you want to work with will conform to some new interface. The best way to build methods based on the presence of a particular member is to write a dynamic method that defers that choice to the runtime. The dynamic implementation will find a proper implementation, use it, and cache for better performance. It's more expensive than a purely statically typed solution, and it's much simpler than parsing expression trees.

Item 39: Use Dynamic to Leverage the Runtime Type of Generic Type Parameters

System.Linq.Enumerable.Cast<T> coerces every object in a sequence to the target type of T. It's part of the framework so that LINQ queries can be used with sequences of IEnumerable (as opposed to IEnumerable<T>). Cast<T> is a generic method, with no constraints on T. That limits the types of conversions available to it. If you use Cast<T> without understanding its limitations, you'll find yourself thinking it doesn't work. In reality, it's working exactly as it should, just not the way you expect. Let's examine its inner workings and limitations. Then, it will be easy to create a different version that does what you expect.

The root of the problem lies with the fact that Cast<T> is compiled into MSIL without any knowledge of T beyond the fact that T must be a managed type that derives from System.Object. Therefore, it does its work only using the functionality defined in System.Object. Examine this class:

```
public class MyType
{
    public String StringMember { get; set; }

    public static implicit operator String(MyType aString)
    {
        return aString.StringMember;
    }
}
```

```
    public static implicit operator MyType(String aString)
    {
        return new MyType { StringMember = aString };
    }
}
```

See Item 28 for why conversion operators are bad; however, a user-defined conversion operator is key to this issue. Consider this code (assume that GetSomeStrings() returns a sequence of strings):

```
var answer1 = GetSomeStrings().Cast<MyType>();
try
{
    foreach (var v in answer1)
        Console.WriteLine(v);
}
catch (InvalidCastException)
{
    Console.WriteLine("Cast Failed!");
}
```

Before starting this item, you may have expected that GetSomeStrings() .Cast<MyType>() would correctly convert each string to a MyType using the implicit conversion operator defined in MyType. Now you know it doesn't; it throws an InvalidCastException.

The above code is equivalent to this construct, using a query expression:

```
var answer2 = from MyType v in GetSomeStrings()
              select v;
try
{
    foreach (var v in answer2)
        Console.WriteLine(v);
}
catch (InvalidCastException)
{
    Console.WriteLine("Cast failed again");
}
```

The type declaration on the range variable is converted to a call to Cast<MyType> by the compiler. Again, it throws an InvalidCastException. Here's one way to restructure the code so that it works:

```
var answer3 = from v in GetSomeStrings()
              select (MyType)v;
foreach (var v in answer3)
   Console.WriteLine(v);
```

What's the difference? The two versions that don't work use Cast<T>(), and the version that works includes the cast in the lambda used as the argument to Select(). Cast<T> cannot access any user-defined conversions on the runtime type of its argument. The only conversions it can make are reference conversions and boxing conversions. A reference conversion succeeds when the `is` operator succeeds (see Item 3). A boxing conversion converts a value type to a reference type and vice versa (see Item 45). Cast<T> cannot access any user-defined conversions because it can only assume that T contains the members defined in System.Object. System.Object does not contain any user-defined conversions, so those are not eligible. The version using Select<T> succeeds because the lambda used by Select() takes an input parameter of `string`. That means the conversion operation defined on MyType.

As I've pointed out before, I usually view conversion operators as a code smell. On occasion, they are useful, but often they'll cause more problems than they are worth. Here, without the conversion operators, no developer would be tempted to write the example code that didn't work.

Of course, if I'm recommending not using conversion operators, I should offer an alternative. MyType already contains a read/write property to store the `string` property, so you can just remove the conversion operators and write either of these constructs:

```
var answer4 = GetSomeStrings().
    Select(n => new MyType { StringMember = n });
var answer5 = from v in GetSomeStrings()
              select new MyType { StringMember = v };
```

Also, if you needed to, you could create a different constructor for MyType. Of course, that is just working around a limitation in Cast<T>(). Now that you understand why those limitations exist, it's time to write a different method that gets around those limitations. The trick is to write the generic method in such a way that it leverages runtime information to perform any conversions.

You could write pages and pages of reflection-based code to see what conversions are available, perform any of those conversions, and return the proper type. You could do that, but it's a waste. Instead, C# 4.0 dynamic can do all the heavy lifting. You're left with a simple Convert<T> that does what you expect:

```
public static IEnumerable<TResult> Convert<TResult>(
    this System.Collections.IEnumerable sequence)
{
    foreach (object item in sequence)
    {
        dynamic coercion = (dynamic)item;
        yield return (TResult)coercion;
    }
}
```

Now, as long as there is a conversion (either implicit or explicit) from the source type to the target type, the conversion works. There are still casts involved, so the possibility for runtime failure exists. That's just part of the game when you are coercing the type system. Convert<T> does work in more situations than Cast<T>(), but it also does more work. As developers, we should be more concerned about what code our users need to create than we are about our own code. Convert<T> passes this test:

```
var convertedSequence = GetSomeStrings().Convert<MyType>();
```

Cast<T>, like all generic methods, compiles with only limited knowledge of its type parameters. That can lead to generic methods not working the way you'd expect. The root cause is almost always that the generic method could not be made aware of particular functionality in the type representing the type parameters. When that happens, a little application of dynamic can enable runtime reflection to make matters right.

Item 40: Use Dynamic for Parameters That Receive Anonymous Types

One of the shortcomings of anonymous types has been that you cannot easily write methods using them as parameters or return types. Because the compiler generated the anonymous type, you could not use them as parameters to methods, or as return values from methods. Any solution to the problem was necessarily limiting. You could use anonymous types as generic type parameters, or you could use them with any method that used System.Object as a parameter. None of those felt particularly satisfying.

Generic methods could only assume the functionality defined in System.Object. System.Object held the same limitations. Of course, at some point, you'll find that you really need a named class with actual behavior. This item discusses what to do when you want to work with different anonymous types that may have properties of the same name but aren't part of your core application and don't warrant the work to create a new named type.

The static type of dynamic enables you to overcome this limitation. Dynamic enables runtime binding and instructs the compiler to generate all the necessary code to work with whatever the runtime type may be.

Suppose you needed to print information for a price list. Further suppose that your price list may be generated from multiple data sources. You may have one database for items in inventory, another for items that are special order, and yet another for items sold through a third-party supplier. Because these are completely different systems, they may all have different abstractions for the product. Those different abstractions may not have the same names for their properties, and they certainly won't have the same base class or implement the same interface. The classic answer is to implement an adapter pattern (see *Design Patterns*, Gamma, Helm, Johnson, & Vlissides, pp. 139-142) for each of the product abstractions, and convert each object to a single type. That's quite a bit work, and you have more work to do every time a new product abstraction is added. However, the adapter pattern stays in the static type system and will have better performance.

Another, lighter-weight solution is to use dynamic to create a method that works with any type that has the pricing information you seek:

```
public static void WritePricingInformation(dynamic product)
{
    Console.WriteLine("The price of one {0} is {1}",
        product.Name, product.Price);
}
```

You can create an anonymous type that matches the properties you chose for your pricing method anywhere in your code where you pull information from one of your data sources:

```
var price = from n in Inventory
            where n.Cost > 20
            select new { n.Name, Price = n.Cost * 1.15M };
```

You can use any projection you need to create an anonymous type that contains all the necessary properties for your dynamic method. As long as you have properties named "Price" and "Name", the WritePricingInformation method will do the job.

Of course, you can use anonymous types that have other properties as well. As long as the properties you have include the pricing information, you're fine:

```
var orderInfo = from n in Ordered
                select new {
                    n.Name,
                    Price = n.Cost * 1.15M,
                    ShippingCost = n.Cost / 10M
                };
```

Plain old C# objects can be used where dynamic is expected. This means your pricing information method can be used with this concrete type that happens to use the correct property names:

```
public class DiscountProduct
{
    public static int NumberInInventory { get; set; }

    public double Price { get; set; }
    public string Name { get; set; }

    public string ReasonForDiscount { get; set; }

    // other methods elided
}
```

You may have noticed that the type of the Price property in DiscountProduct is double where the type of the Price property in the earlier anonymous types was decimal. That's fine as well. WritePricingInformation uses the dynamic static type, so it will figure that out correctly at runtime. Of course, if DiscountProduct derived from a base Product class, and the Product class contained the Name and Price properties, that would work.

The code written above could easily lead you to believe that I'm advocating dynamic more often than I really am. Dynamic invocation is a good way to solve this problem, but don't overuse it. Dynamic invocation means that you are paying some extra overhead. That overhead is worthwhile when it's needed, but when you can avoid it, you should.

You have to make an either/or choice with dynamic and static invocation. You can create overloads of the WritePricingInformation() method that are specific to the Product classes in your object model:

```csharp
public class Product
{
    public decimal Cost { get; set; }
    public string Name { get; set; }

    public decimal Price
    {
        get { return Cost * 1.15M; }
    }
}


// Derived Product class:
public class SpecialProduct : Product
{
    public string ReasonOnSpecial { get; set; }

    // other methods elided
}


// elsewhere
public static void WritePricingInformation(dynamic product)
{
    Console.WriteLine("The price of one {0} is {1}",
        product.Name, product.Price);
}


public static void WritePricingInformation(Product product)
{
    Console.WriteLine("In type safe version");
    Console.WriteLine("The price of one {0} is {1}",
        product.Name, product.Price);
}
```

The compiler will use the specific version for any objects of type Product or SpecialProduct (or any other product-derived class in your object model). For anything else, the compiler will use the version statically typed as dynamic. That includes anonymous types. Internally, the dynamic binder will cache method info for each method it uses. That will minimize the overhead for the likely case that you'll often be calling WritePricingInformation() for the same anonymous type over and over. Once the method binding has been performed on the first call, it will be reused on each subsequent call. It's a nonzero cost, but the dynamic implementation does as much work as possible to minimize the cost of using dynamic.

You may be wondering why none of these methods are extension methods so that they would appear to be members of the anonymous type. Well, that would be great, but it's not legal C#. You are not allowed to create extension methods that extend dynamic objects.

You can leverage dynamic to create methods that are intended to be used with anonymous types. It's a technique to be used sparingly, like strong spices. If you find yourself creating many methods using dynamic invocation that are intended for use with anonymous types, that's a strong indication that you should create a concrete type to represent that concept. It will be much easier to maintain over time, and you'll have better support from the compiler and the type system. However, when you need one or two utility methods that use an anonymous type, dynamic invocation is a simple way to create that behavior.

Item 41: Use DynamicObject or IDynamicMetaObjectProvider for Data-Driven Dynamic Types

One great advantage of dynamic programming is the ability to build types whose public interface changes at runtime, based on how you use them. C# provides that ability through dynamic, the System.Dynamic.DynamicObject base class, and the System.Dynamic.IDynamicMetaObjectProvider interface. Using these tools, you can create your own types that have dynamic capabilities.

The simplest way to create a type with dynamic capabilities is to derive from System.Dynamic.DynamicObject. That type implements the IDynamicMetaObjectProvider interface using a private nested class. This private nested class does the hard work of parsing expressions and forwarding those to one of a number of virtual methods in the DynamicObject class. That makes it a relatively simple exercise to create a dynamic class, if you can derive from DynamicObject.

For example, consider a class that implemented a dynamic property bag. When you first create the DynamicPropertyBag, it doesn't have any items, and therefore it doesn't have any properties. When you try to retrieve any property, it will throw an exception. You can add any property to the bag by calling the setter on that property. After adding the property, you can call the getter and access any of the properties.

```csharp
dynamic dynamicProperties = new DynamicPropertyBag();

try
{
    Console.WriteLine(dynamicProperties.Marker);
}
catch (Microsoft.CSharp.RuntimeBinder.RuntimeBinderException)
{
    Console.WriteLine("There are no properties");
}

dynamicProperties.Date = DateTime.Now;
dynamicProperties.Name = "Bill Wagner";
dynamicProperties.Title = "Effective C#";
dynamicProperties.Content = "Building a dynamic dictionary";
```

The implementation of the dynamic property bag requires overriding the TrySetMember and TryGetMember methods in the DynamicObject base class.

```csharp
class DynamicPropertyBag : DynamicObject
{
    private Dictionary<string, object> storage =
        new Dictionary<string, object>();

    public override bool TryGetMember(GetMemberBinder binder,
        out object result)
    {
        if (storage.ContainsKey(binder.Name))
        {
            result = storage[binder.Name];
            return true;
        }
```

```
        result = null;
        return false;
    }


    public override bool TrySetMember(SetMemberBinder binder,
        object value)
    {
        string key = binder.Name;
        if (storage.ContainsKey(key))
            storage[key] = value;
        else
            storage.Add(key, value);
        return true;
    }


    public override string ToString()
    {
        StringWriter message = new StringWriter();
        foreach (var item in  storage)
            message.WriteLine("{0}:\t{1}", item.Key,
            item.Value);
        return message.ToString();

    }
}
```

The dynamic property bag contains a dictionary that stores the property names and their values. The work is done in TryGetMember and TrySetMember.

TryGetMember examines the requested name (binder.Name), and if that property has been stored in the Dictionary, TryGetMember will return its value. If the value has not been stored, the dynamic call fails.

TrySetMember accomplishes its work in a similar fashion. It examines the requested name (binder.Name) and either updates or creates an entry for that item in the internal Dictionary. Because you can create any property, the TrySetMember method always returns true, indicating that the dynamic call succeeded.

DynamicObject contains similar methods to handle dynamic invocation of indexers, methods, constructors, and unary and binary operators. You can override any of those members to create your own dynamic members.

In all cases, you must examine the Binder object to see what member was requested and perform whatever operation is needed. Where there are return values, you'll need to set those (in the specified out parameter) and return whether or not your overload handled the member.

If you're going to create a type that enables dynamic behavior, using DynamicObject as the base class is the easiest way to do it. Of course, a dynamic property bag is okay, but let's look at one more sample that shows when a dynamic type is more useful.

LINQ to XML made some great improvements to working with XML, but it still left something to be desired. Consider this snippet of XML that contains some information about our solar system:

```xml
<Planets>
  <Planet>
    <Name>Mercury</Name>
  </Planet>
  <Planet>
    <Name>Venus</Name>
  </Planet>
  <Planet>
    <Name>Earth</Name>
    <Moons>
      <Moon>Moon</Moon>
    </Moons>
  </Planet>
  <Planet>
    <Name>Mars</Name>
    <Moons>
      <Moon>Phobos</Moon>
      <Moon>Deimos</Moon>
    </Moons>
  </Planet>
  <!-- other data elided -->
</Planets>
```

To get the first planet, you would write something like this:

```
// Create an XElement document containing
// solar system data:
```

```
var xml = createXML();

var firstPlanet = xml.Element("Planet");
```

That's not too bad, but the farther you get into the file, the more compli-cated the code gets. Getting Earth (the third planet) looks like this:

```
var earth = xml.Elements("Planet").Skip(2).First();
```

Getting the name of the third planet is more code:

```
var earthName = xml.Elements("Planet").Skip(2).
    First().Element("Name");
```

Once you're getting moons, it's really long code:

```
var moon = xml.Elements("Planet").Skip(2).First().
        Elements("Moons").First().Element("Moon");
```

Furthermore, the above code only works if the XML contains the nodes you're seeking. If there was a problem in the XML file, and some of the nodes were missing, the above code would throw an exception. Adding the code to handle missing nodes adds quite a bit more code, just to handle potential errors. At that point, it's harder to discern the original intent.

Instead, suppose you had a data-driven type that could give you dot nota-tion on XML elements, using the element name. Finding the first planet could be as simple as:

```
// Create an XElement document containing
// solar system data:
var xml = createXML();

Console.WriteLine(xml);

dynamic dynamicXML = new DynamicXElement(xml);

// old way:
var firstPlanet = xml.Element("Planet");
Console.WriteLine(firstPlanet);
// new way:
// returns the first planet.
dynamic test2 = dynamicXML.Planet;
```

Getting the third planet would be simply using an indexer:

```
// gets the third planet (Earth)
dynamic test3 = dynamicXML["Planet", 2];
```

Reaching the moons becomes two chained indexers:

```
dynamic earthMoon = dynamicXML["Planet", 2]["Moons", 0].Moon;
```

Finally, because it's dynamic, you can define the semantics so any missing node returns an empty element. That means all of these would return empty dynamic XElement nodes:

```
dynamic test6 = dynamicXML["Planet", 2]
    ["Moons", 3].Moon; // earth doesn't have 4 moons
dynamic fail = dynamicXML.NotAppearingInThisFile;
dynamic fail2 = dynamicXML.Not.Appearing.In.This.File;
```

Because missing elements will return a missing dynamic element, you can continue to dereference it and know that if any element in the composed XML navigation is missing, the final result will be a missing element. Building this is another class derived from DynamicObject. You have to override TryGetMember, and TryGetIndex to return dynamic elements with the appropriate nodes.

```
public class DynamicXElement : DynamicObject
{
    private readonly XElement xmlSource;

    public DynamicXElement(XElement source)
    {
        xmlSource = source;
    }

    public override bool TryGetMember(GetMemberBinder binder,
        out object result)
    {
        result = new DynamicXElement(null);
        if (binder.Name == "Value")
        {
            result = (xmlSource != null) ?
                xmlSource.Value : "";
            return true;
        }
```

```
        if (xmlSource != null)
            result = new DynamicXElement(
                xmlSource.Element(XName.Get(binder.Name)));
        return true;
    }

    public override bool TryGetIndex(GetIndexBinder binder,
        object[] indexes, out object result)
    {
        result = null;
        // This only supports [string, int] indexers
        if (indexes.Length != 2)
            return false;
        if (!(indexes[0] is string))
            return false;
        if (!(indexes[1] is int))
            return false;

        var allNodes = xmlSource.Elements(indexes[0].
            ToString());
        int index = (int)indexes[1];
        if (index < allNodes.Count())
            result = new DynamicXElement(allNodes.ElementAt(
                index));
        else
            result = new DynamicXElement(null);
        return true;
    }

    public override string ToString()
    {
        if (xmlSource != null)
            return xmlSource.ToString();
        else
            return string.Empty;
    }
}
```

Most of the code uses similar concepts to the code you have seen earlier in this item. The TryGetIndex method is new. It must implement the dynamic behavior when client code invokes an indexer to retrieve an XElement.

Using DynamicObject makes it much easier to implement a type that behaves dynamically. DynamicObject hides much of the complexity of creating dynamic types. It has quite a bit of implementation to handle dynamic dispatch for you. Also, sometimes you will want to create a dynamic type and you won't be able to use DynamicObject because you need a different base class. For that reason, I'm going to show you how to create the dynamic dictionary by implementing IDynamicMetaObjectProvider yourself, instead of relying on DynamicObject to do the heavy lifting for you.

Implementing IDynamicMetaObjectProvider means implementing one method: GetMetaObject. Here's a second version of DynamicDictionary that implements IDynamicMetaObjectProvider, instead of deriving from DynamicObject:

```
class DynamicDictionary2 : IDynamicMetaObjectProvider
{
    #region IDynamicMetaObjectProvider Members
    DynamicMetaObject IDynamicMetaObjectProvider.
        GetMetaObject(
        System.Linq.Expressions.Expression parameter)
    {
        return new DynamicDictionaryMetaObject(parameter,
            this);
    }
    #endregion

    private Dictionary<string, object> storage = new
        Dictionary<string, object>();

    public object SetDictionaryEntry(string key,
        object value)
    {
        if (storage.ContainsKey(key))
            storage[key] = value;
        else
            storage.Add(key, value);
        return value;
    }

    public object GetDictionaryEntry(string key)
    {
```

```
        object result = null;
        if (storage.ContainsKey(key))
        {
            result = storage[key];
        }
        return result;
    }


    public override string ToString()
    {
        StringWriter message = new StringWriter();
        foreach (var item in storage)
            message.WriteLine("{0}:\t{1}", item.Key,
                item.Value);
        return message.ToString();
    }
}
```

GetMetaObject() returns a new DynamicDictionaryMetaObject whenever it is called. Here's where the first complexity enters the picture. GetMeta-Object() is called every time any member of the DynamicDictionary is invoked. If you call the same member ten times, GetMetaObject() gets called ten times. Even if methods are statically defined in DynamicDictionary2, GetMetaObject() will be called and can intercept those methods to invoke possible dynamic behavior. Remember that dynamic objects are statically typed as dynamic, and therefore have no compile-time behavior defined. Every member access is dynamically dispatched.

The DynamicMetaObject is responsible for building an Expression Tree that executes whatever code is necessary to handle the dynamic invocation. Its constructor takes the expression and the dynamic object as parameters. After being constructed, one of the Bind methods will be called. Its responsibility is to construct a DynamicMetaObject that contains the expression to execute the dynamic invocation. Let's walk through the two Bind methods necessary to implement the DynamicDictionary: BindSetMember and BindGetMember.

BindSetMember constructs an expression tree that will call Dynamic-Dictionary2.SetDictionaryEntry() to set a value in the dictionary. Here's its implementation:

```csharp
public override DynamicMetaObject BindSetMember(
    SetMemberBinder binder,
    DynamicMetaObject value)
{
    // Method to call in the containing class:
    string methodName = "SetDictionaryEntry";

    // setup the binding restrictions.
    BindingRestrictions restrictions =
        BindingRestrictions.GetTypeRestriction(Expression,
        LimitType);

    // setup the parameters:
    Expression[] args = new Expression[2];
    // First parameter is the name of the property to Set
    args[0] = Expression.Constant(binder.Name);
    // Second parameter is the value
    args[1] = Expression.Convert(value.Expression,
        typeof(object));

    // Setup the 'this' reference
    Expression self = Expression.Convert(Expression,
        LimitType);

    // Setup the method call expression
    Expression methodCall = Expression.Call(self,
            typeof(DynamicDictionary2).GetMethod(methodName),
            args);

    // Create a meta object to invoke Set later:
    DynamicMetaObject setDictionaryEntry = new
        DynamicMetaObject(
        methodCall,
        restrictions);
    // return that dynamic object
    return setDictionaryEntry;
}
```

Metaprogramming quickly gets confusing, so let's walk through this slowly.
The first line sets the name of the method called in the DynamicDictionary,

"SetDictionaryEntry". Notice that SetDictionary returns the right-hand side of the property assignment. That's important because this construct must work:

```
DateTime current = propertyBag2.Date = DateTime.Now;
```

Without setting the return value correctly, that construct won't work.

Next, this method initializes a set of BindingRestrictions. Most of the time, you'll use restrictions like this one, restrictions given in the source expression and for the type used as the target of the dynamic invocation.

The rest of the method constructs the method call expression that will invoke SetDictionaryEntry() with the property name and the value used. The property name is a constant expression, but the value is a Conversion expression that will be evaluated lazily. Remember that the right-hand side of the setter may be a method call or expression with side effects. Those must be evaluated at the proper time. Otherwise, setting properties using the return value of methods won't work:

```
propertyBag2.MagicNumber = GetMagicNumber();
```

Of course, to implement the dictionary, you have to implement BindGet-Member as well. BindGetMember works almost exactly the same way. It constructs an expression to retrieve the value of a property from the dictionary.

```
public override DynamicMetaObject BindGetMember(
    GetMemberBinder binder)
{
    // Method call in the containing class:
    string methodName = "GetDictionaryEntry";

    // One parameter
    Expression[] parameters = new Expression[]
    {
        Expression.Constant(binder.Name)
    };

    DynamicMetaObject getDictionaryEntry = new
        DynamicMetaObject(
        Expression.Call(
            Expression.Convert(Expression, LimitType),
```

```
        typeof(DynamicDictionary2).GetMethod(methodName),
            parameters),
        BindingRestrictions.GetTypeRestriction(Expression,
            LimitType));
    return getDictionaryEntry;
}
```

Before you go off and think this isn't that hard, let me leave you with some thoughts from the experience of writing this code. This is about as simple as a dynamic object can get. You have two APIs: property `get`, property `set`. The semantics are very easy to implement. Even with this very simple behavior, it was rather difficult to get right. Expression trees are hard to debug. They are hard to get right. More sophisticated dynamic types would have much more code. That would mean much more difficulty getting the expressions correct.

Furthermore, keep in mind one of the opening remarks I made on this section: Every invocation on your dynamic object will create a new DynamicMetaObject and invoke one of the Bind members. You'll need to write these methods with an eye toward efficiency and performance. They will be called a lot, and they have much work to do.

Implementing dynamic behavior can be a great way to approach some of your programming challenges. When you look at creating dynamic types, your first choice should be to derive from System.Dynamic.DynamicObject. On those occasions where you must use a different base class, you can implement IDynamicMetaObjectProvider yourself, but remember that this is a complicated problem to take on. Furthermore, any dynamic types involve some performance costs, and implementing them yourself may make those costs greater.

Item 42: Understand How to Make Use of the Expression API

.NET has had APIs that enable you to reflect on types or to create code at runtime. The ability to examine code or create code at runtime is very powerful. There are many different problems that are best solved by inspecting code or dynamically generating code. The problem with these APIs is that they are very low level and quite difficult to work with. As developers, we crave an easier way to dynamically solve problems.

Now that C# has added LINQ and dynamic support, you have a better way than the classic Reflection APIs: expressions and expression trees. Expressions look like code. And, in many uses, expressions do compile down to delegates. However, you can ask for expressions in an Expression format. When you do that, you have an object that represents the code you want to execute. You can examine that expression, much like you can examine a class using the Reflection APIs. In the other direction, you can build an expression to create code at runtime. Once you create the expression tree you can compile and execute the expression. The possibilities are endless. After all, you are creating code at runtime. I'll describe two common tasks where expressions can make your life much easier.

The first solves a common problem in communication frameworks. The typical workflow for using WCF, remoting, or Web services is to use some code generation tool to generate a client-side proxy for a particular service. It works, but it is a somewhat heavyweight solution. You'll generate hundreds of lines of code. You'll need to update the proxy whenever the server gets a new method, or changes parameter lists. Instead, suppose you could write something like this:

```
var client = new ClientProxy<IService>();
var result = client.CallInterface<string>(
    srver => srver.DoWork(172));
```

Here, the ClientProxy<T> knows how to put each argument and method call on the wire. However, it doesn't know anything about the service you're actually accessing. Rather than relying on some out of band code generator, it will use expression trees and generics to figure out what method you called, and what parameters you used.

The CallInterface() method takes one parameter, which is an Expression <Func<T, TResult>>. The input parameter (of type T) represents an object that implements IService. TResult, of course, is whatever the particular method returns. The parameter is an expression, and you don't even need an instance of an object that implements IService to write this code. The core algorithm is in the CallInterface() method.

```
public TResult CallInterface<TResult>(Expression<
    Func<T, TResult>> op)
{
    var exp = op.Body as MethodCallExpression;
    var methodName = exp.Method.Name;
    var methodInfo = exp.Method;
```

```
    var allParameters = from element in exp.Arguments
                        select processArgument(element);
    Console.WriteLine("Calling {0}", methodName);

    foreach (var parm in allParameters)
        Console.WriteLine(
            "\tParameter type = {0}, Value = {1}",
            parm.Item1, parm.Item2);

    return default(TResult);
}


private Tuple<Type, object> processArgument(Expression
    element)
{
    object argument = default(object);
    LambdaExpression l = Expression.Lambda(
        Expression.Convert(element, element.Type));
    Type parmType = l.ReturnType;
    argument = l.Compile().DynamicInvoke();
    return Tuple.Create(parmType, argument);
}
```

Starting from the beginning of CallInterface, the first thing this code does is look at the body of the expression tree. That's the part on the right side of the lambda operator. Look back at the example where I used CallInterface(). That example called it with srver.DoWork(172). It is a MethodCallExpression, and that MethodCallExpression contains all the information you need to understand all the parameters and the method name invoked. The method name is pretty simple: It's stored in the Name property of the Method property. In this example, that would be 'DoWork'. The LINQ query processes any and all parameters to this method. The interesting work in is processArgument.

processArgument evaluates each parameter expression. In the example above, there is only one argument, and it happens to be a constant, the value 172. However, that's not very robust, so this code takes a different strategy. It's not robust, because any of the parameters could be method calls, property or indexer accessors, or even field accessors. Any of the method calls could also contain parameters of any of those types. Instead of trying to parse everything, this method does that hard work by leveraging the LambdaExpression type and evaluating each parameter expression. Every parameter expression, even the ConstantExpression, could be expressed as the return value from a lambda expression. ProcessArgument() converts the parameter to a LambdaExpression. In the case of the constant expression, it would convert to a lambda that is the equivalent of () => 172. This method converts each parameter to a lambda expression because a lambda expression can be compiled into a delegate and that delegate can be invoked. In the case of the parameter expression, it creates a delegate that returns the constant value 172. More complicated expressions would create more complicated lambda expressions.

Once the lambda expression has been created, you can retrieve the type of the parameter from the lambda. Notice that this method does not perform any processing on the parameters. The code to evaluate the parameters in the lambda expression would be executed when the lambda expression is invoked. The beauty of this is that it could even contain other calls to CallInterface(). Constructs like this just work:

```
client.CallInterface(srver => srver.DoWork(
    client.CallInterface(srv => srv.GetANumber())));
```

This technique shows you how you can use expression trees to determine at runtime what code the user wishes to execute. It's hard to show in a book, but because ClientProxy<T> is a generic class that uses the service interface as a type parameter, the CallInterface method is strongly typed. The method call in the lambda expression must be a member method defined on the server.

The first example showed you how to parse expressions to convert code (or at least expressions that define code) into data elements you can use to implement runtime algorithms. The second example shows the opposite direction: Sometimes you want to generate code at runtime. One common problem in large systems is to create an object of some destination type from some related source type. For example, your large enterprise may contain systems from different vendors each of which has a different type defined for a contact (among other types). Sure, you could type methods by hand, but that's tedious. It would be much better to create some kind of type that "figures out" the obvious implementation. You'd like to just write this code:

```
var converter = new Converter<SourceContact,
    DestinationContact>();
DestinationContact dest2 = converter.ConvertFrom(source);
```

You'd expect the converter to copy every property from the source to the destination where the properties have the same name and the source object has a public `get` accessor and the destination type has a public `set` accessor. This kind of runtime code generation can be best handled by creating an expression, and then compiling and executing it. You want to generate code that does something like this:

```
// Not legal C#, explanation only
TDest ConvertFromImaginary(TSource source)
{
    TDest destination = new TDest();
    foreach (var prop in sharedProperties)
        destination.prop = source.prop;
    return destination;
}
```

You need to create an expression that creates code that executes the pseudo code written above. Here's the full method to create that expression and compile it to a function. Immediately following the listing, I'll explain all the parts of this method in detail. You'll see that while it's a bit thorny at first, it's nothing you can't handle.

```
private void createConverterIfNeeded()
{
    if (converter == null)
    {
        var source = Expression.Parameter(typeof(TSource),
            "source");
        var dest = Expression.Variable(typeof(TDest),
            "dest");

        var assignments = from srcProp in
                    typeof(TSource).GetProperties(
                        BindingFlags.Public |
                        BindingFlags.Instance)
                    where srcProp.CanRead
                    let destProp = typeof(TDest).
                        GetProperty(
                        srcProp.Name,
                        BindingFlags.Public |
                        BindingFlags.Instance)
```

```
                    where (destProp != null) &&
                        (destProp.CanWrite)
                    select Expression.Assign(
                        Expression.Property(dest,
                            destProp),
                        Expression.Property(source,
                            srcProp));

    // put together the body:
    var body = new List<Expression>();
    body.Add(Expression.Assign(dest,
        Expression.New(typeof(TDest))));
    body.AddRange(assignments);
    body.Add(dest);

    var expr =
        Expression.Lambda<Func<TSource, TDest>>(
            Expression.Block(
            new[] { dest }, // expression parameters
            body.ToArray() // body
            ),
            source  // lambda expression
        );

    var func = expr.Compile();
    converter = func;
    }
}
```

This method creates code that mimics the pseudo code shown before. First, you declare the parameter:

```
var source = Expression.Parameter(typeof(TSource), "source");
```

Then, you have to declare a local variable to hold the destination:

```
var dest = Expression.Variable(typeof(TDest), "dest");
```

The bulk of the method is the code that assigns properties from the source object to the destination object. I wrote this code as a LINQ query. The source sequence of the LINQ query is the set of all public instance properties in the source object where there is a get accessor:

```
from srcProp in typeof(TSource).GetProperties(
                BindingFlags.Public | BindingFlags.Instance)
            where srcProp.CanRead
```

The `let` declares a local variable that holds the property of the same name in the destination type. It may be null, if the destination type does not have a property of the correct type:

```
let destProp = typeof(TDest).GetProperty(
            srcProp.Name,
            BindingFlags.Public | BindingFlags.Instance)
        where (destProp != null) &&
              (destProp.CanWrite)
```

The projection of the query is a sequence of assignment statements that assigns the property of the destination object to the value of the same property name in the source object:

```
select Expression.Assign(
    Expression.Property(dest, destProp),
    Expression.Property(source, srcProp));
```

The rest of the method builds the body of the lambda expression. The Block() method of the Expression class needs all the statements in an array of Expression. The next step is to create a List<Expression> where you can add all the statements. The list can be easily converted to an array.

```
var body = new List<Expression>();
body.Add(Expression.Assign(dest,
    Expression.New(typeof(TDest))));
body.AddRange(assignments);
body.Add(dest);
```

Finally, it's time to build a lambda that returns the destination object and contains all the statements built so far:

```
var expr =
    Expression.Lambda<Func<TSource, TDest>>(
        Expression.Block(
        new[] { dest }, // expression parameters
        body.ToArray() // body
        ),
        source  // lambda expression
    );
```

That's all the code you need. Time to compile it and turn it into a delegate that you can call:

```
var func = expr.Compile();
converter = func;
```

That is complicated, and it's not the easiest to write. You'll often find compiler-like errors at runtime until you get the expressions built correctly. It's also clearly not the best way to approach simple problems. But even so, the Expression APIs are much simpler than their predecessors in the Reflection APIs. That's when you should use the Expression APIs: When you think you want to use reflection, try to solve the problem using the Expression APIs instead.

The Expression APIs can be used in two very different ways: You can create methods that take expressions as parameters, which enables you to parse those expressions and create code based on the concepts behind the expressions that were called. Also, the Expression APIs enable you to create code at runtime. You can create classes that write code, and then execute the code they've written. It's a very powerful way to solve some of the more difficult general purpose problems you'll encounter.

Item 43: Use Expressions to Transform Late Binding into Early Binding

Late binding APIs use the symbol text to do their work. Compiled APIs do not need that information, because the compiler has already resolved symbol references. The Expression API enables you to bridge both worlds. Expression objects contain a form of abstract symbol tree that represents the algorithms you want to execute. You can use the Expression API to execute that code. You can also examine all the symbols, including the names of variables, methods, and properties. You can use the Expression APIs to create strongly typed compiled methods that interact with portions of the system that rely on late binding, and use the names of properties or other symbols.

One of the most common examples of a late binding API is the property notification interfaces used by Silverlight and WPF. Both Silverlight and WPF were designed to respond to bound properties changing so that user interface elements can respond when data elements change underneath the user interface. Of course, there is no magic; there is only code that you have to implement. In this case, you have to implement two interfaces: INotifyPropertyChanged and INotifyPropertyChanging. These are both very simple interfaces; each supports one event. The event argument for both of these events simply contains the name of the property that's being updated. You can use the Expression API to create extensions that remove the dependency on the property name. The extensions will use the Expression API to parse the name of the property and will execute the expression algorithm to change the property value.

The late binding implementation for these properties is very simple. Your data classes need to declare support for both interfaces. Every property that can be changed needs some extra code to raise those events. Here's a class that displays the amount of memory used by the current program. It automatically updates itself every 3 seconds. By supporting the INotifyPropertyChanged and INotifyPropertyChanging interfaces, an object of this type can be added to your window class, and you can see your runtime memory usage.

```csharp
public class MemoryMonitor : INotifyPropertyChanged,
    INotifyPropertyChanging
{
    System.Threading.Timer updater;

    public MemoryMonitor()
    {
        updater = new System.Threading.Timer((_) =>
            timerCallback(_),
            null, 0, 5000);
    }

    private void timerCallback(object unused)
    {
        UsedMemory = GC.GetTotalMemory(false);
    }

    public long UsedMemory
    {
        get { return mem; }
        private set
        {
```

```
            if (value != mem)
            {
                if (PropertyChanging != null)
                    PropertyChanging(this,
                        new PropertyChangingEventArgs(
                        "UsedMemory"));

                mem = value;
                if (PropertyChanged != null)
                    PropertyChanged(this,
                        new PropertyChangedEventArgs(
                        "UsedMemory"));
            }
        }
    }
    private long mem;

    #region INotifyPropertyChanged Members
    public event PropertyChangedEventHandler
        PropertyChanged;
    #endregion

    #region INotifyPropertyChanging Members
    public event PropertyChangingEventHandler
        PropertyChanging;
    #endregion
}
```

That's all there is to it. But, every time you create an implementation of either of these interfaces, you'll ask yourself if there is an easier way to do this. Every property setter needs to raise an event. There really isn't a good way around that. But, you can see that every setter needs to raise two events: one before it changes the property and one after. What's worse is that the argument to the event parameters uses a string to represent the property name. That's very brittle. Any refactoring is going to break this code. Any typing mistakes create broken code. So let's make this easier, and let's fix this.

The obvious choice is going to be implementing something in an extension method. You're going to want to add these methods with any class that implements INotifyPropertyChanged and INotifyPropertyChanging.

Like many things, making this easy is hard. But the hard code only gets written once, so it is worth the work. The work to be done is boilerplate:

1. See if the new value and the old value are different.
2. Raise the INotifyPropertyChanging event.
3. Change the value.
4. Raise the INotifyPropertyChanged event.

The hard part is determining what string to use for the name of the property. Remember that the point of this exercise is to make the code durable enough so that strings aren't necessary to make the code work properly. I wanted to make an API that is as simple as possible for users but allows the code underlying that simple API to execute whatever magic was necessary to do all the work.

My original goal was to make the extension methods extend either INotifyPropertyChanged or INotifyPropertyChanging, but that made the API worse, primarily because it made raising the events harder. Instead, the method actually extends the PropertyChanged event that is a member of INotifyPropertyChanged. Here's how you would use it in the MemoryMonitor:

```
// MemoryMonitor, using the extension methods
private void timerCallback(object unused)
{
    long updatedValue = GC.GetTotalMemory(false);
    PropertyChanged.SetNotifyProperty(updatedValue,
        () => UsedMemory);
}


public long UsedMemory
{
    get;
    private set;
}
```

This serves the goal of making the implementation of the MemoryMonitor much easier. No magic strings. The UsedMemory is now an automatic property. There are no magic strings inside the code. The code to implement this is a complicated bit that uses reflection and expression trees, so let's walk through it carefully. Here's the full extension method:

```csharp
public static class PropertyNotifyExtensions
{
    public static T SetNotifyProperty<T>(this
        PropertyChangedEventHandler handler,
        T newValue, Expression<Func<T>> oldValueExpression,
            Action<T> setter)
    {
        return SetNotifyProperty(handler, null, newValue,
            oldValueExpression, setter);
    }

    public static T SetNotifyProperty<T>(this
        PropertyChangedEventHandler postHandler,
        PropertyChangingEventHandler preHandler,
        T newValue, Expression<Func<T>> oldValueExpression,
        Action<T> setter)
    {
        Func<T> getter = oldValueExpression.Compile();
        T oldValue = getter();
        if (!oldValue.Equals(newValue))
        {
            var body = oldValueExpression.Body as
                System.Linq.Expressions.MemberExpression;
            var propInfo = body.Member as PropertyInfo;
            string propName = body.Member.Name;

            // Get the target object
            var targetExpression = body.Expression as
                ConstantExpression;
            object target = targetExpression.Value;

            if (preHandler != null)
                preHandler(target, new
                PropertyChangingEventArgs(propName));

            // Use Reflection to do the set:
            // propInfo.SetValue(target, newValue, null);
            //var compiledSetter = setter.Compile();
            setter(newValue);
```

```
            if (postHandler != null)
                postHandler(target, new
                PropertyChangedEventArgs(propName));
        }
        return newValue;
    }
}
```

Before I go through all the code, let me begin with a simple disclaimer. I removed some of the error handling for space. In production code, you'd need to check that the casts worked, and that the property setter was found. You'd also need to handle possible security exceptions in a Silverlight sandbox.

The first course of action is to compile and execute the property get expression and compare that value to the new value. There's no reason to do any work if the old and new values are the same. Just compile the expression and execute it.

The next part is more complicated. This code parses the expression to find the important components needed to set the value and to raise the INotifyPropertyChanging and INotifyPropertyChanged events. That means finding the name of the property, the type of the target object, and accessing the property setter. Remember how this method was called. Here's the expression that maps to the oldValueExpression:

```
() => UsedMemory
```

That's a member access expression. The member expression contains the Member property, which is the PropertyInfo for the property being changed. One of its members is the Name of the property, which is where you get the string "UsedMemory", which you'll need to raise the event. The PropertyInfo object has another use for you: You'll use Reflection APIs on the PropertyInfo object to change the value of the property.

The technique here can be applied to other problems as well where the framework requires string information on methods or properties. In fact, LINQ to SQL and the Entity Framework are built on the System.Linq .Expression APIs. Those APIs allow you to treat code as data. You can examine the code using the Expression APIs. You can change algorithms, create new code, and execute the code. It's a great way to build dynamic systems.

DataBinding, by its very nature, requires that you work with the string representation of your properties. INotifyPropertyChanged, and INotify-

PropertyChanging are no exception. But, it's an important enough feature that you should prefer supporting those interfaces in any class that might be the object of data binding in your applications. It is common enough that it's worth the extra work to create a general solution.

Item 44: Minimize Dynamic Objects in Public APIs

Dynamic objects just don't behave that well in a statically typed system. The type system sees them as though they were instances of System.Object. But they are special instances. You can ask them to do work above and beyond what's defined in System.Object. The compiler generates code that tries to find and execute whatever members you try to access.

But dynamic objects are pushy. Everything they touch becomes dynamic. Perform an operation where any one of the parameters is dynamic, and the result is dynamic. Return a dynamic object from a method, and everywhere that dynamic is used becomes a dynamic object. It's like watching bread mold grow in a petri dish. Pretty soon, everything is dynamic, and there's no type safety left anywhere.

Biologists grow cultures in petri dishes, restricting where they can grow. You need to do the same with dynamic: Do the work with dynamic objects in an isolated environment and return objects that are statically typed as something other than dynamic. Otherwise, dynamic becomes a bad influence, and slowly, everything involved in your application will be dynamic.

This is not to imply that dynamic is universally bad. Other items in this chapter have shown you some of the techniques where dynamic programming is an excellent solution. However, dynamic typing and static typing are very different, with different practices, different idioms, and different strategies. Mixing the two without regard will lead to numerous errors and inefficiencies. C# is a statically typed language, enabling dynamic typing in some areas. Therefore, if you're using C#, you should spend most of your time using static typing and minimize the scope of the dynamic features. If you want to write programs that are dynamic through and through, you should consider a language that is dynamic rather than a static typed language.

If you're going to use dynamic features in your program, try to keep them out of the public interface to your types. That way, you can use dynamic typing in a single object (or type) petri dish without having them escape into the rest of your program, or into all the code developed by developers who use your objects.

One scenario where you will use dynamic typing is to interact with objects created in dynamic environments, such as IronPython. When your design makes use of dynamic objects created using dynamic languages, you should wrap them in C# objects that enable the rest of the C# world to blissfully ignore the fact that dynamic typing is even happening.

You may want to pick a different solution for those situations where you use dynamic to produce duck typing. Look at the usages of the duck typing sample from Item 38. In every case, the result of the calculation was dynamic. That might not look too bad. But, the compiler is doing quite a bit of work to make this work. These two lines of code (see Item 38):

```
dynamic answer = Add(5, 5);
Console.WriteLine(answer);
```

turn into this to handle dynamic objects:

```
// Compiler generated, not legal user C# code
object answer = Add(5, 5);
if (<Main>o__SiteContainer0.<>p__Site1 == null)
{
    <Main>o__SiteContainer0.<>p__Site1 =
        CallSite<Action<CallSite, Type, object>>.Create(
        new CSharpInvokeMemberBinder(
        CSharpCallFlags.None, "WriteLine",
        typeof(Program), null, new CSharpArgumentInfo[]
        {
            new CSharpArgumentInfo(
            CSharpArgumentInfoFlags.IsStaticType |
            CSharpArgumentInfoFlags.UseCompileTimeType,
            null),
            new CSharpArgumentInfo(
                CSharpArgumentInfoFlags.None,
            null)
        }));
}
<Main>o__SiteContainer0.<>p__Site1.Target.Invoke(
    <Main>o__SiteContainer0.<>p__Site1,
    typeof(Console), answer);
```

Dynamic is not free. There's quite a bit of code generated by the compiler to make dynamic invocation work in C#. Worse, this code will be repeated everywhere that you invoke the dynamic Add() method. That's going to have size and performance implications on your application. You can wrap the Add() method shown in Item 38 in a bit of generic syntax to create a version that keeps the dynamic types in a constrained location. The same code will be generated but in fewer places:

```
private static dynamic DynamicAdd(dynamic left,
    dynamic right)
{
    return left + right;
}


// Wrap it:
public static T1 Add<T1, T2>(T1 left, T2 right)
{
    dynamic result = DynamicAdd(left, right);
    return (T1)result;
}
```

The compiler generates all the dynamic callsite code in the generic Add() method. That isolates it into one location. Furthermore, the callsites become quite a bit simpler. Where previously every result was dynamic, now the result is statically typed to match the type of the first argument. Of course, you can create an overload to control the result type:

```
public static TResult Add<T1, T2, TResult>
    (T1 left, T2 right)
{
    dynamic result = DynamicAdd(left, right);
    return (TResult)result;
}
```

In either case, the callsites live completely in the strongly typed world:

```
int answer = Add(5, 5);
Console.WriteLine(answer);


double answer2 = Add(5.5, 7.3);
Console.WriteLine(answer2);
```

```
// Type arguments needed because
// args are not the same type
answer2 = Add<int, double, double>(5, 12.3);
Console.WriteLine(answer);

string stringLabel = System.Convert.ToString(answer);

string label = Add("Here is ", "a label");
Console.WriteLine(label);

DateTime tomorrow = Add(DateTime.Now, TimeSpan.FromDays(1));
Console.WriteLine(tomorrow);

label = "something" + 3;
Console.WriteLine(label);
label = Add("something", 3);
Console.WriteLine(label);
```

The above code is the same example from Item 38. Notice that this version has static types that are not dynamic as the return values. That means the caller does not need to work with dynamically typed objects. The caller works with static types, safely ignoring the machinations you needed to perform to make the operation work. In fact, they don't need to know that your algorithm ever left the safety of the type system.

Throughout the samples in this chapter, you saw that dynamic types are kept isolated to the smallest scope possible. When the code needs to use dynamic features, the samples show a local variable that is dynamic. The methods would convert that dynamic object into a strongly typed object and the dynamic object never left the scope of the method. When you use a dynamic object to implement an algorithm, you can avoid having that dynamic object be part of your interface. Other times, the very nature of the problem requires that a dynamic object be part of the interface. That is still not an excuse to make everything dynamic. Only the members that rely on dynamic behavior should use dynamic objects. You can mix dynamic and static typing in the same API. You want to create code that is statically typed when you can. Use dynamic only when you must.

We all have to work with CSV data in different forms. Reading and parsing the CSV data is a relatively simple exercise, but a general solution is almost always lacking. This snippet of code reads two different CSV files with different headers and displays the items in each row:

```
var data = new CSVDataContainer(
    new System.IO.StringReader(myCSV));
foreach (var item in data.Rows)
    Console.WriteLine("{0}, {1}, {2}",
    item.Name, item.PhoneNumber, item.Label);

data = new CSVDataContainer(
    new System.IO.StringReader(myCSV2));
foreach (var item in data.Rows)
    Console.WriteLine("{0}, {1}, {2}",
    item.Date, item.high, item.low);
```

That's the API style I want for a general CSV reader class. The rows returned from enumerating the data contain properties for every row header name. Obviously, the row header names are not known at compile time. Those properties must be dynamic. But nothing else in the CSVDataContainer needs to be dynamic. The CSVDataContainer does not support dynamic typing. However, the CSVDataContainer does contain APIs that return a dynamic object that represents a row:

```
public class CSVDataContainer
{
    private class CSVRow : DynamicObject
    {
        private List<Tuple<string, string>> values =
            new List<Tuple<string, string>>();
        public CSVRow(IEnumerable<string> headers,
            IEnumerable<string> items)
        {
            values.AddRange(headers.Zip(items,
                (header, value) => Tuple.Create(header,
                    value)));
        }

        public override bool TryGetMember(
            GetMemberBinder binder,
            out object result)
        {
            var answer = values.FirstOrDefault(n =>
                n.Item1 == binder.Name);
            result = answer.Item2;
```

```
                return result != null;
        }
    }
    private List<string> columnNames = new List<string>();
    private List<CSVRow> data = new List<CSVRow>();

    public CSVDataContainer(System.IO.TextReader stream)
    {
        // read headers:
        var headers = stream.ReadLine();
        columnNames =
            (from header in headers.Split(',')
             select header.Trim()).ToList();

        var line = stream.ReadLine();
        while (line != null)
        {
            var items = line.Split(',');
            data.Add(new CSVRow(columnNames, items));
            line = stream.ReadLine();
        }
    }
    public dynamic this[int index]
    {
        get { return data[index]; }
    }
    public IEnumerable<dynamic> Rows
    {
        get { return data; }
    }
}
```

Even though you need to expose a dynamic type as part of your interface, it's only where the dynamicism is needed. Those APIs are dynamic. They must be. You can't support any possible CSV format without having dynamic support for column names. You could have chosen to expose everything using dynamic. Instead, dynamic appears in the interface only where the functionality demands dynamic.

For space purposes, I elided other features in the CSVDataContainer. Think about how you would implement RowCount, ColumnCount,

GetAt(row, column), and other APIs. The implementation you have in your head would not use dynamic objects in the API, or even in the implementation. You can meet those requirements with static typing. You should. You'd only use dynamic in the public interface when it is needed.

Dynamic types are a useful feature, even in a statically typed language like C#. However, C# is still a statically typed language. The majority of C# programs should make the most out of the type system provided by the language. Dynamic programming is still useful, but it's most useful in C# when you keep it confined to those locations where it's needed and convert dynamic objects into a different static type immediately. When your code relies on a dynamic type created in another environment, wrap those dynamic objects and provide a public interface using different static types.

6 | Miscellaneous

Some items don't fit convenient categories. But that does not limit their importance. Understanding exception-handling strategies is important for everyone. Other recommendations are constantly changing because C# is a living language, with an active community and an evolving standard. Still others may feel outdated, and yet still resonate today. This chapter contains those items that just don't fit easy categories.

Item 45: Minimize Boxing and Unboxing

Value types are containers for data. They are not polymorphic types. On the other hand, the .NET Framework was designed with a single reference type, System.Object, at the root of the entire object hierarchy. These two goals are at odds. The .NET Framework uses boxing and unboxing to bridge the gap between these two goals. Boxing places a value type in an untyped reference object to allow the value type to be used where a reference type is expected. Unboxing extracts a copy of that value type from the box. Boxing and unboxing are necessary for you to use value types where the System.Object type is expected. But boxing and unboxing are always performance-robbing operations. Sometimes, when boxing and unboxing also create temporary copies of objects, it can lead to subtle bugs in your programs. Avoid boxing and unboxing when possible.

Boxing converts a value type to a reference type. A new reference object, the box, is allocated on the heap, and a copy of the value type is stored inside that reference object. See Figure 6.1 for an illustration of how the boxed object is stored and accessed. The box contains the copy of the value type object and duplicates the interfaces implemented by the boxed value type. When you need to retrieve anything from the box, a copy of the value type gets created and returned. That's the key concept of boxing and unboxing: A copy of the value goes in the box, and another gets created whenever you access what's in the box.

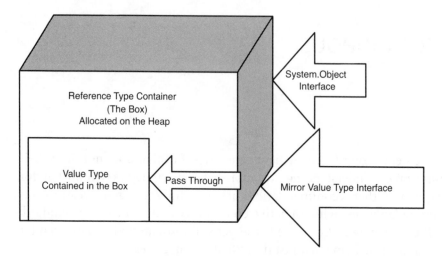

Figure 6.1 Value type in a box. To convert a value type into a System.Object reference, an unnamed reference type is created. The value type is stored inline inside the unnamed reference type. All methods that access the value type are passed through the box to the stored value type.

In many ways, the addition of generics in .NET 2.0 means that you can avoid boxing and unboxing simply by using generic classes and generic methods. That is certainly the most powerful way to create code that uses value types without unnecessary boxing operations. However, there are many locations in the .NET Framework where methods have parameters typed as System.Object. Those APIs will still produce boxing and unboxing operations. It happens automatically. The compiler generates the boxing and unboxing instructions whenever you use a value type where a reference type, such as System.Object, is expected. In addition, the boxing and unboxing operations occur when you use a value type through an interface pointer. You get no warnings—boxing just happens. Even a simple statement such as this performs boxing:

```
Console.WriteLine("A few numbers:{0}, {1}, {2}",
    25, 32, 50);
```

The referenced overload of Console.WriteLine takes an array of System .Object references. ints are value types and must be boxed so that they can be passed to this overload of the WriteLine method. The only way to coerce the three integer arguments into System.Object is to box them. In addition, inside WriteLine, code reaches inside the box to call the ToString() method of the object in the box. In a sense, you have generated this construct:

```
int i = 25;
object o = i; // box
Console.WriteLine(o.ToString());
```

Inside WriteLine, the following code executes:

```
private static void SampleThree()
{
    object firstParm = 5;

    object o = firstParm;
    int i = (int)o; // unbox
    string output = i.ToString();
}
```

You would never write this code yourself. However, by letting the compiler automatically convert from a specific value type to System.Object, you did let it happen. The compiler was just trying to help you. It wants you to succeed. It happily generates the boxing and unboxing statements necessary to convert any value type into an instance of System.Object. To avoid this particular penalty, you should convert your types to string instances yourself before you send them to WriteLine:

```
Console.WriteLine("A few numbers:{0}, {1}, {2}",
    25.ToString(), 32.ToString(), 50.ToString());
```

This code uses the known type of integer, and value types (integers) are never implicitly converted to System.Object. This common example illustrates the first rule to avoid boxing: Watch for implicit conversions to System.Object. Value types should not be substituted for System.Object if you can avoid it.

Another common case in which you might inadvertently substitute a value type for System.Object is when you place value types in .NET 1.x collections. You should use the generic collections added in the 2.0 version of the .NET Base Class Library (BCL) over the 1.x object based collections. However, some components in the .NET BCL still use the 1.x style collections. You should understand the issues and how to avoid them.

The first incarnation of the .NET Framework collections store references to System.Object instances. Anytime you add a value type to a collection, it goes in a box. Anytime you remove an object from a collection, it gets copied from the box. Taking an object out of the box always makes a copy.

That introduces some subtle bugs in your application. The compiler does not help you find these bugs. It's all because of boxing. Start with a simple structure that lets you modify one of its fields, and put some of those objects in a collection:

```
public struct Person
{
    public string Name { get; set; }

    public override string ToString()
    {
        return Name;
    }
}


// Using the Person in a collection:
var attendees = new List<Person>();
Person p = new Person { Name = "Old Name" };
attendees.Add(p);


// Try to change the name:
// Would work if Person was a reference type.
Person p2 = attendees[0];
p2.Name = "New Name";


// Writes "Old Name":
Console.WriteLine(attendees[0].ToString( ));
```

Person is a value type. The JIT compiler creates a specific closed generic type for List<Person> so that Person objects are not boxed, because they are stored in the attendees collection. Another copy gets made when you remove the Person object to access the Name property to change. All you did was change the copy. In fact, a third copy was made to call the ToString() function through the attendees[0] object. For this and many other reasons, you should create immutable value types (see Item 20).

Yes, value types can be converted to System.Object or any interface reference. That conversion happens implicitly, complicating the task of finding them. Those are the rules of the environment and the language. The boxing and unboxing operations make copies where you might not expect. That causes bugs. There is also a performance cost to treating value types polymorphically. Be on the lookout for any constructs that convert value types to either System.Object or interface types: placing values in collections, calling methods defined in System.Object, and casts to System.Object. Avoid these whenever you can.

Item 46: Create Complete Application-Specific Exception Classes

Exceptions are the mechanism of reporting errors that might be handled at a location far removed from the location where the error occurred. All the information about the error's cause must be contained in the exception object. Along the way, you might want to translate a low-level error to more of an application-specific error, without losing any information about the original error. You need to be very thoughtful about when you create your own specific exception classes in your C# applications.

The first step is to understand when and why to create new exception classes, and how to construct informative exception hierarchies. When developers using your libraries write catch clauses, they differentiate actions based on the specific runtime type of the exception. Each different exception class can have a different set of actions taken:

```
try
{
    Foo();
    Bar();
}
catch (MyFirstApplicationException e1)
{
    FixProblem(e1);
}
catch (AnotherApplicationException e2)
{
    ReportErrorAndContinue(e2);
}
catch (YetAnotherApplicationException e3)
{
    ReportErrorAndShutdown(e3);
}
catch (Exception e)
{
```

```
    ReportGenericError(e);
    throw;
}
finally
{
    CleanupResources();
}
```

Different catch clauses can exist for different runtime types of exceptions. You, as an application author, must create or use different exception classes when catch clauses might take different actions. Note that every different exception above is handled in a different way. Developers only want to provide different catch clauses for different exception classes when the handling is different. Otherwise, it's just extra work. Therefore, you should consider creating different exception classes only when you believe developers will take different actions for the problems that cause the exception. If you don't, your users are left with only unappealing options. You can punt and terminate the application whenever an exception gets thrown. That's certainly less work, but it won't win kudos from users. Or, they can reach into the exception to try to determine whether the error can be corrected:

```
private static void SampleTwo()
{
    try
    {
        Foo();
        Bar();
    }
    catch (Exception e)
    {
        switch (e.TargetSite.Name)
        {
            case "Foo":
                FixProblem(e);
                break;
            case "Bar":
                ReportErrorAndContinue(e);
                break;
            // some routine called by Foo or Bar:
            default:
                ReportErrorAndShutdown(e);
```

```
            throw;
        }
    }
    finally
    {
        CleanupResources();
    }
}
```

That's far less appealing than using multiple `catch` clauses. It's very brittle code: If you change the name of a routine, it's broken. If you move the error-generating calls into a shared utility function, it's broken. The deeper into the call stack that an exception is generated, the more fragile this kind of construct becomes.

Before going any deeper into this topic, let me add two disclaimers. First, exceptions are not for every error condition you encounter. There are no firm guidelines, but I prefer throwing exceptions for error conditions that cause long-lasting problems if they are not handled or reported immediately. For example, data integrity errors in a database should generate an exception. The problem only gets bigger if it is ignored. Failure to correctly write the user's window location preferences is not likely to cause far-reaching consequences. A return code indicating the failure is sufficient.

Second, writing a `throw` statement does not mean it's time to create a new exception class. My recommendation on creating more rather than fewer exception classes comes from normal human nature: People seem to gravitate to overusing System.Exception anytime they throw an exception. That provides the least amount of helpful information to the calling code. Instead, think through and create the necessary exceptions classes to enable calling code to understand the cause and provide the best chance of recovery.

I'll say it again: The reason for different exception classes—in fact, the only reason—is to make it easier to take different actions when your users write `catch` handlers. Look for those error conditions that might be candidates for some kind of recovery action and create specific exception classes to handle those actions. Can your application recover from missing files and directories? Can it recover from inadequate security privileges? What about missing network resources? Create new exception classes when you encounter errors that might lead to different actions and recovery mechanisms.

So now you are creating your own exception classes. You do have very specific responsibilities when you create a new exception class. Your exception class must end in "Exception". You should always derive your exception classes from the System.Exception class, or some other appropriate exception class. You will rarely add capabilities to this base class. The purpose of different exception classes is to have the capability to differentiate the cause of errors in `catch` clauses.

But don't take anything away from the exception classes you create, either. The Exception class contains four constructors:

```
// Default constructor
public Exception();


// Create with a message.
public Exception(string);


// Create with a message and an inner exception.
public Exception(string, Exception);


// Create from an input stream.
protected Exception(
    SerializationInfo, StreamingContext);
```

When you create a new exception class, create all four of these constructors. Notice that the last constructor implies that your exception class must be Serializable. Different situations call for the different methods of constructing exceptions. (If you choose to derive from a different exception class, you should include all the appropriate constructors from that particular base class.) You delegate the work to the base class implementation:

```
[Serializable]
public class MyAssemblyException :
  Exception
{
    public MyAssemblyException() :
        base()
    {
    }

    public MyAssemblyException(string s) :
        base(s)
    {
    }
```

```
public MyAssemblyException(string s,
  Exception e) :
    base(s, e)
{
}

protected MyAssemblyException(
  SerializationInfo info, StreamingContext cxt) :
    base(info, cxt)
{
}
}
```

The constructors that take an exception parameter deserve a bit more discussion. Sometimes, one of the libraries you use generates an exception. The code that called your library will get minimal information about the possible corrective actions when you simply pass on the exceptions from the utilities you use:

```
public double DoSomeWork()
{
    // This might throw an exception defined
    // in the third party library:
    return ThirdPartyLibrary.ImportantRoutine();
}
```

You should provide your own library's information when you generate the exception. Throw your own specific exception and include the original exception as its InnerException property. You can provide as much extra information as you can generate:

```
public double DoSomeWork()
{
  try {
    // This might throw an exception defined
    // in the third party library:
    return ThirdPartyLibrary.ImportantRoutine();
  } catch(ThirdPartyException e)
  {
    string msg =
        string.Format("Problem with {0} using library",
          ToString());
```

```
        throw new DoingSomeWorkException(msg, e);
    }
  }
}
```

This new version creates more information at the point where the problem is generated. As long as you have created a proper ToString() method (see Item 5), you've created an exception that describes the complete state of the object that generated the problem. More than that, the inner exception shows the root cause of the problem: something in the third-party library you used.

This technique is called exception translation, translating a low-level exception into a more high-level exception that provides more context about the error. The more information you generate when an error occurs, the easier it will be for users to diagnose and possibly correct the error. By creating your own exception types, you can translate low-level generic problems into specific exceptions that contain all the application-specific information that you need to fully diagnose and possibly correct the problem.

Your application will throw exceptions—hopefully not often, but it will happen. If you don't do anything specific, your application will generate the default .NET Framework exceptions whenever something goes wrong in the methods you call on the core framework. Providing more detailed information will go a long way to enabling you and your users to diagnose and possibly correct errors in the field. You create different exception classes when different corrective actions are possible and only when different actions are possible. You create full-featured exception classes by providing all the constructors that the base exception class supports. You use the InnerException property to carry along all the error information generated by lower-level error conditions.

Item 47: Prefer the Strong Exception Guarantee

When you throw an exception, you've introduced a disruptive event into the application. Control flow has been compromised. Expected actions did not occur. Worse, you've left the cleanup operation to the programmer writing the code that eventually catches the exception. The actions available when you catch exceptions are directly related to how well you manage program state when an exception gets thrown. Thankfully, the C#

community does not need to create its own strategies for exception safety; the C++ community did all the hard work for us. Starting with Tom Cargill's article "Exception Handling: A False Sense of Security," and continuing with writings by Dave Abrahams, Herb Sutter, Scott Meyers, Matt Austern, and Greg Colvin, the C++ community developed a series of best practices that we can adapt to C# applications. The discussions on exception handling occurred over the course of six years, from 1994 to 2000. They discussed, debated, and examined many twists on a difficult problem. We should leverage all that hard work in C#.

Dave Abrahams defined three exception-safe guarantees: the basic guarantee, the strong guarantee, and the no-throw guarantee. Herb Sutter discussed these guarantees in his book *Exceptional C++* (Addison-Wesley, 2000). The basic guarantee states that no resources are leaked and all objects are in a valid state after your exception leaves the function emitting it. That means after any `finally` clauses have run in the method that throws the exception. The strong exception guarantee builds on the basic guarantee and adds that if an exception occurs, the program state did not change. The no-throw guarantee states that an operation never fails, from which it follows that a method does not ever throw exceptions. The strong exception guarantee provides the best tradeoff between recovering from exceptions and simplifying exception handling.

You get some help on the basic guarantee from the .NET CLR. The environment handles memory management. The only way you can leak resources due to exceptions is to throw an exception while you own a resource that implements IDisposable. Item 15 explains how to avoid leaking resources in the face of exceptions. But that's only part of the story. You are still responsible for ensuring that your object's state is valid. Suppose your type caches the size of a collection, along with the collection. You'd need to ensure that the size matches the actual storage after an Add() operation threw an exception. There are countless actions your application may have that if only partially completed would leave your application in an invalid state. These cases are harder to handle, because there are fewer standard idioms for automatic support. Many of these issues can be best solved by adhering to the strong guarantee.

The strong guarantee states that if an operation terminates because of an exception, program state remains unchanged. Either an operation completes or it does not modify program state; there is no middle ground. The advantage of the strong guarantee is that you can more easily continue execution after catching an exception when the strong guarantee is followed. Anytime you catch an exception, whatever operation was attempted did not occur. It did not start, and it did not make some changes. The state of the program is as though you did not start the action.

Many of the recommendations I made earlier will help ensure that you meet the strong exception guarantee. Data elements that your program uses should be stored in immutable value types (see Items 18 and 20). You can also use the functional programming style, such as with LINQ queries. That programming style automatically follows the strong exception guarantee.

Sometimes, you can't use functional programming for styles. If you combine those two items, any modification to program state can easily take place after performing any operation that might throw an exception. The general guideline is to perform any data modifications in the following manner:

1. Make defensive copies of data that will be modified.
2. Perform any modifications to these defensive copies of the data. This includes any operations that might throw an exception.
3. Swap the temporary copies back to the original. This operation cannot throw an exception.

As an example, the following code updates an employee's title and pay using defensive copy:

```
public void PhysicalMove(string title, decimal newPay)
{
    // Payroll data is a struct:
    // ctor will throw an exception if fields aren't valid.
    PayrollData d = new PayrollData(title, newPay,
        this.payrollData.DateOfHire);

    // if d was constructed properly, swap:
    this.payrollData = d;
}
```

Sometimes, the strong guarantee is just too inefficient to support, and sometimes you cannot support the strong guarantee without introducing subtle bugs. The first and simplest case is looping constructs. When the code inside a loop modifies the state of the program and might throw an exception, you are faced with a tough choice: You can either create a defensive copy of all the objects used in the loop, or you can lower your expectations and support only the basic exception guarantee. There are no hard and fast rules, but copying heap-allocated objects in a managed environment is not as expensive as it was in native environments. A lot of time has been spent optimizing memory management in .NET. I prefer to support the strong exception guarantee whenever possible, even if it means copying a large container: The capability to recover from errors outweighs the small performance gain from avoiding the copy. In special cases, it doesn't make sense to create the copy. If any exceptions would result in terminating the program anyway, it makes no sense to worry about the strong exception guarantee. The larger concern is that swapping reference types can lead to program errors. Consider this example:

```
private BindingList<PayrollData> data;
public IBindingList MyCollection
{
    get { return data; }
}


public void UpdateData()
{
    // Unreliable operation might fail:
    var temp = UnreliableOperation();

    // This operation will only happen if
    // UnreliableOperation does not throw an
    // exception.
    data = temp;
}
```

This looks like a great use of the defensive copy mechanism. You've created a copy of your data. Then you grab new data from somewhere to fill the temporary data. Finally, you swap the temporary storage back. It looks great. If anything goes wrong trying to retrieve the data, you have not made any changes.

There's only one problem: It doesn't work. The MyCollection property returns a reference to the data object (see Item 26). All the clients of this class are left holding references to the original BindingList<> after you call UpdateData. They are looking at the old view of the data. The swap trick does not work for reference types—it works only for value types. To fix this, you need to replace the data in the current reference object, and ensure that you do it in such a way that it can never throw an exception. That is difficult, because it is two different atomic operations: removing all the existing objects in the collection and adding all the new objects. You might consider that the risk is small of removing and adding the new items:

```
private BindingList<PayrollData> data;
public IBindingList MyCollection
{
    get
    {
        return data;
    }
}


public void UpdateData()
{
    // Unreliable operation might fail:
    var temp = UnreliableOperation();

    // These operations will only happen if
    // UnreliableOperation does not throw an
    // exception.
    data.Clear();
    foreach (var item in temp)
        data.Add(item);
}
```

That is a reasonable, but not a bulletproof, solution. I mention it because "reasonable" is often the bar you need. However, when you do need bulletproof, you need to do more work. The envelope-letter pattern will hide the internal swapping in an object that enables you to make the swap safely.

The envelope-letter pattern hides the implementation (letter) inside a wrapper (envelope) that you share with public clients of your code. In this example, you'll create a class that wraps the collection and implements the IBindingList<PayrollData>. That class contains the BindingList<PayrollData> and exposes all its methods to class clients.

Your class now works with the envelope class to handle its internal data.

```
private Envelope data;
public IBindingList MyCollection
{
    get
    {
        return data;
    }
}


public void UpdateData()
{
    data.SafeUpdate(UnreliableOperation());
}
```

The Envelope class implements the IBindingList by forwarding every request to the contained BindingList<PayrollData>:

```
public class Envelope : IBindingList
{
    private BindingList<PayrollData> data =
        new BindingList<PayrollData>();

    #region IBindingList Members
    public void AddIndex(PropertyDescriptor property)
      { (data as IBindingList).AddIndex(property); }

    public object AddNew() { return data.AddNew(); }

    public bool AllowEdit { get { return data.AllowEdit; } }

    public bool AllowNew { get { return data.AllowNew; } }

    public bool AllowRemove
        { get { return data.AllowRemove; } }

    public void ApplySort(PropertyDescriptor property,
      ListSortDirection direction)
      { (data as IBindingList).
            ApplySort(property, direction); }
```

```csharp
public int Find(PropertyDescriptor property, object key)
  { return (data as IBindingList).Find(property, key); }

public bool IsSorted
  { get { return (data as IBindingList).IsSorted; } }

private ListChangedEventHandler listChangedHandler;

public event ListChangedEventHandler ListChanged
{
    add { listChangedHandler += value; }
    remove { listChangedHandler -= value; }
}

public void RemoveIndex(PropertyDescriptor property)
  { (data as IBindingList).RemoveIndex(property); }

public void RemoveSort()
    { (data as IBindingList).RemoveSort(); }

public ListSortDirection SortDirection
{ get { return (data as IBindingList).SortDirection; } }

public PropertyDescriptor SortProperty
  {get { return (data as IBindingList).SortProperty;}}

public bool SupportsChangeNotification
  { get { return (data as IBindingList).
      SupportsChangeNotification; } }

public bool SupportsSearching
{get {return (data as IBindingList).SupportsSearching;}}

public bool SupportsSorting
{get {return (data as IBindingList).SupportsSorting;}}
#endregion

#region IList Members
public int Add(object value)
{
```

```
    if (value is PayrollData)
        data.Add((PayrollData)value);
    return data.Count;
}

public void Clear() { data.Clear(); }

public bool Contains(object value)
{
    if (value is PayrollData)
        return data.Contains((PayrollData)value);
    else
        // If the argument isn't the right type,
        // it must not be here.
        return false;
}

public int IndexOf(object value)
{
    if (value is PayrollData)
        return data.IndexOf((PayrollData)value);
    else
        return -1;
}

public void Insert(int index, object value)
{   if (value is PayrollData)
        data.Insert(index, (PayrollData)value); }

public bool IsFixedSize
{ get { return (data as IBindingList).IsFixedSize; } }

public bool IsReadOnly
{ get { return (data as IBindingList).IsReadOnly; } }

public void Remove(object value)
{
    if (value is PayrollData)
        data.Remove((PayrollData)value);
}
```

```csharp
public void RemoveAt(int index)
    { data.RemoveAt(index); }

public object this[int index]
{
    get { return data[index]; }
    set {
        if (value is PayrollData)
            data[index] = (PayrollData)value; }
}
#endregion

#region ICollection Members
public void CopyTo(Array array, int index)
    { (data as System.Collections.ICollection).
        CopyTo(array, index); }

public int Count { get { return data.Count; } }

public bool IsSynchronized
    { get { return (data as
      System.Collections.ICollection).IsSynchronized;}}

public object SyncRoot
    { get { return (data as
        System.Collections.ICollection).SyncRoot; } }
#endregion

#region IEnumerable Members
public System.Collections.IEnumerator GetEnumerator()
    { return data.GetEnumerator(); }
#endregion

public void SafeUpdate(IEnumerable<PayrollData>
    bindingList)
{
    // make the copy:
    BindingList<PayrollData> updates =
    new BindingList<PayrollData>(bindingList.ToList());
```

```
    // swap:
    System.Threading.Interlocked.Exchange
        <BindingList<PayrollData>>(ref data, updates);
    }
}
```

There is a lot of boilerplate code to examine, and much of it is straightforward. However, there are a few important parts that you should examine with a bit more care. First, notice that a number of the members of the IBindingList interface are implemented explicitly by the BindingList<T> class. That is the reason for the casts included throughout many of the methods. Also, I've coded this based on the PayrollData type being a value type. If PayrollData was a reference type, this code would be a bit simpler. I made PayrollData a value type to demonstrate those differences. The type checks are based on that PayrollData being a value type (see Item 20). Finally, notice that the ListChangedEventHandler must be implemented explicitly so that you can forward the event handlers to the contained letter object.

Of course, the point of this exercise was to create and implement the SafeUpdate method. Notice that it does essentially the same work that you did in place before. The only difference is that the swap is now accomplished by a call to Interlocked.Exchange. That guarantees that this code is safe, even in multithreaded applications. The swap cannot be interrupted.

In the general case, you cannot fix the problem of swapping reference types while still ensuring that all clients have the current copy of the object. Swapping works for value types only. That should be sufficient, if you're following the advice of Item 18.

Last, and most stringent, is the no-throw guarantee. The no-throw guarantee is pretty much what it sounds like: A method satisfies the no-throw guarantee if it is guaranteed to always run to completion and never let an exception leave a method. This just isn't practical for all routines in large programs. However, in a few locations, methods must enforce the no-throw guarantee. Finalizers and Dispose methods must not throw exceptions. In both cases, throwing an exception can cause more problems than any other alternative. In the case of a finalizer, throwing an exception terminates the program without further cleanup. Wrapping a large method in a `try`/`catch` block and swallowing all exceptions is how you achieve this no-throw guarantee. Most methods that must satisfy the no-throw guarantee, such as Dispose() and Finalize(), have limited responsibilities.

Therefore, you should be able to write these methods so that they satisfy the no-throw guarantee by writing defensive code.

In the case of a Dispose method throwing an exception, the system might now have two exceptions running through the system. The .NET environment loses the first exception and throws the new exception. You can't catch the initial exception anywhere in your program; it was eaten by the system. This greatly complicates your error handling. How can you recover from an error you don't see?

The last location for the no-throw guarantee is in delegate targets. When a delegate target throws an exception, none of the other delegate targets gets called from the same multicast delegate. The only way around this is to ensure that you do not throw any exceptions from a delegate target. Let's state that again: Delegate targets (including event handlers) should not throw exceptions. Doing so means that the code raising the event cannot participate in the strong exception guarantee. But here, I'm going to modify that advice. Item 24 showed how you can invoke delegates so that you can recover from exceptions. Not everyone does, though, so you should avoid throwing exceptions in delegate handlers. Just because you don't throw exceptions in delegates does not mean that others follow that advice; do not rely on the no-throw guarantee for your own delegate invocations. It's that defensive programming: You should do the best you can because other programmers might do the worst they can.

Exceptions introduce serious changes to the control flow of an application. In the worst case, anything could have happened—or not happened. The only way to know what has and hasn't changed when an exception is thrown is to enforce the strong exception guarantee. Then an operation either completes or does not make any changes. Finalizers, Dispose(), and delegate targets are special cases and should complete without allowing exceptions to escape under any circumstances. As a last word, watch carefully when swapping reference types; it can introduce numerous subtle bugs.

Item 48: Prefer Safe Code

The .NET runtime has been designed so that malicious code cannot infiltrate and execute on a remote machine. Yet some distributed systems rely on downloading and executing code from remote machines. If you might be delivering your software via the Internet or an intranet, or running it directly from the Web, you need to understand the restrictions that the

CLR will place on your assemblies. If the CLR does not fully trust an assembly, it limits the allowed actions. This is called code access security (CAS). On another axis, the CLR enforces role-based security, in which code might or might not execute based on a particular user account's privileges. You'll also see these effects when you create Silverlight applications that run in a browser. The browser model imposes security restrictions on any code running in that environment.

Security violations are runtime conditions; the compiler cannot enforce them. Furthermore, they are far less likely to show up on your development machine; code that you compile is loaded from your hard drive and, therefore, has a higher trust level. Discussing all the implications of the .NET Security model fills volumes, but you can take a small set of reasonable actions to enable your assemblies to interact with the .NET security model more easily. These recommendations apply only if you are creating library components, or components and programs that might be delivered across the Web.

Throughout this discussion, remember that .NET is a managed environment. The environment guarantees a certain amount of safety. The bulk of the .NET Framework library is granted full trust through the .NET config policy when it is installed. It is verifiably safe, which means that the CLR can examine the IL and ensure that it does not perform any potentially dangerous actions, such as accessing raw memory. It does not assert any particular security rights needed to access local resources. You should try to follow that same example. If your code does not need any particular security rights, avoid using any of the CAS APIs to determine your access rights; all you do is decrease performance.

You will use the CAS APIs to access a small set of protected resources that demand increased privileges. The most common protected resources are unmanaged memory and the file system. Other protected resources include databases, network ports, the Windows Registry, and the printing subsystem. In each case, attempting to access those resources fires exceptions when the calling code does not have the proper permissions. Furthermore, accessing those resources might cause the runtime to perform a security stack walk to ensure that all assemblies in the current callstack have the proper permissions. Let's look at memory and the file system, discussing the best practices for a secure and safe program.

You can avoid unmanaged memory access by creating verifiably safe assemblies whenever possible. A safe assembly is one that does not use any pointers to access either the managed or unmanaged heaps. Whether you knew it or not, almost all the C# code that you create is safe. Unless you turn on the /unsafe C# compiler option, you've created verifiably safe code. /unsafe allows the use of pointers, which the CLR cannot verify.

The reasons to use unsafe code are few, with the most common being performance. Pointers to raw memory are faster than safe reference checks. In a typical array, they can be up to ten times faster. But when you use unsafe constructs, understand that unsafe code anywhere in an assembly affects the entire assembly. When you create unsafe code blocks, consider isolating those algorithms in their own assembly (see Item 50). This limits the effect that unsafe code has on your entire application. If it's isolated, only callers who need the particular feature are affected. You can still use the remaining safe functionality in more restrictive environments. You might also need unsafe code to deal with P/Invoke or COM interfaces that require raw pointers. The same recommendation applies: Isolate it. Unsafe code should affect its own small assembly and nothing else.

The advice for memory access is simple: Avoid accessing unmanaged memory whenever possible. When you do need to access unmanaged memory, you should isolate that access in a separate assembly.

The next most common security concern is the file system. Programs store data, often in files. Code that has been downloaded from the Internet does not have access to most locations on the file system—that would be a huge security hole. Yet, not accessing the file system at all would make it far more difficult to create usable programs. This problem is solved by using isolated storage. Isolated storage can be thought of as a virtual directory that is isolated based on the assembly, the application domain, and the current user. Optionally, you can use a more general isolated storage virtual directory that is based on the assembly and the current user.

Partially trusted assemblies can access their own specific isolated storage area but nowhere else on the file system. The isolated storage directory is hidden from other assemblies and other users. You use isolated storage through the classes in the System.IO.IsolatedStorage namespace. The IsolatedStorageFile class contains methods very similar to the System.IO.File class. In fact, it is derived from the System.IO.FileStream class. The code to write to isolated storage is almost the same as writing to any file:

```
IsolatedStorageFile iso =
  IsolatedStorageFile.GetUserStoreForDomain();
```

```
IsolatedStorageFileStream myStream = new
   IsolatedStorageFileStream("SavedStuff.txt",
   FileMode.Create, iso);
StreamWriter wr = new StreamWriter(myStream);
// several wr.Write statements elided
wr.Close();
```

Reading is equally familiar to anyone who has used file I/O:

```
IsolatedStorageFile isoStore =
   IsolatedStorageFile.GetUserStoreForDomain();

string[] files = isoStore.GetFileNames("SavedStuff.txt");
if (files.Length > 0)
{
    StreamReader reader = new StreamReader(new
       IsolatedStorageFileStream("SavedStuff.txt",
       FileMode.Open, isoStore));

    // Several reader.ReadLines( ) calls elided.

    reader.Close();
}
```

You can use isolated storage to persist reasonably sized data elements that enable partially trusted code to save and load information from a carefully partitioned location on the local disk. The .NET environment defines limits on the size of isolated storage for each application. This prevents malicious code from consuming excessive disk space, rendering a system unusable. Isolated storage is hidden from other programs and other users. Therefore, it should not be used for deployment or configuration settings that an administrator might need to manipulate. Even though it is hidden, however, isolated storage is not protected from unmanaged code or from trusted users. Do not use isolated storage for high-value secrets unless you apply additional encryption.

To create an assembly that can live within the possible security restrictions on the file system, isolate the creation of your storage streams. When your assembly might be run from the Web or might be accessed by code run from the Web, consider isolated storage.

You might need other protected resources as well. In general, access to those resources is an indication that your program needs to be fully trusted. The only alternative is to avoid the protected resource entirely. Consider the Windows Registry, for example. If your program needs to access the Registry, you must install your program to the end user's computer so that it has the necessary privileges to access the Registry. You simply can't safely create a Registry editor that runs from the Web. That's the way it should be.

The .NET Security model means that your program's actions are checked against its rights. Pay attention to the rights your program needs and try to minimize them. Don't ask for rights you don't need. The fewer protected resources your assembly needs, the less likely it will generate security exceptions. Avoid using secure resources, and consider alternatives whenever possible. When you do need higher security permissions for some algorithms, isolate that code in its own assembly.

Item 49: Prefer CLS-Compliant Assemblies

The .NET environment is language agnostic: Developers can incorporate components written in different .NET languages without limitations. In practice, it's almost true. You must create assemblies that are compliant with the Common Language Subsystem (CLS) to guarantee that developers writing programs in other languages can use your components.

One of C#'s advantages is that because it was designed to run on the CLR, almost all of your C# assemblies will be CLS compliant. That's not true for many other languages. Many F# constructs do not compile down to CLS-compliant types. DLR languages, such as IronPython and IronRuby, do not create CLS-compliant assemblies in this release. That's one of the reasons C# is an excellent choice for component development in .NET. C# components can be consumed by all the languages that run on the CLR. That's because it's not that hard to create C# components that are CLS compliant.

CLS compliance is a new twist on that least common denominator approach to interoperability. The CLS specification is a subset of operations that every language must support. To create a CLS-compliant assembly, you must create an assembly whose public interface is limited to those features in the CLS specification. Then any language supporting the CLS specification must be capable of using the component. This does not mean you must limit your entire programming palette to the CLS-compliant subset of the C# language, however.

To create a CLS-compliant assembly, you must follow two rules. First, the type of all parameters and return values from public and protected members must be CLS compliant. Second, any non-CLS-compliant public or protected member must have a CLS-compliant synonym.

The first rule is simple to follow: You can have it enforced by the compiler. Add the CLSCompliant attribute to your assembly:

```
[assembly: System.CLSCompliant(true)]
```

The compiler enforces CLS compliance for the entire assembly. If you write a public method or property that uses a construct that is not compliant with CLS, it's an error. That's good because it makes CLS compliance an easy goal. After turning on CLS compliance, these two definitions won't compile because unsigned integers are not compliant with CLS:

```
// Not CLS Compliant, returns unsigned int:
public UInt32 Foo()
{
    return foo;
}


// Not CLS compliant, parameter is an unsigned int.
public void Foo2(UInt32 parm)
{
}
```

Remember that creating a CLS-compliant assembly affects only items that can be seen outside the current assembly. Foo and Foo2 generate CLS compliance errors when declared either public or protected. However, if Foo and Foo2 were internal, or private, they could be included in a CLS-compliant assembly; CLS-compliant interfaces are required only for items that are exposed outside the assembly.

What about this property? Is it CLS compliant?

```
public MyClass TheProperty { get; set; }
```

It depends. If MyClass is CLS compliant and indicates that it is CLS compliant, this property is CLS compliant. On the other hand, if MyClass is not marked as CLS compliant, this property is not CLS compliant. That means that the earlier TheProperty is CLS compliant only if MyClass resides in a CLS-compliant assembly.

You cannot build a CLS-compliant assembly if you have types in your public or protected interface that are not CLS compliant. If, as a component designer, you do not have an assembly marked as CLS compliant, you make it harder for users of your component to create CLS-compliant assemblies. They must hide your types and mirror the functionality in a CLS-compliant wrapper. Yes, this can be done. But, no, it's not a good way to treat the programmers who want to use your components. It's better to strive for CLS-compliant assemblies in all your work: This is the easiest way for clients to incorporate your work in their CLS-compliant assemblies.

The second rule is up to you: You need to make sure that you provide a language-agnostic way to perform all public and protected operations. You also need to make sure that you do not sneak a noncompliant object through your interface using polymorphism.

Operator overloading is a feature that some love and others hate. As such, not every language supports or allows operator overloading. The CLS standard does not take a pro or con stance on the concept of operator overloading. Instead, it defines a function name for each operator: op_equals is the function name created when you write an operator = function. op_add is the name for an overloaded addition operator. When you write an overloaded operator, the operator syntax can be used in languages that support overloaded operators. Developers using a language that does not support operator overloading must use the op_ function name. If you expect these programmers to use your CLS-compliant assembly, you should provide a more convenient syntax. That leads to this simple recommendation: Anytime you overload an operator, create a semantically equivalent function:

```
// Overloaded Addition operator, preferred C# syntax:
public static Foo operator +(Foo left, Foo right)
{
    // Use the same implementation as the Add method:
    return Foo.Add(left, right);
}


// Static function, desirable for some languages:
public static Foo Add(Foo left, Foo right)
{
    return new Foo(left.Bar + right.Bar);
}
```

Finally, watch out for non-CLS types sneaking into an interface when you use polymorphic arguments. It's easy to do with event arguments. You can create a type that is not compliant with CLS and use it where a base type that is CLS-compliant is expected.

Suppose that you created this class derived from EventArgs:

```
public class BadEventArgs : EventArgs
{
    public UInt32 ErrorCode;
}
```

The BadEventArgs type is not CLS compliant; you should not use it with event handlers written in other languages. But polymorphism makes this easy to do. You can declare the event type to use the base class, EventArgs:

```
// Hiding the non-compliant event argument:
public delegate void MyEventHandler(
  object sender, EventArgs args );

public event MyEventHandler OnStuffHappens;

// Code to raise Event:
BadEventArgs arg = new BadEventArgs();
arg.ErrorCode = 24;

// Interface is legal, runtime type is not:
OnStuffHappens(this, arg);
```

The interface declaration, which uses an EventArgs argument, is CLS compliant. However, the actual type you substituted in the event arguments was not. The end result is a type that some languages cannot use. Developers trying to use those types will not be able to call the methods in your assembly. Their language may even hide the visibility of those APIs. Or, they may show that the APIs exist but not provide a way to access them.

This discussion of CLS compliance ends with how CLS-compliant classes implement compliant or noncompliant interfaces. It can get complicated, but we'll simplify it. Understanding CLS compliance with interfaces also will help you fully understand what it means to be CLS compliant and how the environment views compliance.

This interface is CLS compliant if it is declared in a CLS-compliant assembly:

```
[assembly: CLSCompliant(true)]
public interface IFoo
{
    void DoStuff(Int32 arg1, string arg2);
}
```

You can implement that interface in any CLS-compliant class. However, if you declare this interface in an assembly that is not marked as CLS compliant, the IFoo interface is not CLS compliant. In other words, an interface is CLS compliant only if it is defined in a CLS-compliant assembly; conforming to the CLS spec is not enough. The reason is compiler performance. The compilers check CLS compliance on types only when the assembly being compiled is marked as CLS compliant. Similarly, the compilers assume that types declared in assemblies that are not CLS compliant actually are not CLS compliant. However, the members of this interface have CLS-compliant signatures. Even if IFoo is not marked as CLS compliant, you can implement IFoo in a CLS-compliant class. Clients of this class could access DoStuff through the class reference, but not through the IFoo reference.

Consider this small variation:

```
public interface IFoo2
{
    // Non-CLS compliant, Unsigned int
    void DoStuff(UInt32 arg1, string arg2);
}
```

A class that publicly implements IFoo2 is not CLS compliant. To make a CLS-compliant class that implements IFoo2, you must use explicit interface implementation:

```
public class MyClass2 : IFoo2
{
    // explicit interface implementation.
    // DoStuff() is not part of MyClass's public interface
    void IFoo2.DoStuff(UInt32 arg1, string arg2)
    {
        // content elided.
    }
}
```

MyClass has a CLS-compliant public interface. Clients expecting the IFoo2 interface must access it through the non-CLS-compliant IFoo2 pointer.

Complicated? No, not really. Creating a CLS-compliant type mandates that your public interfaces contain only CLS-compliant types. It means that your base class must be CLS compliant. All interfaces that you implement publicly must be CLS compliant. If you implement a non-CLS compliant interface, you must hide it from your public interface using explicit interface implementation.

CLS compliance does not force you to adopt a least common denominator approach to your designs and implementations. It means carefully watching the publicly accessible interfaces of your assembly. For any public or protected class, any type mentioned in these constructs must be CLS compliant:

- Base classes
- Return values for public and protected methods and properties
- Parameters for public and protected methods and indexers
- Runtime event arguments
- Public interfaces, declared or implemented

The compiler tries to enforce a compliant assembly. That makes it easy for you to provide some minimum level of CLS support. With a bit of extra care, you can create an assembly that anyone using any language can use. The CLS specification tries to ensure that language interoperability is possible without sacrificing the constructs in your favorite language. You just need to provide alternatives in the interface.

CLS compliance requires you to spend a little time thinking about the public interfaces from the standpoint of other languages. You don't need to restrict all your code to CLS-compliant constructs; just avoid the non-compliant constructs in the interface. The payback of interlanguage operability is worth the extra time.

Item 50: Prefer Smaller, Cohesive Assemblies

This item should really be titled "Build Assemblies That Are the Right Size and Contain a Small Number of Public Types." But that's too wordy, so I titled it based on the most common mistake I see: developers putting everything but the kitchen sink in one assembly. That makes it hard to reuse components and harder to update parts of a system. Many smaller assemblies make it easier to use your classes as binary components.

The title also highlights the importance of cohesion. Cohesion is the degree to which the responsibilities of a single component form a meaningful unit. Cohesive components can be described in a single simple sentence. You can see this in many of the .NET FCL assemblies. Two examples are: The System.Core assembly provides types and algorithms that support LINQ, and the System.Windows.Forms assembly provides classes that model Windows controls. Web Forms and Windows Forms are in different assemblies because they are not related. You should be able to describe your own assemblies in the same fashion using one simple sentence. No cheating: The MyApplication assembly provides everything you need. Yes, that's a single sentence. But it's also lazy, and you probably don't need all of that functionality in My2ndApplication. (Though you'd probably like to reuse some of it. That "some of it" should be packaged in its own assembly.)

You should not create assemblies with only one public class. You do need to find the middle ground. If you go too far and create too many assemblies, you lose some benefits of encapsulation: You lose the benefits of internal types by not packaging related public classes in the same assembly. The JIT compiler can perform more efficient inlining inside an assembly than across assembly boundaries. This means that packaging related types in the same assembly is to your advantage. Your goal is to create the best-sized package for the functionality you are delivering in your component. This goal is easier to achieve with cohesive components: Each component should have one responsibility.

In some sense, an assembly is the binary equivalent of class. We use classes to encapsulate algorithms and data storage. Only the public classes, structs, and interfaces are part of the official contract, so only the public types are visible to users. (Remember that interfaces cannot be declared protected.) In the same sense, assemblies provide a binary package for a related set of classes. Only public and protected classes are visible outside an assembly. Utility classes can be internal to the assembly. Yes, they are more visible than private nested classes, but you have a mechanism to share a common implementation inside that assembly without exposing that implementation to all users of your classes. Partitioning your application into multiple assemblies encapsulates related types in a single package.

Splitting functionality into assemblies implies having more code than you would have in a short essay like an Effective Item. Rather than write an entire new application, I'll discuss a variety of enhancements to the dynamic CSV class from Item 44. You need to determine if the new features belong with the core capabilities you've already delivered, or if it's an option that a smaller set of your users will appreciate. The version I created returns all data in the CSV file as strings. You could create adapters that would convert the strings to numeric values when the column supported it. That would probably be something that most users would want. Those adapters should be in the same assembly. Another addition might be supporting more than one level of headers. That would enable nested headers, like Excel pivot tables. That feels like something you'd put into a different assembly. Only some of your users would use that feature. The most common usage would be the version containing the single headers. That means it makes the most sense to put the multiple header functionality in a different assembly. It may depend on the core assembly, but it should not be in the same location.

What about internationalization? That one doesn't have a simple answer. You may be creating applications for multinational enterprises, and multiple language support is critical for everyone. Or, you may be writing a simple utility for local soccer leagues. Or, your expected audience could be anywhere in between. If most of your users will be in one language, whatever that might be, separating multiple languages into a separate assembly (or even one assembly per language) might make sense. On the other hand, if your user base will often need to use CSV files in a variety of languages, multiple languages should be part of the core functionality. You need to decide if this new functionality is going to be useful to an overwhelming majority of users for your core functionality. If it is, then you should add the new functionality to the same assembly. On the other hand, if this new functionality is expected to be used only in some of the more complicated examples, then you should separate that functionality into a separate deliverable unit.

Second, using multiple assemblies makes a number of different deployment options easier. Consider a three-tiered application, in which part of the application runs as a smart client and part of the application runs on the server. You supply some validation rules on the client so that users get feedback as they enter or edit data. You replicate those rules on the server and combine them with other rules to provide more robust validation. The complete set of business rules is implemented at the server, and only a subset is maintained at each client.

Sure, you could reuse the source code and create different assemblies for the client and server-side business rules, but that would complicate your delivery mechanism. That leaves you with two builds and two installations to perform when you update the rules. Instead, separate the client-side validation from the more robust server-side validation by placing them in different assemblies. You are reusing binary objects, packaged in assemblies, rather than reusing object code or source code by compiling those objects into the multiple assemblies.

An assembly should contain an organized library of related functionality. That's an easy platitude, but it's much harder to implement in practice. The reality is that you might not know beforehand which classes will be distributed to both the server and client portions of a distributed application. Even more likely, the set of server- and client-side functionality will be somewhat fluid; you'll move features between the two locations. By keeping the assemblies small, you'll be more likely to redeploy more easily on both client and server. The assembly is a binary building block for your application. That makes it easier to plug a new component into place in a working application. If you make a mistake, make too many smaller assemblies rather than too few large ones.

I often use Legos as an analogy for assemblies and binary components. You can pull out one Lego and replace it easily; it's a small block. In the same way, you should be able to pull out one assembly and replace it with another assembly that has the same interfaces. The rest of the application should continue as if nothing happened. Follow the Lego analogy a little farther. If all your parameters and return values are interfaces, any assembly can be replaced by another that implements the same interfaces (see Item 22).

Smaller assemblies also let you amortize the cost of application startup. The larger an assembly is, the more work the CPU does to load the assembly and convert the necessary IL into machine instructions. Only the routines called at startup are JITed, but the entire assembly gets loaded and the CLR creates stubs for every method in the assembly.

Time to take a break and make sure we don't go to extremes. This item is about making sure that you don't create single monolithic programs, but that you build systems of binary, reusable components. You can take this advice too far. Some costs are associated with a large program built on too many small assemblies. You will incur a performance penalty when program flow crosses assembly boundaries. The CLR loader has a little more work to do to load many assemblies and turn IL into machine instructions, particularly resolving function addresses.

Extra security checks also are done across assembly boundaries. All code from the same assembly has the same level of trust (not necessarily the same access rights, but the same trust level). The CLR performs some security checks whenever code flow crosses an assembly boundary. The fewer times your program flow crosses assembly boundaries, the more efficient it will be.

None of these performance concerns should dissuade you from breaking up assemblies that are too large. The performance penalties are minor. C# and .NET were designed with components in mind, and the greater flexibility is usually worth the price.

So how do you decide how much code or how many classes go in one assembly? More important, how do you decide which code goes in an assembly? It depends greatly on the specific application, so there is not one answer. Here's my recommendation: Start by looking at all your public classes. Combine public classes with common base classes into assemblies. Then add the utility classes necessary to provide all the functionality associated with the public classes in that same assembly. Package related public interfaces into their own assemblies. As a final step, look for classes that are used horizontally across your application. Those are candidates for a broad-based utility assembly that contains your application's utility library.

The end result is that you create a component with a single related set of public classes and the utility classes necessary to support it. You create an assembly that is small enough to get the benefits of easy updates and easier reuse, while still minimizing the costs associated with multiple assemblies. Well-designed, cohesive components can be described in one simple sentence. For example, "Common.Storage.dll manages the offline data cache and all user settings" describes a component with low cohesion. Instead, make two components: "Common.Data.dll manages the offline data cache. Common.Settings.dll manages user settings." When you've split those up, you might need a third component: "Common.EncryptedStorage.dll manages file system IO for encrypted local storage." You can update any of those three components independently.

Small is a relative term. mscorlib.dll is roughly 2MB; System.Web .RegularExpressions.dll is merely 56KB. But both satisfy the core design goal of a small, reusable assembly: They contain a related set of classes and interfaces. The difference in absolute size has to do with the difference in functionality: mscorlib.dll contains all the low-level classes you need in every application. System.Web.RegularExpressions.dll is very specific; it contains only those classes needed to support regular expressions in Web controls. You will create both kinds of components: small, focused assemblies for one specific feature and larger, broad-based assemblies that contain common functionality. In either case, make them as small as is reasonable but no smaller.

Index

Symbols and Numbers

+ (addition) operator, in dynamic
programming, 228–229

==() operator
defined, 44
hash value equality, 45–46

0 (null)
ensuring valid state for value types,
110–114
initialization of nonserializable
members, 159–160
initializing object to, 75

A

Abrahams, Dave, 285

Abstract base classes, 129–131

Access
compile-time vs. runtime constants, 8
security, 294–298

Accessible data members, 1–7

Accessors
event, 149
inclining property, 66–67
property, 4–5, 7

Action<>, 144

Adapter patterns, 240

Add()
limitations of dynamic
programming, 228–236
minimizing dynamic objects in
public APIs, 268–270

AggregateExceptions, 220–225

Algorithms, parallel
constructing with exceptions in
mind, 203–215
PLINQ implementation of, 203–215

Allocations
distinguishing between value types
and reference types, 107–108
minimizing, 94–98

Amdahl's law, 214

Annotation of named parameters, 63

Anonymous types, 239–243

APIs (application programming
interfaces)
avoiding conversion operators in,
56–60
CAS, 295
large-grain internet service, 166–171
making use of expression, 254–261
minimizing dynamic objects in
public, 267–273
transforming late binding to early
binding with expressions, 262–267